Human Rights Due Diligence and Labour Governance

OXFORD LABOUR LAW

Series Editors: Professor Alan Bogg (University of Bristol Law School), Professor Anne Davies (University of Oxford, Faculty of Law), Professor Keith Ewing (School of Law, King's College London), and Mark Freedland (University of Oxford, Faculty of Law).

The *Oxford Labour Law* series (formerly known as the *Oxford Monographs on Labour Law* series) has come to represent a significant contribution to the literature of British, European, and international labour law. The series recognizes the arrival not only of a renewed interest in labour law generally, but also the need for fresh approaches to the study of labour law following a period of momentous change in the UK and Europe. The series is concerned with all aspects of collective labour law and individual employment law, including the growing role of human rights and discrimination in employment. It is concerned also with the influence of politics and economics in shaping labour law, as well as the importance of legal theory and international labour standards. Recent titles address developments in multiple jurisdictions.

ALSO AVAILABLE IN THE SERIES

Catholic Social Teaching and Labour Law
An Ethical Perspective on Work
Mark Bell

Structural Injustice and Workers' Rights
Virginia Mantouvalou

Reforming Age Discrimination Law
Beyond Individual Enforcement
Alysia Blackham

Putting Human Rights to Work
Labour Law, The ECHR, and The Employment Relation
Philippa Collins

Strike Ballots, Democracy, and Law
Breen Creighton, Catrina Denvir, Richard Johnstone,
Shae McCrystal, Alice Orchiston

Living Wage
Regulatory Solutions to Informal and
Precarious Work in Global Supply Chains
Shelley Marshall

A Purposive Approach to Labour Law
Guy Davidov

Human Rights Due Diligence and Labour Governance

INGRID LANDAU

OXFORD
UNIVERSITY PRESS

OXFORD
UNIVERSITY PRESS

Great Clarendon Street, Oxford, OX2 6DP,
United Kingdom

Oxford University Press is a department of the University of Oxford.
It furthers the University's objective of excellence in research, scholarship,
and education by publishing worldwide. Oxford is a registered trade mark of
Oxford University Press in the UK and in certain other countries

First Edition published in 2023

Published in the United States of America by Oxford University Press
198 Madison Avenue, New York, NY 10016, United States of America

British Library Cataloguing in Publication Data
Data available

Library of Congress Control Number: 2023946375

ISBN 978–0–19–887606–9

DOI: 10.1093/oso/9780198876069.001.0001

Printed and bound by
CPI Group (UK) Ltd, Croydon, CR0 4YY

For Ada and Albs

General Editors' Preface

This is an important book which we warmly welcome to the series. The question of corporate compliance with human rights standards has proved to be intractable. Yet, there is an urgent need to ensure compliance and an urgent need to ensure that corporations take responsibility for the conduct of their contractors and suppliers. Rana Plaza—where more than a thousand workers were killed and more than twice as many were injured—is a stain on the global economy that will never be removed. But although the most serious in recent years, it is not the only one. We are reminded on a regular basis of corporate disregard—directly or indirectly—for workers' rights specifically and human rights more broadly.

The *Oxford Labour Law* series has covered a wide range of issues, thereby emphasising the broad range of the discipline. Dr Landau's impressively executed study addresses the role of human rights due diligence (HRDD) as a tool for the protection of labour rights. HRDD is one of a number of key initiatives addressed to transnational companies to ensure that they comply with international human rights obligations throughout their operations and their supply chains. It is an initiative stimulated by the UN Guiding Principles on Business and Human Rights (UNGPs), which include corporate due diligence requirements. These were adopted in 2011, two years before Rana Plaza.

In what is a fascinating volume, Dr Landau traces the origins of the UNGPs and examines in detail some of the problems to have arisen in relation to the operation of HRDD in particular. The author points out that HRDD is an 'ambiguous transnational labour norm' and that its meaning is contested by state, non-state, and hybrid actors and institutions at multiple levels. The author's account of the different expectations of employers and trade unions about what HRDD requires is informed by her wide range of research methods, including some very revealing interviews with key actors. While trade unions see HRDD as a means of worker empowerment, businesses see HRDD differently, as a practical tool for risk management.

This difference of approach is fully explored by Dr Landau, and its troubling implications from a labour rights perspective are fully examined. So, too, is the approach to HRDD in the work of international agencies, including the Organisation for Economic Co-operation and Development (OECD) and the International Labour Organization (ILO). The former has embedded HRDD in its Guidelines for Multinational Enterprises, revised in 2011, a revision designed, in part, to encourage companies to adopt a 'risk-based due diligence' approach to all labour and human rights. The latter, in contrast, has been much slower to respond, with the result that the OECD has emerged as the dominant interpreter of HRDD, reinforcing the business-orientated approach in the latter's construction.

Apart from shining much needed light on the work of the OECD in relation to HRDD, the study also deals with HRDD initiatives at the national level. Here, Dr Landau explores two contrasting responses in legislation, comparing the approach of those countries (such as Australia, the United Kingdom, and the United States) where the law effectively defers to managerial interpretations of HRDD with those countries (such as France) where the law is used to elaborate standards in the design and evaluation of due diligence processes, as well as imposing some accountability for the quality of the due diligence undertaken. It is clear that the role of the state in these ways is very much at an early stage of development.

Nevertheless, as is powerfully argued in this study, it is also clear that HRDD has failed to meet the expectations initially accorded to it by the international trade union movement and other labour rights activists. The author nevertheless takes a pragmatic approach to HRDD's retention, arguing persuasively for its reorientation in the direction of labour rights protection. This would require active intervention by states, with Dr Landau laying out in the concluding chapters a clear agenda for reform, as well as advancing the case for the improvement of OECD procedures. The latter will be critical if the OECD continues to develop its much underestimated role in transnational labour law.

ALB, ACLD, KDE, and MRF
14 July 2023

Preface

When I commenced research for this study in 2015, there were no human rights due diligence (HRDD) laws in place and only a handful of relevant scholarly articles. In the country from which I hail, Australia, very few people were familiar with the concept. One of the greatest privileges, but also greatest challenges, of undertaking this research has been keeping pace with HRDD's rapid institutionalisation in transnational governance. Difficult choices have had to be made concerning upon which sites of contest to focus and at what point to cease chronicling and examining new developments and new literature. It is thus important to acknowledge that, while this book captures and critiques developments that have occurred during a critical period in the evolution of HRDD (the first decade or so of its existence), these processes of transnational norm elaboration and contestation continue to unfold at a rapid pace.

Ingrid Landau
Melbourne
12 September 2023

Acknowledgements

I am grateful to the activists, practitioners, policymakers, and scholars on various continents who agreed to participate in this research and share their time and insights with me. I also wish to acknowledge those who, many years ago now, introduced me to the compelling world of international labour rights: Colin Fenwick, Alison Tate, and Sharan Burrow.

This book draws on doctoral research supported by Melbourne Law School Research Support Funds, a Melbourne Research Scholarship, and an Australian Government Research Training Scholarship. In the early stages of this research, I also benefited from financial support from host organisations to attend workshops organised by Harvard Law School's Institute for Global Law and Policy and jointly by New York University's Stern Centre for Business and Human Rights and University of St Gallen's Institute of Business Ethics.

I have benefited immensely from feedback on this research provided by colleagues in both the labour law and the business and human rights communities. I gratefully acknowledge the guidance and support provided at various stages by Dorothée Baumann-Pauly, John Howe, Shelley Marshall, Richard Mitchell, Jill Murray, Justine Nolan, and John Tobin.

I wish to express my gratitude to the editors of this series, Alan Bogg, Anne Davies, Keith Ewing, and Mark Freedland, for supporting this publication. It is an immense privilege to have my work published here. I also wish to thank the three anonymous referees who provided comments on the draft manuscript.

Without the support of Carolyn Sutherland in the Department of Business Law and Taxation at Monash Business School, I would not have been able to complete this project alongside my teaching and other research commitments. I am also forever grateful to colleagues Andrew Moshirnia and Adriana Orifici for their encouragement and friendship throughout.

Finally, I acknowledge those who, no doubt, will never read this book but without whom it could not have been written. My mother, and David, Gayle, and Chris Samuel have always been supportive of my work. I am forever grateful to, and for, my sisters and my children: Imogen (Clare), Rose, Ada, and Albert. Getting this done would not have been possible without their love, tolerance, support, and humour.

Contents

Table of Legislation

List of Abbreviations

ACT	Action, Collaboration, Transformation
AFL–CIO	American Federation of Labor and Congress of Industrial Organizations
BAFA	Federal Office for Economic Affairs and Export Control
BIAC	Business and Industry Advisory Council to the OECD
BWI	Building and Wood Workers' International
CCC	Clean Clothes Campaign
CSR	corporate social responsibility
DRC	Democratic Republic of Congo
EU	European Union
ECCHR	European Center for Constitutional and Human Rights
ECCJ	European Coalition for Corporate Justice
EFFAT	European Federation of Food, Agriculture and Tourism
ERC	European Research Council
ETI	Ethical Trading Initiative
ETUC	European Trade Union Confederation
EY	Ernst & Young
FIDH	International Federation for Human Rights
FIFA	Fédération Internationale de Football Association
GSCs	global supply chains
GUF	global union federation
HRC	United Nations Human Rights Council
HRDD	human rights due diligence
HRW	Human Rights Watch
IBA	International Bar Association
ICCPR	International Covenant on Civil and Political Rights
ICESCR	International Covenant on Economic, Social and Cultural Rights
IFA	international framework agreement
IFHR	International Federation for Human Rights
IGO	intergovernmental organisation
ILC	International Labour Conference
ILO	International Labour Organization
IO	international organisation
IOE	International Organisation of Employers
ITUC	International Trade Union Confederation
IUF	International Union of Food, Agricultural, Hotel, Restaurant, Catering, Tobacco and Allied Workers' Associations
LEAH	Labour Equality and Human Rights
MNE	multinational enterprise
MSA AUS	Modern Slavery Act 2018 (Aust)

MSA UK	Modern Slavery Act 2015 (UK)
MSI	multi-stakeholder initiative
NBIM	Norges Bank Investment Management
NCP	national contact point
NGO	non-governmental organisation
OECD	Organisation for Economic Co-operation and Development
OHCHR	Office of the High Commissioner for Human Rights
PSF	professional services firm
PwC	Pricewaterhouse Coopers
RBC	responsible business conduct
RMIT	Royal Melbourne Institute of Technology
SEC	US Securities Exchange Commission
SEIU	Service Employees International Union
SRSG	UN Special Representative of the Secretary-General on Human Rights and Transnational Corporations and Other Business Enterprises
TCA	transnational company agreement
TIRA	transnational industrial relations agreement
TLAN	transnational labour activist network
TUAC	Trade Union Advisory Committee to the OECD
TUC	Trade Union Congress
UGT	União Geral dos Trabalhadores
UN	United Nations
UNCTC	UN Centre on Transnational Corporations
UNGA	United Nations General Assembly
UNGPs	United Nations Guiding Principles on Business and Human Rights
WPRBC	OECD Working Party on Responsible Business Conduct

1

Introduction

The Rise of a New Concept in Transnational Labour Governance

In June 2016, following years of political wrangling, government, employer, and worker members of the International Labour Organization met at the annual International Labour Conference in Geneva to discuss the challenge of achieving decent work in global supply chains.[1] For the international trade union movement and a number of international labour and human rights non-governmental organisations, this discussion was seen as a significant opportunity to advance efforts to achieve greater legal accountability of multinational enterprises for labour rights abuses that occur in the production of their goods and services.[2] In the lead-up to the event, the International Trade Union Confederation, Human Rights Watch, and others intensified efforts to elevate the issue on the global policy agenda by drawing attention to the ongoing and systematic exploitation of workers in sectors as diverse as agriculture, garment and footwear, mining, construction, and electronics.[3] They called for a new international convention to be adopted by the UN agency responsible for the world of work that would help address the 'governance gaps'[4] that continued to facilitate and enable exploitation and poor working conditions for millions of workers engaged within global supply chains (GSCs).[5]

There are many aspects of these demands, and the dynamics that underpin them, that are long familiar to those concerned with the protection and promotion

[1] See Chapter 5.

[2] See eg Clean Clothes Campaign, 'Position Paper on Human Rights Due Diligence' (March 2016) 5 <https://archive.cleanclothes.org/resources/publications/position-paper-on-human-rightsdue-diligence/view> accessed 7 October 2022; HRW (Human Rights Watch), 'Human Rights in Supply Chains: A Call for a Binding Global Standard on Due Diligence' (2016) <www.hrw.org/report/2016/05/30/human-rights-supply-chains/call-binding-global-standard-due-diligence> accessed 7 October 2022; AFWA (Asia Floor Wage Alliance) and others, 'Precarious Work in the Gap Global Value Chain' (2016) <www.globallaborjustice.org/wp-content/uploads/2018/05/Precarious-Work-in-the-GAP-Global-Value-Chain.pdf> accessed 20 September 2018.

[3] See also Huw Thomas and Mark Anner, 'Dissensus and Deadlock in the Evolution of Labour Governance: Global Supply Chains and the International Labour Organisation (ILO)' (2023) 184 Journal of Business Ethics 33, 43.

[4] Andrew Crane, Dirk Matten, and Jeremy Moon, *Corporations and Citizenship: Business, Responsibility and Society* (CUP 2008) 205.

[5] According to International Labour Organization (ILO) estimates, an estimated 450 million people work in global supply chains, with more than one in five jobs today linked to GSCs: ILO, 'World Employment and Social Outlook 2015' (ILO 2015).

Human Rights Due Diligence and Labour Governance. Ingrid Landau, Oxford University Press. © Ingrid Landau 2023.
DOI: 10.1093/oso/9780198876069.003.0001

of workers' rights in the global economy. Since at least the 1970s, activists, civil society, and scholars have called for stronger intergovernmental standard-setting and cooperation to secure responsible business conduct by companies that have operations or supply chains that extend across national jurisdictions. They have also consistently pointed to the persistent and well-documented failures of existing public and private regulatory approaches that rely on voluntary adoption and implementation of standards by companies to effectively address these problems. Indeed, there is now a rich multidisciplinary literature documenting the emergence and evolution of contests over the scope and nature of corporate accountability for labour rights in the global economy.[6] Much has also been written on the need for nation-states—both individually and collectively—to address the formidable legal and practical barriers that impede efforts by workers and others to hold businesses to account for violations of workers' internationally recognised rights associated with the production of their goods and services.

Yet, there was something in the calls by the international union movement and civil society organisations in 2016 that was novel and, until recently, has largely gone overlooked by scholars of transnational labour law. This lay in the way in which the proposed solution was framed. In the lead-up to the International Labour Conference in 2016, trade unions and labour and human rights non-governmental organisations (NGOs) were not simply calling on states to adopt a legally binding instrument to address the challenges of decent work in GSCs, but they were also calling for an instrument that would embody a specific response. They were calling for a convention that would oblige states to require companies domiciled in their jurisdictions to conduct *human rights due diligence*.

It is this phenomenon—the rise to prominence of human rights due diligence (HRDD) as a way of conceptualising and operationalising corporate responsibility for working conditions in GSCs—that is the subject of this book. Introduced into the global lexicon through the UN Guiding Principles on Business and Human Rights (UNGPs) in 2011, HRDD is offered as a way for business enterprises to give effect to their overarching responsibility to respect human rights.[7] It is a process through which an enterprise assesses actual and potential human rights impacts, integrates and acts upon the findings, tracks the effectiveness of responses, and communicates externally on these efforts. According to the UNGPs, HRDD should cover human rights impacts that an enterprise may cause or contribute to through its own activities or which may be directly linked to its operations, products, or services by business relationships. Human rights to be considered during the HRDD process should include, at a minimum, those rights enumerated in the

[6] See Chapter 2.

[7] UN OHCHR (United Nations Office of the High Commissioner for Human Rights), 'Guiding Principles on Business and Human Rights: Implementing the United Nations 'Protect, Respect, and Remedy' Framework' (2011) Guiding Principle 15 (hereafter UNGPs).

International Bill of Human Rights (the Universal Declaration of Human Rights and the main instruments through which it has been codified; the International Covenant on Civil and Political Rights; and the International Covenant on Economic, Social and Cultural Rights) and the ILO Declaration on Fundamental Principles and Rights at Work.[8]

The 2016 calls by the international labour movement and NGOs for a binding instrument on HRDD at the ILO is just one manifestation of the 'irresistible rise'[9] of this concept in transnational labour governance over the past decade. At the global level, HRDD has now been integrated into the two major 'soft law' transnational instruments on corporate responsibility and workers' rights: the Organisation for Economic Co-operation and Development (OECD) Guidelines for Multinational Enterprises[10] and the ILO 'Tripartite Declaration of Principles Concerning Multinational Enterprises and Social Policy'.[11] It is found in the ILO's Protocol of 2014 to the Forced Labour Convention, 1930[12] and in the ILO's Violence and Harassment Convention, 2019 (No 190).[13] The concept has influenced the approaches of numerous multi-stakeholder initiatives (MSIs) that deal in whole or in part with labour issues.[14] As noted above, the international trade union movement has proven a strong supporter of the concept, joining many human rights organisations in calling for binding international instruments mandating HRDD not only at the ILO[15] but also at the United Nations.[16]

At the national level, HRDD is being embraced by civil society actors and others in a number of OECD countries. In recognition that voluntary approaches to HRDD have failed to deliver broad and meaningful change, an increasing number of countries are now adopting laws mandating due diligence with respect to certain labour rights, or at least reporting on such efforts. These types of laws now exist

8 ibid 17–24.

9 Holly Cullen, 'The Irresistible Rise of Human Rights Due Diligence: Conflict Minerals and Beyond' (2016) 48 George Washington International Law Review 743.

10 OECD, *OECD Guidelines for Multinational Enterprises* (OECD Publishing 2011).

11 ILO, *Tripartite Declaration of Principles Concerning Multinational Enterprises and Social Policy* (5th edn, ILO 2017).

12 Protocol of 2014 to the Forced Labour Convention, 1930 (103rd Session Geneva 11 June 2014 art 2(e). This Protocol supplements the Forced Labour Convention, 1930 (No 29) (opened for signatures 28 June 1930, entered into force 1 May 1932) 39 UNTS 55.

13 Violence and Harassment Convention, 2019 (No 190) (entered into force 25 June 2021) art 4(2), 9(a), 9(c).

14 See e.g. ETI (Ethical Trading Initiative), 'Human Rights Due Diligence Framework' (19 May 2016) <www.ethicaltrade.org/resources/human-rights-due-diligence-framework> accessed 28 September 2022; Shift, 'Implications of the UN Guiding Principles on Business and Human Rights for the Fair Labor Association' (2012) <https://shiftproject.org/resource/implications-of-the-guiding-principles-for-the-fair-labor-association> accessed 28 September 2022.

15 Sharan Burrow, 'Global Supply Chains: What Does Labour Want?' (*OpenDemocracy* 31 May 2016) <www.opendemocracy.net/en/beyond-trafficking-and-slavery/global-supply-chains-what-does-labour-want>> accessed 28 September 2022.

16 ITUC (International Trade Union Confederation), 'Global Unions Welcome Next Steps in Binding Treaty Process to End Corporate Impunity' (*Media Release* 11 December 2020) <www.ituc-csi.org/global-unions-welcome-treaty-next-step> accessed 28 September 2022.

in Australia, France, Germany, the Netherlands, Norway, the United Kingdom, and the United States. The introduction of mandatory human rights due diligence is being debated in other jurisdictions, and the European Union (EU) is in the process of adopting a Directive on the subject.[17] These trends are only likely to continue, with transnational activist networks strongly advocating for further legalisation of the concept.[18]

How has a concept—coined only a decade or so ago and that has its origins in human rights discourse and in corporate practice—emerged as such a dominant frame through which to conceptualise and operationalise business responsibility when it comes to workers' rights in global supply chains? How has the concept been able to garner such broad-based support among actors in the global North? And what does the rise of HRDD mean for transnational labour governance as a field of activism, policymaking, and scholarship? This book explores these questions through the adoption of a socio-legal and empirical lens. Proceeding from the observation that HRDD as presented in the UNGPs is open to multiple interpretations, it examines contests that have taken place globally over the role and meaning of the concept as it relates to workers' rights. It also explores how the embrace of a new frame and HRDD's subsequent legalisation has led to subtle but important shifts in configurations of actors and institutions in transnational labour governance.

In this introductory chapter, I provide an overview of this book. I explain how this study builds on existing critiques of HRDD by way of situating the concept within transnational labour governance and transnational labour law. I outline the theoretical framework and method used and conclude with an overview of the chapters.

I. Overview of This Book

This monograph examines HRDD as a tool of transnational labour law. It is argued that the fact that HRDD originated from, and is being shaped by, actors and institutions that do not fall within the traditional bailiwick of labour governance should not blind us to its growing significance. In effect, what is occurring is an extension of the scope of transnational labour market governance, not through what

[17] See Chapter 6.

[18] This book adopts Abbott and others' understanding of 'legalisation' as referring to a particular form of institutionalisation characterised by three components: obligation (the extent to which a rule binds actors), precision (the extent to which a rule unambiguously defines the conduct it requires, authorises, or proscribes), and delegation (the extent to which third parties have been granted authority to implement, interpret, and apply the rule). Legalisation can thus be understood as a continuum, ranging from 'hard' legalisation (where all three components are high), to multiple forms of 'soft' legalisation, through to the complete absence of legalisation. Kenneth W Abbott and others, 'The Concept of Legalization' (2000) 54 International Organization 401.

we would conventionally understand to constitute labour regulation. New actors are emerging, and the locus of interpretive authority in public labour governance is shifting. This book explains these developments and demonstrates why they should be of concern to transnational labour law.

The book begins by contextualising the arrival of HRDD within an already crowded and highly contested field. Drawing on critiques directed at the veneer of consensus surrounding the adoption of the UNGPs[19] and the ambiguity inherent in HRDD,[20] it is suggested that the concept of HRDD as articulated in the UNGPs enjoyed broad support in transnational labour governance because it was a concept capable of being interpreted and operationalised in very diverse ways. Christine Parker and John Howe have suggested that it was ambiguous because it was intended to be so.[21] In developing the concept, Professor John Ruggie, acting as United Nations Special Representative of the Secretary-General on the Issue of Human Rights and Transnational Corporations and Other Business Enterprises (SRSG), was acutely aware of the need to avoid generating a political stalemate akin to that which had led, only several years earlier, to the demise of the Draft UN Norms on the Responsibilities of Transnational Corporations and Other Business Enterprises with Regard to Human Rights (Draft Norms).[22] The SRSG's determination to enrol business in his project led to the development of a concept inspired by enterprise risk management practices and deeply sympathetic to the practicalities of business and to managerial orientations and values. At the same time, however, 'principled pragmatism'[23] and the need to maintain the support of other stakeholders, such as NGOs, led to the embedding within the UNGPs of vague terms and strategic ambiguities.

Drawing on documentary analysis and interviews, this study reveals that these ambiguities enabled the coexistence of significantly divergent understandings within transnational labour governance as to what HRDD required of business and states. Two distinct interpretations of the concept arose as a consequence of actors

[19] Surya Deva, 'Treating Human Rights Lightly: A Critique of the Consensus Rhetoric and the Language Employed by the Guiding Principles' in Surya Deva and David Bilchitz (eds), *Human Rights Obligations of Business: Beyond the Responsibility to Respect* (CUP 2012).

[20] Christine Parker and John Howe, 'Ruggie's Diplomatic Project and Its Missing Regulatory Infrastructure' in Radu Mares (ed), *The UN Guiding Principles on Business and Human Rights: Foundations and Implementation* (Martinus Nijhoff 2012). For discussion of ambiguity in international law more generally, see eg John Tobin, 'Seeking to Persuade: A Constructive Approach to Human Rights Treaty Interpretation' (2010) 23 Harvard Human Rights Journal 1; Christine Bell and Kathleen Cavanaugh, '"Constructive Ambiguity" or Internal Self-Determination? Self-Determination, Group Accommodation, and the Belfast Agreement' (1998) 22 Fordham International Law Journal 1345.

[21] Parker and Howe (n 20).

[22] UN Sub-Commission on the Promotion and Protection of Human Rights, 'Norms on the Responsibilities of Transnational Corporations and Other Business Enterprises with Regard to Human Rights' (26 August 2003) UN Doc E/CN.4/Sub.2/2003/12/Rev.2.

[23] John G Ruggie, *Just Business: Multinational Corporations and Human Rights* (WW Norton & Company 2013) xlii–xlvi.

in the field filtering the concept through divergent logics. Labour and human rights activists interpreted the concept through a logic emphasising rights; empowerment of workers and trade unions; and principles of transparency, participation, and accountability. Business actors interpreted the concept through a logic emphasising managerial discretion, corporate risk management, and internal control over corporate systems and processes. When mediated through these two irreconcilable logics, HRDD has taken on two very different forms. The former logic positioned HRDD as a corrective to many of the well-documented deficiencies of private transnational labour governance. The latter logic positioned the concept overwhelmingly as a managerial innovation and a practical tool through which to better organise and manage internal and external business risks.

Socio-legal and transnational governance scholars have long pointed out that ambiguity in international standards means that much of the 'action' in determining what constitutes compliance occurs after the standard has been adopted.[24] This book investigates contests that have taken place transnationally over what the concept of HRDD requires of businesses and states. Informed by understandings of transnational rulemaking as an iterative and recursive process,[25] it examines these contests at several different levels: the international, regional, and national. At the international level, HRDD has been contested at multiple sites, including at IGOs such as the ILO and the OECD. At the regional and national levels, these struggles are manifesting themselves in civil society campaigns for mandatory HRDD laws across Europe and in the Anglo-American world. This analysis reveals that there is little, to date, to suggest that HRDD is being legalised transnationally in a way that renders it a potent mechanism of transnational labour law. To the extent that the concept has been successfully elaborated upon internationally, public norm-making to date has been limited to the production of guidance that fails to articulate or in any way enforce any clear minimum standards of corporate conduct. At the national level, HRDD is being legalised in ways that narrow the concept, circumscribe its potential, and tend to legitimise rather than challenge existing corporate practices.

This book also explores implications of the concept's ascension for the configuration of actors and institutions in transnational labour governance. As socio-legal scholars remind us, the ascension of a new idea or frame can have far-reaching and unanticipated implications for the configuration of actors within a field and the goals, tactical repertoires, and discursive positions these various actors adopt.[26]

[24] Lauren B Edelman and Shauhin A Talesh, 'To Comply or Not to Comply - That Isn't the Question: How Organizations Construct the Meaning of Compliance' in Christine Parker and Vibeke Lehmann Nielsen (eds), *Explaining Compliance: Business Responses to Regulation* (Edward Elgar 2011); Terence C Halliday, 'Recursivity of Global Normmaking: A Sociolegal Agenda' (2009) 5 Annual Review of Law and Society 263.

[25] Halliday (n 24).

[26] See eg Sally Engle Merry, *Human Rights and Gender Violence: Translating International Law into Local Justice* (Chicago UP 2006); Margaret Keck and Kathryn Sikkink, *Activists beyond Borders: Advocacy Networks in International Politics* (Cornell University Press 1998).

Reframing may also 'redefine the political space and channel activism in subtle but consequential ways'.[27] Such dynamics are not unfamiliar to international labour law, with scholars pointing to the transformative impact on the field of the adoption of 'core labour standards'[28] and human rights discourse to promote and protect workers' rights.[29] HRDD's reframing of questions around corporate accountability and labour rights in terms of due diligence and risk management, along with its legalisation, is impacting transnational labour governance as a field of law, activism, and scholarship in significant but largely underappreciated ways. By privileging technical and professional expertise, HRDD is facilitating the expansion in the field of for-profit actors. Professional management consultancies, risk advisory services, and law firms are rapidly expanding and diversifying their services in this area, in response to growing corporate demand for due diligence-related services and products. National courts are being positioned to play a greater role in determining the nature and scope of corporate responsibility with respect to workers' rights transnationally. The OECD is consolidating its role as the pre-eminent IGO in the area of corporate accountability and labour rights at the expense of the ILO. This study explains these developments and explores their implications.

There is little to suggest that the considerable momentum towards legalisation of HRDD at international, regional, and national levels will abate in the near future. For this reason, the message this book seeks to convey is largely a cautionary one. It does not advance the argument that HRDD is necessarily unhelpful or that it should be forsaken as a tool of transnational labour law. But it does raise concerns to the effect that HRDD is largely being legalised in ways that lend a technical and apolitical veneer to questions around corporate accountability and labour rights. The rise of the concept also appears to be reinforcing, rather than challenging, extant private labour governance approaches that have long been viewed as inadequate by labour activists and scholars. This is despite the fact that the concept's diffusion has been welcomed—indeed, in part, driven—by actors who believe it will broaden and more deeply embed respect for workers' rights within internal corporate processes and legal frameworks.

This book is thus a call for scholars and activists to be attentive to the hazards as well as the promise of the concept's increasing prominence. It would be unwise to presume that stronger legalisation of HRDD per se will necessarily strengthen transnational labour governance. This book calls for a greater attentiveness to the

[27] Tim Bartley, 'How Foundations Shape Social Movements: The Construction of an Organizational Field and the Rise of Forest Certification' (2007) 54(3) Social Problems 229, 234.

[28] See eg Phillip Alston, '"Core Labour Standards" and the Transformation of the International Labour Rights Regime' (2004) 15 European Journal of International Law 457; Anke Hassel, 'The Evolution of a Global Labor Governance Regime' (2008) 21 Governance 231.

[29] See eg Judy Fudge, 'The New Discourse of Labor Rights: From Social to Fundamental Rights?' (2007) 29 Comparative Labor Law & Policy Journal 29; Kevin Kolben, 'Labor Rights as Human Rights?' (2010) 50 Virginia Journal of International Law 449; Colin Fenwick and Tonia Novitz (eds), *Human Rights at Work: Perspectives on Law and Regulation* (Hart Publishing 2010).

design of HRDD regulatory interventions so as to ensure they are crafted in a way that broadens, rather than narrows, spaces for workers and labour and human rights activists to challenge and seek to reshape state and corporate approaches to regulating working conditions in global supply chains. The final substantive chapter of this book begins the task of considering how this could be done.

II. What Does It Mean to Consider HRDD as Transnational Labour Law?

Despite longstanding and extensive engagement by transnational labour law scholars with the question of how to regulate transnational supply chains to improve respect for labour rights, scholarship that examines HRDD from a labour perspective remains limited. What exists has largely been tentative in nature[30] or has been concerned with assessing the adequacy of the UNGPs more broadly as a normative framework through which to prevent and remedy unjust working conditions currently prevailing in global supply chains.[31] This is not to say, however, that the concept of HRDD has gone without academic scrutiny. Indeed, while literature on HRDD is relatively new, it is already substantial. It consists of a diverse range of primary materials and scholarship from various disciplines, including human rights law,[32] business ethics,[33] transnational governance,[34] and business regulation and compliance.[35] Much of this literature is drawn upon to help build the arguments in this book, in particular, scholarship that has questioned the

[30] Anne Trebilcock, 'Due Diligence on Labour Issues: Opportunities and Limits of the UN Guiding Principles on Business and Human Rights' in Adelle Blackett and Anne Trebilcock (eds), *Research Handbook on Transnational Labour Law* (Edward Elgar 2015); Ingrid Landau, 'Game Changer? Human Rights Due Diligence and Corporate Respect for Workers' Rights in a Global Economy' in John Howe, Anna Chapman, and Ingrid Landau (eds), *The Evolving Project of Labour Law* (Federation Press 2017); Nicolas Bueno, 'Multinational Enterprises and Labour Rights: Concepts and Implementation' in Janice R Bellace and Beryl ter Haar (eds), *Research Handbook on Labour, Business and Human Rights* (Edward Elgar 2019).

[31] Yossi Dahan, Hannah Lerner, and Faina Milman-Sivan, 'The Guiding Principles for Business and Human Rights: Labour Violations and Shared Responsibility' (2016) 34 International Journal of Comparative Labour Law and Industrial Relations 425; Rashmi Venkatesan, 'The UN Framework on Business and Human Rights: A Workers' Rights Critique' (2019) 157 Journal of Business Ethics 635.

[32] See eg Deva and Bilchitz (n 19); Robert McCorquodale and Justine Nolan, 'The Effectiveness of Human Rights Due Diligence for Preventing Business Human Rights Abuses' (2021) 68 Netherlands International Law Review 455; Gabriela Quijano and Carlos Lopez, 'Rise of Mandatory Human Rights Due Diligence: A Beacon of Hope or a Double-Edged Sword?' (2021) 6 Business and Human Rights Journal 241.

[33] Björn Fasterling and Geert Demuijnck, 'Human Rights in the Void? Due Diligence in the UN Guiding Principles on Business and Human Rights' (2013) 116 Journal of Business Ethics 799.

[34] Mark Taylor, 'The Ruggie Framework: Polycentric Regulation and the Implications for Corporate Social Responsibility' (2011) 5 Nordic Journal of Applied Ethics 9; Karin Buhmann, 'Public Regulators and CSR: The "Social Licence to Operate" in Recent United Nations Instruments on Business and Human Rights and the Juridification of CSR' (2016) 136 Journal of Business Ethics 699.

[35] See eg Mares (n 20); Ingrid Landau, 'Human Rights Due Diligence and the Risk of Cosmetic Compliance' (2019) 20 Melbourne Journal of International Law 221.

façade of consensus masking the UNGPs,[36] HRDD's marriage of human rights and risk management discourse,[37] and the absence of appropriate regulatory architectures.[38] However, the overriding aim of this study is not to conceptually or empirically critique HRDD but to understand the implications of its emergence as an instrument of transnational labour law. In order to achieve this objective, this book locates HRDD in *transnational labour governance* and examines the promises and perils of the concept through a *transnational labour law* lens. Each of these concepts is explained briefly below.

A. Transnational Labour Governance

Transnational labour governance is conceptualised throughout this book as both a regulatory regime and a field. As a regulatory regime, the term refers to the assemblage of 'actors, institutions, norms and rules that are of importance for the process and the outcome' of regulating working conditions in global supply chains.[39] As in many other areas of transnational governance, recent decades have seen a shift away from seeing regulation as state-centric and towards seeing regulatory spaces as more fragmented and polycentric.[40] A plethora of public, private, and hybrid standards and initiatives have emerged in recent decades to address governance challenges arising from the globalisation of production. Transnational labour governance as a regulatory regime encompasses public governance, understood as regulatory activities implicitly associated with the state. It also includes private governance, understood as various structures of oversight 'in which non-state actors—whether for-profit companies, NGOs, or a mix of the two—adopt and to some degree enforce rules for other organisations, such as their suppliers or clients'.[41] There is now a rich interdisciplinary literature on the evolution and dynamics of the emergent transnational labour governance regime. It encompasses, but is significantly broader than, traditional labour law institutions and actors at the workplace, sectoral, national, and international level. It is 'transnational' in that it comprises actors, networks, and initiatives that span national boundaries but are not global in the sense of encompassing the whole world. The term 'governance' recognises the polycentric nature of the regulatory regime and the existence of

[36] See Chapter 2.
[37] See Chapter 3.
[38] See Chapters 3 and 8.
[39] This definition of a 'regime' is drawn from Burkard Eberlein and Edgar Grande, 'Beyond Delegation: Transnational Regulatory Regimes and the EU Regulatory State' (2005) 12 Journal of European Public Policy 89, 91.
[40] Mathias Koenig-Archibugi, 'Global Regulation' in Robert Baldwin, Martin Cave, and Martin Lodge (eds), *The Oxford Handbook of Regulation* (OUP 2010); Peter Drahos, 'Regulatory Globalisation' in Peter Drahos (ed), *Regulatory Theory: Foundations and Applications* (ANU Press 2017).
[41] Tim Bartley, *Rules without Rights: Land, Labor and Private Authority in the Global Economy* (OUP 2018) 7.

public and private arrangements and of 'hard' and 'soft' forms of regulation. States and intergovernmental organisations remain important actors in labour governance but have been joined by many others—multinational enterprises, industry organisations, NGOs, and various professions—with a stake in the form or outcome of a regulatory standard or arrangement.[42] These actors perform a range of regulatory tasks, from the construction of transnational norms to norm interpretation, dissemination, monitoring, implementation, and enforcement. Actors may perform these tasks unilaterally, but they may also work together in private-sector, civil society, multi-stakeholder, or hybrid public–private regulatory arrangements. The various initiatives interact with each other and with public actors and regulatory arrangements at various levels and in diverse and complex ways.[43]

As a field, transnational labour governance comprises a semi-autonomous and socially constructed space or 'arena that brings a number of different actors (often with different interests, ideologies, and organisational forms) into routine contact with one another, under a common frame of reference, in pursuit of an at least partially shared project'.[44] The field is concerned with the regulation of work in the transnational sphere[45] and overlaps (conceptually and in practice) with other semi-autonomous fields, such as business and human rights. While 'loosely networked', the field 'consists of several centres of activity that monitor each other',[46] with these centres being geographic (mainly North America and Western Europe) and institutional. The field is populated by many actors, including inter-governmental organisations (IGOs), nation-states, businesses and business representative organisations, NGOs, trade unions and for-profit private actors offering services such as management advisory services, legal advice, and social auditing. Though connected by common networks and sharing 'field frames',[47] the actors in this field have diverse interests, discourses, values, and beliefs and establish and take part in institutions that take varied forms and perform various regulatory functions.[48] Actors also have varying degrees of authority, legitimacy, and regulatory capacities.[49] Finally, conceiving of transnational labour governance as a 'field' hints at the existence of a space in which there is a great deal of cooperation and competition.[50]

42 Marie-Laure Djelic and Kerstin Sahlin-Andersson, 'Reordering the World: Transnational Regulatory Governance and Its Challenges' in David Levi-Faur (ed), *The Oxford Handbook of Governance* (OUP 2012).

43 Burkard Eberlein and others, 'Transnational Business Governance Interactions: Conceptualization and Framework for Analysis' (2014) 8 Regulation & Governance 1.

44 Bartley, 'How Foundations Shape Social Movements' (n 27) 233.

45 Bob Hepple, *Labour Laws and Global Trade* (Hart Publishing 2005) 3.

46 Bartley, 'How Foundations Shape Social Movements' (n 27) 232.

47 ibid 233.

48 Eberlein and others (n 43).

49 Djelic and Sahlin-Andersson (n 42) 745.

50 Yves Dezalay and Bryant G Garth, 'Legitimating the New Legal Orthodoxy' in Yves Dezalay and Bryant G Garth (eds), *Global Prescriptions: The Production, Exportation and Importation of a New Legal Orthodoxy* (University of Michigan Press 2002) 309.

As Yves Dezalay and Bryant Garth have observed, international fields are generally not occupied by actors 'happily coexisting together in [an] effort to produce new and emancipatory global norms' but by various actors engaged in struggle over the power to shape emergent rules and practices.[51]

B. Transnational Labour Law

Whereas defining the term 'transnational labour governance' is necessary to clarify the scope and focus of this book, defining transnational labour law is necessary to explain its perspective and normative orientation. As a field of scholarship and activism, transnational labour law has a unique set of concerns and approaches influenced by its origins in national labour movements and labour law scholarship.[52] These features, which distinguish the field from the overlapping but distinct field of human rights, are explored briefly below.

Labour law recognises the core importance of work to human dignity. Although people enter the market system in their capacity as factors of production, labour is not a commodity to be bought and sold in response to supply and demand. Labour law has long intervened to 'mediate' labour's participation in the market and to 'infuse' it with a dignity that the market alone cannot provide.[53] As Adelle Blackett explains,

> While there is a clear logic to dealing with a range of social responsibility considerations together ... labor is simply different because of the relational dimensions of the workplace and the risk of enlarging the scope of management power in a relationship of subordination.[54]

A key objective of labour law is to be a countervailing force to the inequality of bargaining power inherent in the employment relationship.[55] This inequality has traditionally been conceived of in terms of an employee's subordination to his or her direct employer within the context of a vertically integrated firm. As Adelle Blackett and Anne Trebilcock note, globalisation has challenged, if not undermined, the compact that was struck in the post-war period. Political and economic developments have complicated the task of responding, conceptually and

[51] ibid 318.

[52] Adelle Blackett and Anne Trebilcock, 'Conceptualizing Transnational Labour Law' in Blackett and Trebilcock, *Research Handbook on Transnational Labour Law* (n 30) 3.

[53] Adelle Blackett, 'Global Governance, Legal Pluralism and the Decentered State: A Labor Law Critique of Codes of Corporate Conduct' (2001) 8 Indiana Journal of Global Legal Studies 401, 418.

[54] ibid 445.

[55] Otto Kahn-Freund, *Labour and the Law* (3rd edn, Stevens 1972) 18. For a discussion of the enduring principle at the transnational level, see Blackett and Trebilcock, 'Conceptualizing Transnational Labour Law' (n 52) 12.

in practice, to the asymmetries of power that exist between workers and those who benefit from their labour. These developments have not, however, challenged or rendered obsolete labour law's concern with redefining and rebalancing these relationships, 'however diffuse both the legal order and the owners of capital have become'.[56] The underpinning values of labour law have largely remained intact.[57]

Transnational labour law shares labour law's enduring commitment to the objectives of worker protection, worker agency, and social justice.[58] Worker protection is seen as necessary to prevent working people from suffering unfair and unjust treatment at the hands of those who engage their labour and the various detrimental social and economic outcomes arising from liberal labour markets.[59] It includes both protective rights (those affording statutory protection to individual workers) and facilitative rights (those allowing or encouraging unionisation and the collective negotiation of workers' terms and conditions).[60] Historically, these rights have taken the form of statutory guarantees backed by the coercive power of the state. However, recent decades have also seen the worker protective function—in the form of both setting standards and securing compliance—being undertaken (albeit in a limited and patchy fashion) by an increasingly diverse set of actors and regulatory mechanisms.[61]

Traditionally in labour law, worker agency has been conceptualised in terms of industrial democracy, with workers being active architects rather than passive beneficiaries of workplace norms and their application.[62] Along with the recognition of the unequal power relationship between the individual worker and their employer, it is this concern with worker agency that has motivated labour law's enduring focus on the fundamental rights to freedom of association and to collective bargaining. In more recent years, rising concern with employer non-compliance with minimum labour standards has also led to a broader understanding of worker agency and voice. As Tess Hardy points out, for many non-unionised or vulnerable workers, 'voice may be less about improving or influencing conditions at the workplace, and more about simply ensuring that the existing standards are respected and upheld'.[63] In this way, worker agency in transnational labour law extends to

[56] Blackett and Trebilcock, 'Conceptualizing Transnational Labour Law' (n 52) 13.

[57] ibid 7.

[58] ibid 12. It should be noted that the goals of labour law are by no means uncontested: indeed, there is a rich scholarly debate on the idea or goals of labour law. See eg Guy Davidov, *The Idea of Labour Law* (OUP 2016); Ruth Dukes, *The Labour Constitution: The Enduring Idea of Labour Law* (OUP 2014).

[59] Kolben (n 29) 469.

[60] ibid 470.

[61] See Chapter 2.

[62] Harry W Arthurs, 'Corporate Self-Regulation: Political Economy, State Regulation and Reflexive Labour Law' in Cynthia Estlund and Brian Bercusson (eds), *Regulating Labour in the Wake of Globalisation* (Hart Publishing 2007) 19.

[63] Tess Hardy, '"It's Oh So Quiet?" Employee Voice and the Enforcement of Employment Standards in Australia' in Alan Bogg and Tonia Novitz (eds), *Voices at Work: Continuity and Change in the Common Law World* (OUP 2014).

comprise voice in relation to the monitoring and enforcement of compliance with minimum employment standards.

Transnational labour law also shares labour law's concern with social justice and, most specifically, with distributive justice to ensure that workers gain a fair distribution of resources in the context of the individual working relationship and broader economic arrangements.[64] Again, this is reflected in the importance afforded to freedom of association and collective bargaining rights, which are recognised as critical to enabling workers to engage on more equal terms with those who benefit from their labour. For many scholars, these emphases on matters of redistribution and economic justice render labour law as a field of scholarship and activism distinct from human rights.[65] As David Kennedy has argued, human rights may, indeed, function more to legitimise than to challenge prevailing patterns of redistribution.[66]

Labour law also brings distinct approaches or modes of operation. These include an emphasis on *collectivism* over individualism, on *process* rights over outcome standards, and on *negotiation and bargaining* over law.[67] In contrast to what is often described as the individualism of human rights, the labour movement regards 'the collective as the means of individual emancipation'.[68] It is this ethos that leads to a positioning of freedom of association and collective bargaining rights as the 'linchpin'[69] of labour rights. Labour law (and transnational labour law) places a strong emphasis on rights that facilitate a *process* of organising and collective negotiation of working conditions.[70] These types of rights are seen as just as important, if not more so, than rights to specific employment conditions in areas such as health and safety, working hours, and minimum wages (often termed 'outcome rights').'[71] Finally, labour law values *collective negotiation* and bargaining with employers with a view to workers together negotiating to achieve specifically desired economic and non-economic outcomes.[72] Law—in the form of statute and adjudication—is important (increasingly so) but remains a second-best solution, compensating for weaknesses in bargaining power.[73] This logic has carried into the transnational

[64] On distributional justice in labour law, see Guy Davidov, 'Distributive Justice and Labour Law' in Hugh Collins, Gillian Lester, and Virginia Mantouvalou (eds), *Philosophical Foundations of Labour Law* (OUP 2018). In the context of global supply chains, this concern with distributive justice is manifest, for example, in the goal of a living wage. See eg Shelley Marshall, *Living Wage: Regulatory Solutions to Informal and Precarious Work in Global Supply Chains* (OUP 2019).

[65] See eg Kolben (n 29).

[66] David Kennedy, 'The International Human Rights Movement: Part of the Problem?' (2001) 3 European Human Rights Law Review 245, 261.

[67] Kolben (n 29); Guy Mundlak, 'Human Rights and Labor Rights: Why Don't the Two Tracks Meet?' (2012) 34 Comparative Labour Law and Policy Journal 217.

[68] Kolben (n 29) 471.

[69] ibid. See also Blackett and Trebilcock, 'Conceptualizing Transnational Labour Law' (n 52) 13–16.

[70] Mark Anner, 'Corporate Social Responsibility and Freedom of Association Rights: The Precarious Quest for Legitimacy and Control in Global Supply Chains' (2012) 40 Politics & Society 609.

[71] Kolben (n 29) 471–72.

[72] Mundlak (n 67).

[73] ibid 229.

sphere, with collective representation remaining transnational labour law's 'core method'.[74] Again, the focus on negotiated solutions is seen as an important distinction between labour and human rights as fields of scholarship and activism, with human rights often seen as placing a greater emphasis on the protection of individual rights by way of litigation, lobbying, and social awareness.[75]

It is important to acknowledge that the conceptual and methodological distinctions between labour and human rights as fields of law, scholarship, and activism identified above have eroded to a significant extent in recent years.[76] The two fields no longer run on 'parallel tracks'.[77] For example, labour scholars and movements have increasingly embraced human rights discourse and advocacy strategies to protect rights and advance interests.[78] Nonetheless, as Blackett and Trebilcock emphasise, transnational labour law retains a distinctive set of concerns and methods.[79]

To date, transnational labour law's perspective, normative concerns, and approaches have been brought to bear on many aspects of transnational governance. This includes on the use of specific frames and language to promote workers' rights and on specific regulatory mechanisms and initiatives. This book builds on this body of work by applying a transnational labour law lens to HRDD. It also seeks to contribute to the discipline through its empirical investigation of a stage in the regulatory process that tends to be overlooked in transnational labour law scholarship: how an international labour norm, subsequent to its adoption, is shaped, translated, and contested; by whom; and with what implications.

III. Approach and Method

In examining the rise of HRDD in transnational labour governance, this study adopts a socio-legal and empirical approach. Socio-legal scholarship seeks to go beyond a traditional doctrinal approach to consider the context in which legal texts are formed and are 'used, abused, avoided and so on'.[80] For socio-legal scholars working in international law, 'texts' are broadly defined: encompassing hard and soft forms of law, conventions and best practices, model laws or legislative guides,

74 Blackett and Trebilcock, 'Conceptualizing Transnational Labour Law' (n 52) 8.
75 Mundlak (n 67).
76 Kolben (n 29) 450.
77 Virginia Leary, 'The Paradox of Workers' Rights as Human Rights' in Lance Compa and Stephen Diamond (eds), *Human Rights, Labor Rights and International Trade* (University of Pennsylvania Press 2003) 22.
78 Kolben (n 29).
79 Blackett and Trebilcock, 'Conceptualizing Transnational Labour Law' (n 52) 3.
80 Amanda Perry-Kessaris, 'What Does It Mean to Take a Socio-Legal Approach to International Economic Law?' in Amanda Perry-Kessaris (ed), *Socio-Legal Approaches to International Economic Law: Text, Context, Subtext* (Routledge 2013) 6.

and prescriptive and diagnostic standards.[81] Consideration of the context involves recognising the politics of a text and confronting 'who crafts the text, what form it takes, and how it is carried into global and national arenas of economic activity'.[82] Socio-legal scholarship is inescapably interdisciplinary, drawing on analytical concepts and methods from the social sciences.[83] This study draws on theories and insights from sociology, international law and politics, and regulation and compliance. As explained below, it also employs empirical methods used widely in the social sciences. This book draws specifically on two overlapping strands of socio-legal scholarship. The first focuses on how norms are formed and contested in transnational governance. The second theorises how compliance with ambiguous norms is constructed and by whom.

Applying a socio-legal perspective to HRDD's arrival in global governance is helpful as it reveals the politically contested, iterative, and endogenous nature of transnational lawmaking. Global norm-making is seen as an 'exercise of power, a struggle among competing actors in global arenas'.[84] This political dimension of global norm-making permeates the norm-making process: how a norm is framed, in which arenas or fora norm-making occurs, which actors are included or excluded from the norm-making exercises,[85] and why some regulatory approaches and possibilities are settled upon while others are foreclosed.[86] The increasingly technocratic nature of global norm-making—in the form of technical and managerial language or the use of numerical indicators—may obfuscate, but does not remove, the political dimension.[87] Scholars have drawn attention to the fact that competition and contestation in the transnational domain involves not just actors that overtly participate in political processes such as states, business, and civil society. Transnational norm-making also involves competition between and within groups of experts with competing normative and regulatory agendas and values.[88] These contests may arise between actors with 'different expertises and know-how' and occur in relation to not only the form of the rules but also the particular type of expertise the rules require and the value of that particular currency in relation to other competitors in the field.[89]

[81] Terence C Halliday and Susan Block-Lieb, 'Global Duelists: The Recursive Politics of the Text in International Trade Law' in Perry-Kessaris, *Socio-Legal Approaches to International Economic Law* (n 80) 77.

[82] ibid 78.

[83] Perry-Kessaris, 'What Does It Mean to Take a Socio-Legal Approach to International Economic Law?' (n 80) 10–15.

[84] Halliday (n 24) 268–69.

[85] ibid.

[86] Tim Bartley, 'Certifying Forests and Factories: States, Social Movements, and the Rise of Private Regulation in the Apparel and Forest Products Fields' (2003) 31 Politics & Society 433.

[87] Tim Büthe and Walter Mattli, *The New Global Rulers: The Privatization of Regulation in the World Economy* (Princeton UP 2011) 12.

[88] Yves Dezalay and Bryant G Garth, 'Introduction: Constructing Transnational Justice' in Yves Dezalay and Bryant G Garth (eds), *Lawyers and the Construction of Transnational Justice* (Routledge 2012) 13.

[89] Dezalay and Garth, 'Legitimating the New Orthodoxy' (n 50) 307–8, 381.

Socio-legal perspectives on global norm-making emphasise the iterative nature of the process. As transnational legal theorist Terence Halliday explains, theoretical and empirical accounts of the emergence of global norms in a range of areas demonstrate that 'global norms do not spring into fully formed global regulatory regimes. Norms evolve dynamically, through iterations among transnational state and non-state organisations, between global and national actors.'[90] There may be years of judicial and/or quasi-judicial clarification between the time a new concept is introduced into global or national governance and the time it settles. Indeed, where a norm exhibits certain features, it may not settle at all.[91] Over time, global norms may change in form (eg from soft to hard forms of law or vice versa), may be embraced by various actors (eg they may begin as forms of industry self-regulation but later be adopted by states),[92] and are shaped by cycles of lawmaking at different levels.[93]

Finally, socio-legal scholarship recognises the endogenous nature of law. Law is not exogenous to those organisations it seeks to influence: it is not formulated and defined outside of organisations and prior to reaching organisational domains.[94] Rather, at national and international levels, business actors play influential roles in shaping the rules that are designed to regulate them. This influence is exerted not only in contests leading up to the formal adoption of a law but also, subsequently, as private actors construct and influence the meaning of compliance with rules or norms with which they are expected to comply. These later processes of norm renegotiation are rendered more likely where the original norm exhibited certain features. These include where it has used vague and ambiguous language, where it shifts responsibility for interpreting what compliance means to the regulated entity, where it is politically contested, and where it is accompanied by weak enforcement mechanisms.[95]

Subsequent scholarship has expanded legal endogeneity theory in two important ways. While the theory originally developed in the domestic context,[96] these theories have been applied to analyse transnational legal processes.[97] In addition, socio-legal scholars have shown that it is not just regulated actors that

[90] Halliday (n 24) 274.

[91] Halliday and Block-Lieb (n 81) 82.

[92] John Braithwaite and Peter Drahos, *Global Business Regulation* (CUP 2000) 481.

[93] ibid.

[94] Edelman and Talesh (n 24) 103. See also Sharon Gilad, 'Beyond Endogeneity: How Firms and Regulators Co-Construct the Meaning of Regulation' (2014) 36 Law & Policy 134.

[95] Lauren B Edelman, 'Legal Ambiguity and Symbolic Structures; Organizational Mediation of Civil Rights Law' (1992) 97 American Journal of Sociology 1531; Lauren B Edelman, *Working Law: Courts, Corporations and Symbolic Civil Rights* (Chicago UP 2016); Sharon Gilad, 'It Runs in the Family: Meta-Regulation and Its Siblings' (2010) 4 Regulation & Governance 485.

[96] The theory has been applied in a range of legal areas, including civil rights, consumer-rights, and insurance: see Edelman and Talesh (n 24).

[97] Terence C Halliday and Bruce G Carruthers, 'The Recursivity of Law: Global Norm Making and National Lawmaking in the Globalization of Corporate Insolvency Regimes' (2007) 112 American Journal of Sociology 1135, 1144–45.

shape the meaning of compliance with specific norms. Intermediaries—such as lawyers, auditors, and other business practitioners—may also be involved in co-constructing and mediating understandings of compliance.[98] Transnationally, these actors mediate between global and local through translating, advising, and implementing on international norms in domestic settings.[99] The roles played by these mediating actors are often not neutral. Rather, they may extract a price in the process of mediating norms from the global to the national or local levels.[100]

This study has employed a mixed-method research design, involving multi-sited fieldwork and analysis of primary and secondary sources. Multi-sited fieldwork entails field-intensive study using a range of qualitative methods such as participant observation, interviewing, field note-taking, archival and document analysis, and sustained interactions with participants.[101] While this type of fieldwork is most often associated with the discipline of anthropology, it has been adapted successfully by regulatory scholars to gain in-depth understanding of the complex transnational dimensions of governance arrangements in areas as wide-ranging as global environmental politics,[102] international sport,[103] and international mining standards.[104] It is an approach that has proven particularly fruitful in understanding the emergence and development of new regulatory regimes that do not have clear boundaries or map neatly on to global, national, or local levels.[105] It is also useful because it enables researchers to engage with different perspectives, spaces, and actors[106] and to make sense of 'how pluralistic orders come together and diverge'.[107] Multi-sited fieldwork encourages researchers to be sensitive to the fact that regulatory pluralism does not always lead to convergence: multiple meanings and approaches may emerge at multiple sites.[108]

The primary sources of data for this project have been publicly available documents and semi-structured interviews. Archival material relating to the mandate

[98] Lauren B Edelman, Steven E Abraham, and Howard S Erlanger, 'Professional Construction of Law: The Inflated Threat of Wrongful Discharge' (1992) 26 Law & Society Review 47; Shauhin Talesh, 'Rule-Intermediaries in Action: How State and Business Stakeholders Influence the Meaning of Consumer Rights in Regulatory Governance Arrangements' (2015) 37 Law & Policy 1.

[99] Kenneth W Abbott, David Levi-Faur, and Duncan Snidal, 'Theorizing Regulatory Intermediaries: The RIT Model' (2017) 670 Annals of the American Academy of Political and Social Sciences 14; Merry (n 26).

[100] Halliday (n 24) 286.

[101] Kathryn Henne, 'Multi-Sited Fieldwork in Regulatory Studies' in Drahos, *Regulatory Theory* (n 40).

[102] Christian Downie, *The Politics of Climate Change Negotiations: Strategies and Variables in Prolonged International Negotiations* (Edward Elgar 2014).

[103] Kathryn Henne, *Testing for Athletic Citizenship: Regulating Doping and Sex in Sport* (Rutgers International Press 2015).

[104] Hevina S Dashwood, *The Rise of Global Corporate Social Responsibility: Mining and the Spread of Global Norms* (CUP 2012).

[105] Henne, 'Multi-Sited Fieldwork' (n 101) 104.

[106] ibid 108.

[107] ibid 111.

[108] ibid 106–07.

of the former SRSG was examined to generate a historical account of the development of the concept. Documentary sources included submissions to international consultation processes and policy and advocacy material produced by interviewees' organisations during the period 2011 to 2022. These were supplemented by the author's participation in, and/or public records of, the UN Annual Forum on Business and Human Rights and the OECD Forum on Responsible Business Conduct in the years 2015–2018 (inclusive) and the ILO's International Labour Conference in 2016.

Documentary analysis was supplemented by thirty-two semi-structured interviews conducted between June 2015 and April 2017. Interviews were conducted in person at five international sites: Geneva, Paris, London, Washington, and New York.[109] These sites were selected because the most prominent actors engaged in interpreting the concept are based in these cities.[110] These sites also covered the three jurisdictions (France, the United Kingdom, and the United States) in which most progress towards legalisation of HRDD at the national level had occurred at that time. Interviews were conducted with five categories of participants: business or business representative organisations, trade unions and NGOs, IGOs, governments, and intermediaries (such as advisors and consultants). Interviewees were identified using a combination of purposive, niche, and snowball and stratified sampling methods.[111] Interviews lasted between thirty minutes and two hours, and all were conducted by the author.

Interviewees were asked to explain what they understood HRDD to entail and its purpose. Interview questions also covered the four stages of HRDD and the perceived role of various actors (including external stakeholders and the state) with respect to the process. Substantially similar questions were posed to all actors to explore areas of consensus and contestation. However, interviewees were encouraged to present their views in their own terms, and effort was made to follow the interviewee's emphasis as to what developments were important and for what reasons. All interviews except one were digitally recorded and transcribed with the consent of the research subjects.[112] Interviews were anonymised and each interview allocated an identifier according to a basic classification scheme. Transcripts were coded thematically using Nvivo qualitative data analysis software.

It is important to acknowledge the limitations to the focus and methods of this study. This book has sought to investigate how HRDD has been understood, contested, and institutionalised in transnational labour governance and to explore the implications of the concept's ascension for the field. The questions posed and

[109] Two interviews were done by Skype as the interviewees were unable to meet in person.
[110] As Terence Halliday has observed, global norms are, somewhat paradoxically, often crafted by a very small number of actors: Halliday (n 24) 286.
[111] John David Lofland, 'Analytic Ethnography: Features, Failings, and Futures' (1995) 24 Journal of Contemporary Ethnography 30.
[112] One interviewee declined to be recorded so written notes were taken during the interview.

answered in this book do not go directly to whether HRDD as an approach is empirically capable of furthering the protection and promotion of workers' rights in a global economy. Nor does it explore in detail how specific regulatory frameworks can best be designed and/or improved to incentivise effective HRDD. While these are critical questions, they are beyond the scope of this book.

While this study examines contests underway with respect to HRDD as a contested transnational norm, it has been impossible, within the scope of the project, to examine all institutions and actors in the relevant regulatory regime. Choices have had to be made. Effort was taken to interview highly influential actors within transnational labour governance and to select public sites of international law-making (the OECD and the ILO) that, despite the increasing presence of private actors, continue to play a significant role in norm diffusion and elaboration in transnational governance.[113] A decision was taken early on not to focus on norm elaboration processes at the UN by way of ongoing negotiations for a business and human rights treaty on the basis that these negotiations were likely to be protracted and to deal with HRDD in only general terms.[114] In Chapter 7, I identify other actors whose influence on HRDD as an emerging transnational norm merits further empirical examination.

It is also important to note that while multi-sited fieldwork is well suited to studying transnational governance dynamics, there are risks associated with the method. These include an insufficient depth of information and insight being obtained due to the multiplicity of sites under examination or that connections between sites and actors may be presumed.[115] Efforts taken to minimise these risks included supplementing interviews and fieldwork with extensive document collection and analysis of primary and secondary material. Ongoing feedback from actors within the field as to the conclusions drawn was also solicited by way of informal communications, as well as formal presentations at international workshops and academic conferences.

IV. Chapter Overview

This book is organised into nine chapters. Following this introductory chapter, Chapters 2 and 3 provide historical and conceptual background. To understand the actual and potential impact of HRDD on transnational labour governance, it is necessary to have a sense of the regulatory landscape in which it has been embedded.

[113] Michael N Barnett and Martha Finnemore, 'The Politics, Power, and Pathologies of International Organizations' (1999) 53 International Organization 699, 713–15.

[114] Justine Nolan has described waiting for a comprehensive treaty holding corporations to account for human rights abuses as akin to waiting for Godot: Justine Nolan, 'The Corporate Responsibility to Respect Human Rights: Soft Law or Not Law?' in Deva and Bilchitz (n 19) 143.

[115] Henne, 'Multi-Sited Fieldwork' (n 101) 97.

Chapter 2 begins by sketching the broad contours of transnational labour governance prior to the mandate of the SRSG. This landscape was a complex and crowded one, in which a bewildering array of public, private, and hybrid regulatory initiatives sought to regulate working conditions in global supply chains in various ways, including through the setting of minimum standards and the monitoring and/or certifying of compliance. It was also a fiercely contested landscape, in which different stakeholder groups diverged significantly in their views on the extent to which, and how, corporate actors should be held accountable for their commitments and the role of workers, trade unions, and other stakeholders in private labour governance initiatives. The chapter then traces the emergence of HRDD. The political nature of the SRSG's mandate and his determination to enrol business in the project led to the development of a concept that was deeply sympathetic to the practicalities of business and to business orientations and values. At the same time, however, his commitment to 'principled pragmatism' and the imperative of keeping other stakeholders (particularly civil society) on board led to the embedding within the UNGPs of strategic ambiguities. These ambiguities are found within HRDD itself and in the relationship between HRDD and the state. In effect, the UNGPs postponed, rather than resolved, genuine agreement until some future date and forum.[116]

Chapter 3 provides a conceptual analysis of HRDD. It is suggested that, to understand the nature of contests underway, it is necessary to unpack HRDD on three levels. At the level of the enterprise, it can be understood as *risk management*. It calls for business professionals to engage in a comfortingly familiar process of risk identification, assessment, prioritisation, and mitigation. Conceptualised in this way, HRDD is very much the domain of those well versed in the art of risk management, such as risk officers, lawyers, management consultancies, and global risk-advisory practices. Yet, HRDD is more than just a managerial innovation; it is also a regulatory one. Conceiving HRDD as *business regulation* reveals both the stakes involved in contests over its legalisation and the extent to which some regulatory possibilities have eventuated and others foreclosed. Seeing HRDD as business regulation also helps expose the overt and subtle processes through which understandings of the concept are being shaped. Finally, this study conceptualises HRDD as an emerging *transnational norm*. It is a norm that is being diffused at multiple levels (global, regional, and national) through multiple instruments and mechanisms and by multiple actors. This diffusion—and the norm's legalisation—is well underway but very incomplete.

Chapters 4–6 examine how the meaning of HRDD has been understood and contested subsequent to adoption of the UNGPs in 2011. Chapter 4 explores how HRDD was received by actors within the field of transnational labour

[116] Bell and Cavanaugh (n 20).

governance. Drawing on in-depth interviews and document analysis, I show that HRDD has played an important function in enabling a shared frame and language between diverse stakeholders. However, this shared language did not equate to shared understandings of the concept. Actors interpreted HRDD in divergent ways. I suggest that these divergences in interpretation arise largely from the fact that actors filtered the concept through divergent logics. I identify two basic stylised logics within transnational labour governance: a transnational labour logic and a managerial one. When mediated through these competing logics, HRDD takes on different characteristics and implications. While the former logic led to a robust interpretation of HRDD that challenges extant business models and approaches, the latter logic led to an interpretation that demands significantly less from companies and presents much less of a challenge to existing practices.

Chapter 5 examines how the contests between these two logics have played out at the international level. I focus on two prominent intergovernmental organisations in transnational labour governance: the OECD and the ILO. While not traditionally seen as a key player in transnational labour governance, the OECD has enthusiastically embraced HRDD as a means of promoting more responsible business governance when it comes to labour rights in global supply chains. It has revised its key instrument on corporate accountability, the OECD Guidelines for Multinational Enterprises, to encourage companies to adopt a 'risk-based due diligence' approach to all labour and human rights. The organisation has also vigorously pursued a 'Proactive Agenda' to promote and elaborate upon what HRDD entails with respect to labour rights. The OECD's working style and composition have enabled it to embrace HRDD in a way that the ILO has not been able to do due to its more cumbersome (and democratic) structure and methods. The OECD has also been successful in garnering broad support for its work, particularly among the global business community, largely by deferring to a managerial interpretation of due diligence and minimising the political nature of its standard-setting activities.

Engagement with HRDD by the second inter-governmental organisation examined in Chapter 5—the ILO—has been slower and more fraught. Certain constituents of the tripartite organisation, including the Workers' Group and some member states, have sought to use the ILO as a forum through which to secure a transnational-labour-oriented interpretation of HRDD. To date, however, these efforts have been met with strong opposition by the organisation's employer constituency. While the Employers' Group has not resisted the involvement of the ILO with HRDD per se, it has encouraged the organisation to focus on the responsibilities of nation-states, rather than multinationals directly, and to limit its role to the provision of information on labour rights risks and best practice. The ILO continues to struggle to find its role and voice with respect to the concept and what it means for business as well as for states and workers.

Chapter 6 considers how HRDD is being institutionalised and interpreted at the national and regional level. Consistent with the iterative and recursive nature of international lawmaking, states are employing the concept of due diligence to promote greater corporate responsibility for adverse labour rights impacts. For national regulators, many of whom have 'been as perplexed in the past by business and human rights challenges as business itself',[117] HRDD has offered a practical way forward. In a number of jurisdictions, HRDD has 'hardened' into legal obligation, and this trend is anticipated to continue. The chapter identifies and discusses HRDD-related regulatory initiatives before categorising them into two distinct approaches. The first approach, found largely in Anglo-Saxon liberal economies such as the United States, the United Kingdom, and Australia, essentially consolidates, rather than challenges, managerial interpretations of HRDD and extant private labour governance. While the second approach, found in continental Europe, is broader in scope (ie with respect to the rights covered) and imposes more substantive obligations on companies, it remains too early to tell whether those obligations will be implemented in a manner that strengthens transnational labour law.

Chapters 7–9 pull together the findings from earlier chapters and draw out their significance for labour activism and scholarship. Chapter 7 argues that HRDD is consolidating, if not driving, important but largely underappreciated reconfigurations in the relative prominence of three sets of actors in transnational labour governance. These emerging developments in the field demand further recognition, reflection, dissection, and discussion among labour activists who are prioritising HRDD as a strategic objective and international labour scholars. First, by privileging risk and professional expertise, the concept is leading to the growth of a market for due diligence-related services and products. This demand is being met (and, indeed, in part driven) by an increasingly influential subset of regulatory intermediaries that has received relatively little attention by scholars of labour regulation. Professional management consultancies and law firms are rapidly expanding and diversifying their services in this area. On a fee-for-service basis, companies are offered an ever-increasing array of products related to the design and implementation of labour rights due diligence. The chapter discusses the positive aspects and risks associated with this increased role of intermediaries in transnational labour governance. Second, the chapter considers the implications (arising from legalisation of the concept described in Chapter 6) of a more active role for courts in determining the nature and scope of corporate accountability for workers' rights transnationally. Finally, with respect to intergovernmental organisations, and building on the discussion in Chapter 5, the chapter argues that the

[117] Michael Connor, 'Interview with John Ruggie' (*Business Ethics* 30 October 2011) <https://business-ethics.com/2011/10/30/8127-un-principles-on-business-and-human-rights-interview-with-john-ruggie> accessed 30 September 2022.

concept has consolidated the position of the OECD in transnational labour governance, potentially at the expense of the ILO.

In a bid to prompt further reflection and debate among scholars and activists, Chapter 8 begins the task of envisaging an alternative trajectory for HRDD as transnational labour law. It discusses a set of measures that could help to steer HRDD towards an institutional form that opens up, rather than forecloses, spaces for workers and trade unions to challenge extant corporate practices where these cause or contribute to labour rights violations in transnational supply chains. Chapter 9, the conclusion, summarises the key arguments advanced and explores questions for further research.

2
Situating HRDD in Transnational Labour Governance

I. Introduction

To understand the contests that have taken place with respect to human rights due diligence (HRDD) in transnational labour governance after the adoption of the UN Guiding Principles on Business and Human Rights (UNGPs) in 2011,[1] it is important to appreciate the landscape in which the concept has been embraced and embedded. This chapter begins with an overview of the evolution of transnational labour governance. It then traces the emergence of the concept of HRDD from the failed UN Norms on the Responsibilities of Transnational Corporations and Other Business Enterprises (the draft Norms)[2] through to the adoption of the UNGPs. Finally, it explains how the concept came to prominence in the field.

This chapter shows that broad-based support for the UNGPs in 2011 did not indicate the resolution of key issues of contention in transnational labour governance. Rather, the United Nations Special Representative of the Secretary-General on the Issue of Human Rights and Transnational Corporations and Other Business Enterprises (SRSG) Professor John Ruggie secured support for the concept by using two devices long familiar to international legal scholars: reframing and strategic ambiguity. Business support for HRDD was generated by reframing human rights in a way that was familiar to, and resonated with, business and by avoiding the imposition of substantive constraints on managerial prerogative. At the same time, however, Ruggie was able to generate support for the concept in the international labour and human rights movements by the use of vague language. In critical areas, the language used to explain HRDD neither imposed a requirement nor foreclosed a possibility. Because of this ambiguity, in the eyes of many labour and human rights activists, the concept carried the potential for the further opening up of corporate practices to contestation and political leverage. It also offered a

[1] UN OHCHR (United Nations Office of the High Commissioner for Human Rights), 'Guiding Principles on Business and Human Rights: Implementing the United Nations "Protect, Respect, and Remedy" Framework' (2011) (hereafter UNGPs).

[2] UN Sub-Commission on the Promotion and Protection of Human Rights, 'Norms on the Responsibilities of Transnational Corporations and Other Business Enterprises with Regard to Human Rights' (26 August 2003) UN Doc E/CN.4/Sub.2/2003/12/Rev.2 (hereafter Draft Norms).

Human Rights Due Diligence and Labour Governance. Ingrid Landau, Oxford University Press. © Ingrid Landau 2023.
DOI: 10.1093/oso/9780198876069.003.0002

promising channel through which greater accountability of companies for labour rights abuses could be secured in law.

II. The Contested Terrain of Transnational Labour Governance

In this section, I summarise the evolution of transnational labour governance in the late decades of the twentieth century and the early 2000s. The account begins by foregrounding the problems that transnational labour governance has emerged to address. It then provides a brief overview of its evolution. This overview is important because it reveals the crowded and contested nature of the field, in which actors disagreed over many fundamental questions and jostled for regulatory influence. This section also identifies key areas of contest within transnational labour governance that existed at the time HRDD emerged as a concept.

A. The Rise of Global Supply Chains and Governance Gaps

The emergence of transnational labour governance is generally located in the late twentieth century and described as a response to the expansion of global markets and the changing character of the global firm.[3] During this time, in many industries, production went 'global', dispersed across national jurisdictions. Often, this dispersion involved the shift of production and manufacturing functions from developed to developing countries.[4] Production not only dispersed but also fragmented. Large companies moved towards network-based and supply-chain models of production, involving multiple corporate entities spread across numerous countries. By their very nature, these networks and supply chains entailed the divestment of direct control of operations by the lead firm in favour of negotiated relationships.[5] In many sectors (such as apparel, electronics, food, and toys), these value chains consist of large firms domiciled in developed countries ('lead firms') coordinating and working with a multitude of independent suppliers, often located in developing countries.

[3] There are examples of transnational private labour governance dating back to the early twentieth century; however, it expanded significantly in the 1980s and 1990s. See Tim Bartley, *Rules without Rights: Land, Labor and Private Authority in the Global Economy* (OUP 2018) 8.

[4] Frederick Mayer and Gary Gereffi, 'Regulation and Economic Globalization: Prospects and Limits of Private Governance' (2010) 12 Business and Politics 1.

[5] Beth Kytle and John Gerard Ruggie, 'Corporate Social Responsibility as Risk Management: A Model for Multinationals' (2005) Corporate Social Responsibility Initiative Working Paper No 10, 2 <www.hks.harvard.edu/sites/default/files/centers/mrcbg/programs/cri/files/workingpaper_10_kytle_ruggie.pdf> accessed 3 October 2022.

These changes in the loci and organisation of production delivered efficiency dividends for lead firms, as well as employment opportunities, much needed investment, and technology transfer to developing countries. However, the same changes also began to expose and exacerbate 'governance deficits' in the global economy.[6] This included in the area of labour protection. National labour law frameworks—conventionally regarded as the primary source of formal protection for workers—proved incapable of adequately protecting workers. The scope of labour laws was often too narrow to afford protection to all workers, or the substantive protections offered by the laws were inadequate to ensure decent working conditions. Labour laws were not enforced in practice due to factors such as lack of institutional capacity and corruption. At the same time, these workplaces remained out of reach of the (often more robust) regulatory frameworks in developed countries. The failure of regulatory frameworks to adequately address these gaps in protection left many workers within these global supply chains with little regulatory protection against violations of internationally recognised workers' rights, including unsafe and unhealthy working conditions, low wages, excessive working hours, child and forced labour, discrimination, and repression of rights to organise and bargain collectively.[7] The traditional state-based system of international labour law, comprising International Labour Organization (ILO) conventions and recommendations, backed up by the ILO's regular supervision and 'special procedures' systems, proved incapable of addressing these labour governance deficits.

B. Early Intergovernmental Regulatory Responses

In the 1970s, attention began to focus on the role and responsibilities of multinational enterprises (MNEs) more directly, including by way of attempts to formulate public international standards on responsible business conduct. The earliest but least successful attempt occurred with the establishment, in 1974, of the UN Centre on Transnational Corporations (UNCTC).[8] In 1976, the intergovernmental Commission tasked with overseeing the activities of the UNCTC established an Intergovernmental Working Group on a Code of Conduct to develop a global code of conduct for multinational corporations. While a draft text was produced in 1986,[9]

[6] Gary Gereffi and Frederick Mayer, 'Globalization and the Demand for Governance' in Gary Gereffi (ed), *The New Offshoring of Jobs and Global Development* (ILO 2006) 45–49.

[7] See ILO, 'Decent Work in Global Supply Chains' (*ILC* 2016) 105/IV.

[8] This body was established by the UN Economic and Social Council in 1974 and formally dissolved in 1992. For an account of the UNCTC's activities, see Khalil Hamdani and Lorraine Ruffing, 'Lessons from the UN Centre on Transnational Corporations for the Current Treaty' in Surya Deva and David Bilchitz (eds), *Building a Treaty on Business and Human Rights: Context and Contours* (CUP 2017).

[9] UNCTC, The United Nations Code of Conduct on Transnational Corporations (1986).

further progress was stymied by political and ideological differences among United Nations (UN) member states.[10]

The failure of this endeavour provided an opportunity for another intergovernmental organisation—the Organisation for Economic Co-operation and Development (OECD)—to step in and fill the gap.[11] In 1976, the OECD adopted its own Guidelines on Multinational Enterprises (OECD Guidelines for MNEs). Annexed to the OECD Declaration on International Investment and Multinational Enterprises, these guidelines set standards for responsible business conduct in a range of domains, from taxation through to science and technology, industrial relations, and employment.[12] The main purpose of the OECD Guidelines for MNEs was to facilitate the resolution of disputes concerning alleged non-compliance with the instrument through mediation and conciliation. While the Guidelines constitute non-binding recommendations from the OECD member states to MNEs, they impose binding obligations on states that adhere to the OECD Declaration on International Investment and Multinational Enterprises or otherwise endorse the Guidelines. These states are obliged to promote the OECD Guidelines for MNEs, including through the establishment of National Contact Points (NCPs) to receive complaints over their application and interpretation.

In 1977, the ILO adopted its own instrument directed at governments and private actors: the Tripartite Declaration of Principles Concerning Multinational Enterprises and Social Policy (ILO Tripartite Declaration). This Declaration sought to engage MNEs in the task of compliance with ILO conventions and recommendations. Both the OECD Guidelines for MNEs and the ILO Tripartite Declaration have endured to the present day and emerged as significant sites of contest with respect to HRDD. They are discussed further in Chapter 5.

C. The Expansion of Private Transnational Labour Governance

The failure of public governance at both domestic and international levels to respond adequately to growing concerns over the regulation of working conditions in the transnational operations and supply chains of MNEs led, in the 1990s, to the expansion of private governance responses.[13] Following the shift of production of goods such as garments, footwear, and toys from North America and Europe to developing countries, activists and the media began to expose poor working

[10] Hamdani and Ruffing (n 8) 33–34.

[11] Lucio Baccaro and Valentina Mele, 'For Lack of Anything Better? International Organizations and Global Corporate Codes' (2011) 89 Public Administration 451, 454.

[12] OECD, 'OECD Declaration on International Investment and Multinational Enterprises' (adopted 21 June 1976, amended 25 May 2011) OECD/LEGAL/0144, Annex 1.

[13] Luc Fransen, *Corporate Social Responsibility and Global Labor Standards: Firms and Activists in the Making of Private Regulation* (Routledge 2012).

conditions in supplier factories and demand that brands and lead firms accept some responsibility for workers in their supply chains, despite the absence of direct ownership or direct legal responsibilities. These campaigns were carried out and coordinated by a variety of actors, including trade unions, faith-based groups, student activists, feminist groups, and development-orientated and human rights non-governmental organisations (NGOs), often via 'transnational labor activist networks' (TLANs).[14] Campaigns often took the form of public demonstrations and consumer boycotts, directed at pressurising large Western-domiciled businesses to take some responsibility for working conditions in their supply chains.[15] These campaigns represented a shift from seeing the regulation of labour standards in global supply chains as the exclusive responsibility of governments and a growing recognition of the responsibilities of MNEs themselves, along with a desire for companies to be held directly accountable for their adverse social impacts.

Acceptance by brands and lead firms of some degree of responsibility for working conditions was initially institutionalised through voluntarily assumed corporate codes of conduct. In their most rudimentary form, these unilateral private governance initiatives involved the adoption by a lead firm of a code of conduct stipulating minimum labour standards in areas such as wages, working hours, and workplace health and safety. Suppliers of the firm were required to sign up to these codes. Throughout the 1990s, ongoing demands by TLANs on MNEs to improve the quality and implementation of these codes of conduct led to the gradual systemisation by firms of efforts to monitor and secure compliance.[16] These monitoring efforts have overwhelmingly been undertaken by way of auditing social conditions in supplier factories.[17] Initially, audits were undertaken internally, with lead firms using their own employees to monitor suppliers' compliance with their codes of conduct. This approach soon came under criticism from trade unions, NGOs, and scholars for lacking independence and credibility.[18] Firms then began to engage external compliance auditors to monitor labour practices. This use of the audit to evaluate working conditions (often referred to as 'social auditing') remains the dominant form globally for verifying labour standards in supply chains.[19] It is discussed further below and in Chapters 4 and 7.

[14] Margaret Keck and Kathryn Sikkink, *Activists beyond Borders: Advocacy Networks in International Politics* (Cornell UP 1998).

[15] ibid.

[16] Richard Locke, *The Promise and Limits of Private Power: Promoting Labor Standards in a Global Economy* (CUP 2013) 11.

[17] Genevieve LeBaron, Jane Lister, and Peter Dauvergne, 'Governing Global Supply Chain Sustainability through the Ethical Audit Regime' (2017) 14 Globalizations 958, 962.

[18] See eg Dara O'Rourke, 'Monitoring the Monitors: A Critique of PricewaterhouseCoopers Labor Monitoring' (*Massachusetts Institute of Technology* 2000) <https://nature.berkeley.edu/orourke/PDF/pwc.pdf> accessed 3 October 2022.

[19] Jolyon Ford and Justine Nolan, 'Regulating Transparency on Human Rights and Modern Slavery in Corporate Supply Chains: The Discrepancy between Human Rights Due Diligence and the Social Audit' (2020) 26 Australian Journal of Human Rights 27, 28.

D. Multi-Stakeholder Initiatives and International Framework Agreements

Persisting concerns among TLANs about both the content and accountability mechanisms associated with corporate codes of conduct led, in the mid-to-late 1990s, to the emergence of the multi-stakeholder initiative (MSI). MSIs that focused on labour governance in transnational supply chains first emerged in the US garment industry in the 1990s before rapidly spreading to other industries and regions.[20] From early on, disagreements between stakeholders over the design of MSIs—including issues such as governance arrangements and the nature and level of independent oversight—led to splintering of the emergent field and the creation of alternative initiatives.[21] Today, while most MSIs are similar in that they bring together multiple stakeholders to work together to achieve objectives collectively, they diverge significantly with respect to their structure, membership, governance, transparency, monitoring, and reporting procedures.[22] Some MSIs have developed and operated with the participation of trade union organisations or NGOs, while others have been established and governed by corporations only. There are MSIs focused on dialogue between stakeholders (eg the UK-based Ethical Trading Initiative and the UN Global Compact) and learning platforms and others (such as the US-based Fair Labor Association and Workers' Rights Consortium) that engage in compliance-related activities. Some issue certification or labels for those organisations that comply with their standards, for example, the UK-based Fair Trade and Social Accountability International. Despite early expectations to the contrary, these MSIs have not converged over time, continuing to exhibit significant differences in their approaches.[23]

Dissatisfaction among labour activists and trade unions with private governance initiatives adopted unilaterally by multinationals also manifested itself in the development of International Framework Agreements (IFAs), sometimes referred to as Global Framework Agreements or Transnational Industrial Relations Agreements, in the late 1980s.[24] These agreements, negotiated directly between MNEs and

[20] While definitions of MSIs vary, the term generally refers to 'initiatives governing social and/or environmental standards of production that have participants from both business and societal interest groups as members and governance structures': Luc Fransen, 'Multi-Stakeholder Governance and Voluntary Programme Interactions: Legitimation Politics in the Institutional Design of Corporate Social Responsibility' (2012) 10 Socio-Economic Review 163, 166.

[21] Jennifer Bair and Florence Palpacuer, 'The Institutionalisation of Supply Chain CSR' in Kiyoteru Tsutsui and Alwyn Lim (eds), *Corporate Social Responsibility in a Globalizing World* (CUP 2015).

[22] See Fransen, 'Multi-Stakeholder Governance and Voluntary Programme Interactions' (n 20).

[23] Luc Fransen and Brian Burgoon, 'A Market for Worker Rights: Explaining Business Support for International Private Labour Regulation' (2011) 19 Review of International Political Economy 236, 240.

[24] Sarah Ashwin and others, 'Spillover Effects across Transnational Industrial Relations Agreements: The Potential and Limits of Collective Action in Global Supply Chains' (2020) 73 Industrial and Labour Relations Review 995, 996.

global union federations (GUFs),[25] provide for the joint regulation of labour relations and standards. In most cases, the standards set in such agreements extend beyond the formal organisational boundaries of the signatory MNEs to cover parts of their supply chains. From a trade union perspective, IFAs have been seen as a more legitimate means of promoting better working conditions than other forms of private labour governance because of their emphasis on social dialogue, labour representation, and collective bargaining.[26] Since the 1980s, IFAs have evolved in their level of sophistication with respect to the standards and mechanisms of implementation, monitoring, and dispute resolution. However, they continue to be limited largely to European-based companies[27] and to suffer from limitations in scope and implementation.[28]

E. The Contested Nature of Transnational Labour Governance

The very brief description of transnational labour governance's evolution above shows that, by the early twenty-first century, the field was a crowded and contested one. Public governance initiatives (such as the OECD Guidelines for MNEs and the ILO Tripartite Declaration) existed alongside, and interacted with, a panoply of private governance arrangements. While there had been some progress towards convergence in the field in the form of a shared understanding that multinational firms had *some* responsibility for working conditions in their supply chains, the nature of this responsibility (whether voluntarily assumed or legal) remained a subject of contention. The extent of responsibility also remained disputed. Contention also surrounded questions concerning the extent to which it was desirable and/or necessary to include workers (directly and/or collectively through trade unions) and other civil society organisations in their governance and implementation of private labour governance for these initiatives to be legitimate and effective. These divergences in views manifested themselves in ongoing contestation within the field as to the legitimacy of specific approaches and initiatives. Below, I briefly elaborate upon what are widely regarded by labour and human rights activists, and

[25] GUFs are the international umbrella organisations that represent national sectoral trade union federations in key industries. See further Michele Ford and Michael Gillan, 'The Global Union Federations in International Industrial Relations: A Critical Review' (2015) 57 Journal of Industrial Relations 456.

[26] Felix Hadwiger, 'Global Framework Agreements: Achieving Decent Work in Global Supply Chains?' (2015) 7 International Journal of Labour Research 8.

[27] According to Sydow and others, only 17 of the over 100 agreements negotiated by the end of 2013 were concluded with non-European MNEs: Jörg Sydow and others, 'Implementation of Global Framework Agreements: Towards a Multi-Organizational Practice Perspective' (2014) 20 Transfer 489, 491.

[28] ibid. See Markus Helfen and Jörg Sydow, 'Negotiating as Institutional Work: The Case of Labor Standards and International Framework Agreements' (2013) 34 Organization Studies 1073; Konstantinos Papadakis (ed), *Shaping Global Industrial Relations: The Impact of International Framework Agreements* (ILO Publication/Palgrave Macmillan 2011).

many scholars, to be three key deficiencies in the transnational labour governance regime. These issues are important to understanding the attraction of HRDD to certain actors in the field (as elaborated upon in Chapter 4). The issues are the selectivity of standards, dominance of the social audit, and the absence of effective enforcement mechanisms.

Throughout the 1990s and 2000s, labour activists and trade unions voiced concern over the perceived selectivity of standards displayed by private labour governance initiatives. This selectivity was initially demonstrated in the formulation of the standards themselves and, later, in the monitoring of supplier performance with respect to certain standards but not others.[29] In short, these initiatives have been shown to lead to some improvements in outcome standards (specific employment conditions such as health and safety, working hours, and minimum wages) but not in process rights such as freedom of association and the right to collective bargaining.[30] Tim Bartley explains:

> In large part, this is because the expansion of collective rights is usually unpalatable to both local elites and to transnational corporations charged with enforcing private rules. For lead firms, having collectively organized workers and communities in their supply chains increases the threat of disruption and decreases managerial flexibility of their suppliers. Brands and retailers routinely adopt rules that call for collective rights to be respected, but rarely demand rigorous definitions of compliance or prioritise these rules over others.[31]

For many labour activists, this selectivity in addressing labour rights is highly problematic in light of their conviction that sustainable improvements in working conditions in global supply chains are only achievable through the empowerment of workers.[32]

A second and related area of contest concerned the role of the social audit. As noted above, this voluntary, privatised system of workplace inspection has long been used unilaterally by firms as well as by many MSIs (such as the Fair Labor Association and Social Accountability International). This approach has come under sustained criticism for being an ineffective means of monitoring and verifying corporate practices.[33] Labour activists and scholars have identified critical shortcomings in social audits. While audit-based compliance programs may generate some positive outcomes, these outcomes are limited in scope and often

29 Axel Marx and Jan Wouters, 'Redesigning Enforcement in Private Labour Regulation: Will It Work?' (2015) 155 International Labour Review 435.

30 Niklas Egels-Zandén and Jeroen Merk, 'Private Regulation and Trade Union Rights: Why Codes of Conduct Have Limited Impact on Trade Union Rights' (2014) 123 Journal of Business Ethics 461.

31 Bartley (n 3) 64.

32 Marx and Wouters, 'Redesigning Enforcement' (n 29) 441.

33 Axel Marx and Jan Wouters, 'Rule Intermediaries in Global Labor Governance' (2017) 670 Annals of the American Academy of Political and Social Science 189.

not sustained.[34] Social audits have been shown to fail to detect or correct many instances of labour violations in global supply chains.[35] The audit scope and methodology are often confined and selective—with the focus on outcome standards (such as health and safety and working hours) rather than process rights (such as freedom of association and non-discrimination).[36] Auditors frequently adopt a checklist approach, which allows for quantification of conditions on a given day and makes for easier tracking and comparison. However, standardised audits can miss crucial information which is essential for sustained compliance, for example, whether workers are engaged via labour providers or contractors, whether there are collective forms of worker voice, or whether there are avenues for raising complaints and remediating breaches.[37]

Trade unions and labour activists have been particularly strong critics of the social audit. Summarising its longstanding views on the subject in 2013, the peak trade union confederation in the United States, the American Federation of Labour and Congress of Industrial Organizations (AFL–CIO), observed that social auditing practices have contributed to a multi-billion dollar 'CSR [corporate social responsibility] certification and social auditing industry' that has delivered for management and corporations but not for workers as the claimed beneficiaries of these practices.[38] For many critics, to be credible, monitoring systems must 'move beyond social audits' and place worker empowerment and union engagement at the centre of monitoring efforts.[39]

The absence of rigorous *enforcement* of standards—in the context of public and/or private labour governance—has been another enduring concern of labour activists and scholars in the field. As the overview of transnational labour governance above reveals, recent years have seen a proliferation of public and private governance initiatives. However, public international instruments, such as the OECD Guidelines for MNEs, have been overwhelmingly 'soft' in nature. It remains up to the individual MNE to determine whether, and the extent to which, it adheres to these recommended standards. While some MNEs have responded to pressures by TLANs by adopting their own forms of self or co-regulation, adoption of, or participation in, such initiatives has tended to be limited to those firms that have faced significant public pressure to do so. Moreover, MNEs face mixed incentives to enforce relevant standards, desiring assurances of decent working conditions from

34 Richard Locke, Matthew Amengual, and Akshay Mangla, 'Virtue Out of Necessity? Compliance, Commitment, and the Improvement of Labor Conditions in Global Supply Chains' (2009) 37 Politics & Society 319, 329.

35 Jill Esbenshade, *Monitoring Sweatshops: Workers, Consumers, and the Global Apparel Industry* (Temple UP 2004);Marx and Wouters, 'Rule Intermediaries' (n 33).

36 Brian Finnegan, 'Responsibility Outsourced: Social Audits, Workplace Certification and Twenty Years of Failure to Protect Workers Rights' (*American Federation of Labor–Congress of Industrial Organizations* 2013) .

37 LeBaron, Lister, and Dauvergne (n 17) 958.

38 Finnegan (n 36) 4.

39 ibid 28.

suppliers in order to protect their public reputations, while also seeking high levels of flexibility and ever lower prices.[40] MSIs met similar dilemmas with respect to enforcement of standards, needing to balance membership generation and maintenance with external demands for legitimacy and effectiveness.[41] The significant and persisting gap between international labour standards (whether embodied in public or private initiatives) and their implementation has long prompted calls from labour and human rights activists for binding rules—at national and international levels—rather than voluntary norms.[42]

In summary, the landscape of transnational labour governance by the early twenty-first century was crowded and contested. The emergence of global supply chains had rendered national labour laws and global non-binding standards set by intergovernmental organisations inadequate because authority had become dispersed not only across national jurisdictions but also among global buyers and their myriad suppliers. Private governance arrangements emerged to address these regulatory voids. These private initiatives have come to dominate the field and to interact in complex ways with various forms of public governance. While some degree of rule-making and oversight of suppliers by multinationals had become nearly universal by the early twenty-first century,[43] private initiatives continued to exhibit great diversity. Disagreements persisted as to the nature and scope of a multinational company's responsibility with respect to workers in its transnational supply chains as well as the desirability and efficacy of different approaches to monitoring and enforcement. Actors in the field also disagreed over the adequacy of private governance initiatives and the extent to which greater public regulation was necessary to make corporations accountable for poor working conditions and violations of labour rights in global supply chains.

III. The Pursuit of Corporate Accountability through the United Nations

While labour and human rights activists continued their efforts throughout the 2000s to both challenge and strengthen private labour governance, they had not given up hope of achieving higher corporate accountability standards at the intergovernmental level. This included seeking stronger business and human rights standards through the UN. This section studies relevant developments leading up to the endorsement by the UN Human Rights Council of the HRDD concept in

[40] Bartley (n 3) 31.
[41] Dorothée Baumann-Pauly and others, 'Industry-Specific Multi-Stakeholder Initiatives That Govern Corporate Human Rights Standards: Legitimacy Assessments of the Fair Labor Association and the Global Network Initiative' (2017) 143 Journal of Business Ethics 771.
[42] Bartley (n 3) 281.
[43] ibid 10.

2011. It begins by briefly discussing the development of the draft Norms in the late 1990s and the politics surrounding their demise. While this effort to develop legally binding international human rights standards for companies proved unsuccessful, it played an important role in shaping the political environment in which the UNGPs were subsequently developed and adopted. Finally, this section provides an overview of the UNGPs and explain how HRDD features within this framework.

A. The Rise and Fall of the Draft Norms

Produced by a Sub-Commission of the UN Commission on Human Rights, the draft Norms first appeared in 2000 and were adopted by the Sub-Commission on the Promotion and Protection of Human Rights in August 2003.[44] While maintaining the position under international law that states have primary responsibility for ensuring that business respects human rights,[45] they proposed imposing a positive obligation to respect human rights on corporations and other enterprises under international law for the first time. In doing so, they reflected the conviction held by many that the absence of clear and direct human rights obligations on corporations continued to be a key obstacle to more responsible corporate human rights practice. They also required transnational corporations to adopt internal structures and monitoring mechanisms to ensure that they, and those with which they had business relationships, complied with the draft Norm's requirements. The draft Norms quickly became the subject of debate, which intensified until their demise in 2005.[46]

The draft Norms have been widely characterised as a political failure.[47] They quickly created sharp divisions between and within key stakeholder groups, including companies, national and international business organisations, human rights and labour NGOs, trade unions, states, lawyers, and academics.[48] These divisions were not necessarily along expected lines: for example, a number of companies and business groups supported the Norms and the International Trade Union Confederation (ITUC) and some human rights NGOs expressed concern over the draft instrument. Nonetheless, it remained the case that the draft Norms were the subject of strong and broad criticism from a range of stakeholders.

[44] Draft Norms (n 2).

[45] ibid art 1.

[46] Larry Catá Backer, 'Multinational Corporations, Transnational Law: The United Nation's Norms on the Responsibilities of Transnational Corporations as Harbinger of Corporate Responsibility in International Law' (2006) 37 Columbia Human Rights Law Review 287, 331–32.

[47] David Kinley, Justine Nolan, and Natalie Zerial, 'The Politics of Corporate Social Responsibility: Reflections on the United Nations Human Rights Norms for Corporations' (2007) 25 Companies and Securities Law Journal 30.

[48] ibid.

Criticism related to a number of features. These included the manner in which the Norms had been produced (with states, companies, and business groups complaining of inadequate consultation), the proposal to impose obligations directly on companies under international law, and their intended legal status. The draft Norms were also criticised for the use of vague and ambiguous concepts.[49] Ongoing and vehement criticism of the draft Norms ultimately led to their abandonment by the UN Commission on Human Rights.

Despite their ultimate demise, the draft Norms laid the basis for subsequent developments in important ways. They placed business and human rights squarely on the agenda of the UN and raised the hopes of many that the global organisation's involvement could quicken the pace of development of human rights standards for businesses.[50] They also prompted the UN to seek an alternative approach to break the policy paralysis which had arisen around questions on business and human rights. The change of approach came in the form of a request by the Commission on Human Rights in 2005 that the UN Secretary-General appoint the SRSG.[51]

B. Protect, Respect, and Remedy

Appointed to the position of SRSG in 2005, Professor John Ruggie of the Kennedy School of Government at Harvard University was acutely aware, from the commencement of his mandate, that the task before him was not only conceptual but also political and diplomatic.[52] This sensitivity to the political nature of his task was reflected early through his setting up of multi-stakeholder consultations and his abandonment of any proposal to base corporate liability on direct obligation. He was particularly cognisant of the need to consult more extensively with the corporate sector and to ensure that proffered solutions were palatable to this important stakeholder group.[53] Adopting an approach described by the SRSG himself as 'principled pragmatism',[54] the Special Representative set about developing a

49 Backer (n 46) 214.

50 Kinley, Nolan, and Zerial (n 47) 31.

51 There is an alternative view: as Voiculescu explains, while '[s]ome regarded the 2005 appointment of the SRSG to map out the human rights responsibilities of business organisations as a response to the standstill over the UN Norms ..., others saw it as attempt to bring the Norms to a standstill': Aurora Voiculescu, 'Human Rights, Corporate Social Responsibility and International Economic Law: Strong Answers to Strong Questions?' in Amanda Perry-Kessaris (ed), *Socio-Legal Approaches to International Economic Law* (Taylor and Francis 2013) 226.

52 John G Ruggie, *Just Business: Multinational Corporations and Human Rights* (WW Norton & Company 2013).

53 ibid. See also UN, 'Report of the Special Representative of the Secretary-General on the Issue of Human Rights and Ttransnational Corporations and Other Business Enterprises, Interim Report of the Special Representative of the Secretary-General on the Issue of Human Rights and Transnational Corporations and Other Business Enterprises' (22 February 2006) UN Doc E/CN.4/2006/97, [54]–[81] (hereafter 2006 Interim Report).

54 The SRSG defined principled pragmatism as 'an unflinching commitment to the principle of strengthening the promotion and protection of human rights as it relates to business, coupled with a

conceptual and policy framework to anchor the business and human rights debate and to help guide all relevant actors.

The SRSG began by diagnosing the nature of the business and human rights problem facing the global community, concluding that the problem lay in 'governance gaps created by globalization—between the scope and impact of economic forces and actors, and the capacity of societies to manage their adverse consequences'.[55] Firms increasingly operated globally, but the world's social fabric and political institutions had largely remained national in focus. While it was clear that, under international law, states had a duty to protect against non-state human rights abuses, this was often not translated into adequate efforts to regulate and adjudicate corporate actors. The SRSG also recognised problems posed by the rise of supply-chain models of business organisation, which increased the probability that a company would, in some manifestation or other, breach its own corporate principles or community expectations of responsible corporate behaviour. In this context, '[t]he core challenge of business and human rights ... lies in devising instruments of corporate and public governance to contain and reduce these tendencies'.[56] While the focus of the SRSG extended significantly beyond labour rights, violations of such rights featured prominently in his work. Research conducted by the SRSG during his first mandate found that violations of labour rights account for approximately 45 per cent of all corporate human rights violations. Indirect labour rights violations (ie violations by actors with which a company is connected) constitute about 41 per cent of the overall cases of human rights violations, with most occurring in developing countries.[57]

Adopted by the UN Human Rights Council (HRC) in June 2008, the 'Protect, Respect and Remedy' Framework consists of three complementary and interdependent pillars.[58] The first is the state duty to protect against human rights abuses by third parties, including business enterprises, through appropriate policies, regulation, and adjudication. The second is the corporate responsibility to respect human rights, which means that business enterprises should act with due diligence to avoid infringing on the human rights of others and to address adverse impacts with which they are involved. The third is the need for greater access by

pragmatic attachment to what works best in creating change where it matters most—in the daily lives of people': 2006 Interim Report (n 53) [81].

[55] UN, 'Report of the Special Representative of the Secretary-General on the Issue of Human Rights and Transnational Corporations and Other Business Enterprises, Protect, Respect and Remedy: A Framework for Business and Human Rights' (7 April 2008) UN Doc A/HRC/8/5 [3] (hereafter Protect, Respect and Remedy Framework). For a critique of the proposition that the problem lies in governance gaps, see Sally Wheeler, 'Corporate Respect for Human Rights: As Good as It Gets?' in Perry-Kessaris (n 51).

[56] Protect, Respect and Remedy Framework (n 55) [23].

[57] Ruggie (n 52) 20–27.

[58] Protect, Respect and Remedy Framework (n 55).

victims to effective remedy, judicial and non-judicial. These pillars are to act as 'mutually reinforcing parts of a dynamic, interactive system to advance the enjoyment of human rights'.[59] The HRC 'welcomed' the Framework and extended the SRSG's mandate for a further three years, with the task of providing more concrete guidance on its implementation.

The culmination of the SRSG's extended mandate—the UNGPs—were adopted by the HRC in July 2011.[60] The Council's unanimous endorsement was widely recognised as a significant diplomatic and political achievement.[61] It was also characterised as a breakthrough in global governance. For the first time, the UN member states had adopted a common position laying down standards of expected behaviour from business with regard to human rights.[62] The normative significance of the UNGPs lay not in the creation of new international law obligations but in their elaboration of 'the implications of existing standards and practices for states and businesses' and integration of these 'within a single, logically coherent and comprehensive template'.[63] In addition to endorsing the UNGPs, the HRC established a follow-up to the SRSG's mandate. This included a Working Group consisting of five independent experts of balanced geographical representation to promote and disseminate the UNGPs and an annual multi-stakeholder Forum on Business and Human Rights.[64]

C. The UN Guiding Principles on Business and Human Rights

The UNGPs consist of thirty-one foundational and operational principles, each with supporting commentary which explicates the principle's meaning and its implications for law, policy, and practice. Ten of the principles elaborate on the state duty to protect human rights, fourteen on the corporate responsibility to respect human rights, and seven on access to remedy.

[59] UN, 'Report of the Special Representative of the Secretary-General on the Issue of Human Rights and Transnational Corporations and Other Business Enterprises, Business and Human Rights: Further Steps towards the Operationalization of the 'Protect, Respect and Remedy' Framework (9 April 2010) UN Doc A/HRC/14/27 [2].

[60] Human Rights Council, 'Human Rights and Transnational Corporations and Other Business Enterprises' (6 July 2011) UN Doc A/HRC/RES/17/4 (hereafter Resolution 17/4).

[61] Karin Buhmann, 'The Development of the "UN Framework": A Pragmatic Process Towards a Pragmatic Output' in Radu Mares (ed), *The UN Guiding Principles on Business and Human Rights: Foundations and Implementation* (Koninklijke Brill 2012).

[62] Radu Mares, 'Business and Human Rights after Ruggie: Foundations, the Art of Simplification and the Imperative of Cumulative Progress' in Mares, *The UN Guiding Principles on Business and Human Rights* (n 61) 2.

[63] UN, 'Report of the Special Representative of the Secretary-General on the Issue of Human Rights and Transnational Corporations and Other Business Enterprises, John Ruggie, "Guiding Principles on Business and Human Rights: Implementing the United Nations "Protect, Respect and Remedy" Framework' (21 March 2011) UN Doc A/HRC/17/31, [14] (hereafter 'Guiding Principles').

[64] Resolution 17/4 (n 60) [6]–[18].

Guiding Principles 11–24 deal with the corporate responsibility to respect human rights. The baseline responsibility of companies is 'that they should avoid infringing on the human rights of others and should address adverse human rights impacts with which they are involved'.[65] This responsibility exists independently of the ability or willingness of the state to fulfil its own human rights obligations and over and above compliance with national laws and regulations.[66] The responsibility applies to all enterprises, irrespective of size, sector, operational context, ownership, and structure.[67] In contrast to the state duty to protect human rights, this corporate responsibility is a 'global standard of expected conduct' rather than a legal obligation.[68]

Guiding Principle 13 recognises three ways in which a business may be involved with adverse human rights impacts and makes clear that what is required of business depends on which of these three types of involvement applies. Business enterprises should avoid *causing* or *contributing to* adverse human rights impacts through their own activities and address such impacts when they occur. Business enterprises should also seek to prevent or mitigate adverse human rights impacts that are *directly linked* to their operations, products, or services by their business relationships, even if they have not contributed to those impacts.[69]

The UNGPs identify three measures that business enterprises should have in place to meet their responsibility to respect human rights.[70] First is a policy commitment to meet that responsibility. Second is an HRDD process to identify, prevent, mitigate, and account for how they manage their potential adverse human rights impacts. Finally, businesses should have a remediation process to address any adverse human rights impacts which they cause or to which they contribute.

Human rights due diligence is offered in the UNGPs as a process by which business enterprises can identify, prevent, mitigate, and account for how they address their human rights impacts.[71] It consists of four components:

(a) *Identifying and assessing* any actual or potential adverse human rights impacts with which the business may be involved either through its own activities or as a result of business relationships;
(b) *Integrating findings* from impact assessments across relevant internal functions and processes, and taking appropriate action;
(c) *Tracking the effectiveness* of measures and processes to address adverse human rights impacts to verify whether they are being addressed; and

65 UNGPs (n 1) 13–14, Guiding Principle 11.
66 ibid 13, Commentary on Guiding Principle 11.
67 ibid 15, Guiding Principle 14.
68 ibid 13, Commentary on Guiding Principle 11.
69 ibid 14–15, Guiding Principle 13.
70 ibid 15–16, Guiding Principle 15. These three measures are detailed in Guiding Principles 16–22.
71 ibid 17, Guiding Principle 17.

(d) *Communicating externally* on how impacts are being addressed, particularly when concerns are raised by or on behalf of affected stakeholders.[72]

According to the UNGPs, HRDD should extend to cover adverse human rights impacts that business enterprises 'may cause or contribute to through its own activities, or which may be directly linked to its operations, products or services by its business relationships'.[73] The scope and complexity of HRDD will depend on the size of the business enterprise, the risk of 'severe human rights impacts', and the nature and context of its operations.[74] The UNGPs provide further guidance for companies on how to prioritise actions to address actual and potential adverse human rights impacts (where it is necessary to do so)[75] and in what circumstances companies should disclose information to stakeholders and in what form.[76]

The UNGPs make clear that HRDD is not the same as other forms of business due diligence. First and foremost, this is because the focus of HRDD is on risks to human rights, not to the company. This stands in contrast to, for example, 'social risk', which refers to the leverage that people, or groups of people, with a negative perception of corporate activity have on the business enterprise's value.[77] Unlike transactional due diligence, HRDD is to be ongoing in recognition of the fact that human rights risks may change over time as the business enterprise's operations and operating context evolves.[78] Yet another important distinction is that due diligence should involve consultation with stakeholders,[79] including in assessing impacts, tracking performance, and handling grievances. Finally, companies should be prepared to communicate externally on HRDD. This may include, but not necessarily involve, formal reporting.[80]

IV. Securing Support through Reframing and Ambiguity

While support for the UNGPs was by no means unanimous or unqualified,[81] the concept of HRDD was welcomed by a broad range of stakeholders. International

[72] ibid 19–24, Guiding Principles 18–21.
[73] ibid 17–18, Guiding Principle 17.
[74] ibid.
[75] ibid 26, Guiding Principle 24.
[76] ibid 23–24, Guiding Principle 21.
[77] Björn Fasterling, 'Human Rights Due Diligence as Risk Management: Social Risk Versus Human Rights Risk' (2017) 2 Business and Human Rights Journal 1.
[78] UNGPs (n 1) 18, Guiding Principle 17.
[79] ibid 19–24, Guiding Principles 18–21.
[80] ibid 23–24, Guiding Principle 21.
[81] See eg HRW (Human Rights Watch), 'UN Human Rights Council: Weak Stance on Business Standards'(*Statement* 16 June 2011) <www.hrw.org/news/2011/06/16/un-human-rights-council-weak-stance-business-standards> accessed 5 October 2022; Amnesty International and others, 'Joint Civil Society Statement on the Draft Guiding Principles on Business and Human Rights' (*Statement* January 2011) <www.fidh.org/IMG/pdf/Joint_CSO_Statement_on_GPs.pdf> accessed 5 October 2022.

business associations saw the concept as 'practical and achievable'.[82] The international labour movement also proved strongly supportive. The ITUC described the expectation that business conduct due diligence with respect to human rights as 'logical and appropriate'[83] and HRDD as a concept 'with great potential'.[84] The Council of Global Unions observed that the 'emphasis on due diligence with respect to established standards of human rights offers a more satisfactory basis for addressing the responsibility of business for its impacts on society'.[85] Even global human rights NGOs such as Amnesty International, heavily critical of the UNGPs as a whole, described HRDD as 'clearly an important component in preventing corporate-related human rights abuses'.[86] Below, I argue that the SRSG was successful in generating and maintaining broad-based support for HRDD by way of two mechanisms. The first involved reframing human rights as a form of business risk management. Through this reframing process, the SRSG was able to present a concept to business that resonated with managerial perspectives and practices. The second involved the use of ambiguity. The SRSG's 'principled pragmatism' and the imperative of keeping important stakeholders (such as the labour movement and NGOs) on board with the project led to the embedding within the UNGPs of certain strategic ambiguities. The use of these mechanisms effectively enabled the SRSG to circumvent significant areas of contestation in the field. I introduce these two mechanisms below and explore their implications in subsequent chapters.

A. From Rights to Risks

As noted above, in light of the failure of the draft Norms, the SRSG was acutely aware of the need to sustain business support for his project.[87] As he explained in 2011, the approaches proposed in the UNGPs, including HRDD, 'have to make

[82] IOE (International Organisation of Employers), International Chamber of Commerce, and BIAC (Business and Industry Advisory Council to the OECD), 'Joint Statement on Business and Human Rights to the United Nations Human Rights Council' (*Statement* 30 May 2011) (on file with author).

[83] ITUC (International Trade Union Confederation), 'The United Nations "Protect, Respect, Remedy" Framework for Business and Human Rights and the United Nations Guiding Principles for Business and Human Rights: A Guide for Trade Unionists' (*Version 1.0* May 2012) 12 <www.ituc-csi.org/IMG/pdf/12-04-23_ruggie_background_fd.pdf> accessed 5 October 2022.

[84] Sharon Burrow, 'Letter from Sharan Burrow to John G Ruggie' (*ITUC* 27 May 2011) 1 <www.ituc-csi.org/IMG/pdf/Letter_to_Mr_John_G_Ruggie_.pdf> accessed 5 October 2022.

[85] Global Unions, 'Draft Guiding Principles for the Implementation of the United Nations' "Protect, Respect and Remedy" Framework: Global Unions' Response' (January 2011)1 <https://media.business-humanrights.org/media/documents/files/media/documents/ruggie/global-unions-response-re-guiding-principles-jan-2011.pdf> accessed 10 September 2020.

[86] Amnesty International, 'Comments in Response to the UN Special Representative of the Secretary General on Transnational Corporations and Other Business Enterprises: Guiding Principles—Proposed Outline' (*Statement* 4 October 2010) 3 <www.amnesty.org/en/documents/IOR50/001/2010/en> accessed 10 September 2020.

[87] Ruggie (n 52) 144–45.

sense inside of a company. Otherwise, it is not going to get done.'[88] Ruggie achieved these twin objectives of political palatability and operational feasibility through the act of *reframing* human rights issues for companies as risks. From early on in the SRSG's mandate, business-related human rights issues were routinely expressed in terms of risk and risk management.[89] The four elements of HRDD presented in the UNGPs closely reflect existing enterprise risk management practices, particularly with regard to the management of social and environmental risk.[90] Through the process of reframing or 'frame alignment', the SRSG was able to present human rights—a concept that was largely unfamiliar and challenging to business—within an interpretive frame that was meaningful and persuasive.[91] The implications of this reframing exercise are discussed further in subsequent chapters.

B. Strategic Ambiguity

The SRSG also needed the support of the labour and human rights movements. The SRSG secured the support of these important stakeholders for a concept that was deeply sympathetic to business orientation and practices by the strategic use of ambiguity.[92] As Deva has argued, the SRSG stepped around, rather than confronted, criticisms and concerns from NGOs and others during the drafting process.[93] Disagreement on key issues was masked by way of a text using weak and imprecise language. This ambiguity enabled the SRSG to position HRDD in a way that encompassed both sides of the debate.[94] Below, I identify key areas in which HRDD, as presented in the UNGPs, uses vague and ambiguous language. These are: first, the breadth and scope of the HRDD process; second, the extent to which businesses are expected to be transparent and consultative when engaging in HRDD; and finally, the role of the state with respect to incentivising or requiring corporate HRDD.

The first strategic ambiguity embedded in HRDD concerns the breadth and scope of the exercise. On the one hand, the UNGPs purport to resolve these two

88 'Business and Human Rights: Together at Last? A Conversation with John Ruggie' (2011) 35 Fletcher Forum of World Affairs 117, 121.

89 Fasterling (n 77) 227.

90 ibid 229.

91 Sociological concepts of frame alignment are well recognised in organisational studies and transnational regulation. See Robert D Benford and David A Snow, 'Framing Processes and Social Movements: An Overview and Assessment' (2000) 26 Annual Review of Sociology 211; Ryan Goodman and Derek Jinks, *Socializing States: Promoting Human Rights through International Law* (OUP 2013).

92 Christine Parker and John Howe, 'Ruggie's Diplomatic Project and Its Missing Regulatory Infrastructure' in Mares, *The UN Guiding Principles on Business and Human Rights* (n 61). See also Wheeler (n 55).

93 Surya Deva, 'Treating Human Rights Lightly: A Critique of the Consensus Rhetoric and the Language Employed by the Guiding Principles' in Surya Deva and David Bilchitz (eds), *Human Rights Obligations of Business: Beyond the Responsibility to Respect* (CUP 2012).

94 Parker and Howe (n 92) 279.

controversial matters and in a manner that appeals to worker and human rights activists. They clarify that HRDD is to cover, at a minimum, 'all internationally proclaimed human rights', including those in the ILO's Declaration of Fundamental Principles and Rights at Work.[95] With respect to scope, the process should cover adverse human rights impacts that the business enterprise may cause or contribute to through its own activities or that may be directly linked to its operations, products, or services by its business relationships.[96]

In both these areas, however, the SRSG addressed the concern of business that expectations would not be unreasonable by using vague language that preserves scope for managerial discretion. It is recognised that the HRDD process may 'vary in complexity with the size of the business enterprise, the risk of severe human rights impacts, and the nature and context of its operations'.[97] While business enterprises should address all their adverse human rights impacts, 'it may not always be possible to address them simultaneously'.[98] It is also recognised that '[w]here business enterprises have large numbers of entities in their value chains it may be unreasonably difficult to conduct due diligence for adverse human rights impacts across them all'.[99] Where this is the case, business enterprises should identify 'general areas where the risk of adverse human rights impacts is most significant, whether due to certain suppliers' or clients' operating context, the particular operations, products or services involved, or other relevant considerations' and prioritise these for HRDD.[100]

A second strategic ambiguity relates to the extent to which businesses are required to be consultative and transparent with respect to HRDD. Again, on their face, the UNGPs emphasise the importance of these processes. It is recommended, for example, that business enterprises engage in 'meaningful consultation with potentially affected groups and other stakeholders' when identifying and assessing actual or potential adverse human rights impacts.[101] However, this is followed by the caveat that consultation is to be 'appropriate to the size of the business enterprise and the nature and context of the operation'.[102] Despite the urging from global unions and others for more precise language,[103] the term 'stakeholder' is left undefined, and there is no mention of trade unions, or workers' representatives more generally, in the UNGPs. Consultation is neither required nor recognised as a right.[104]

95 UNGPs (n 1) 13, Guiding Principle 12.
96 ibid 17, Guiding Principle 17.
97 ibid.
98 ibid 26, Commentary to Guiding Principle 24.
99 ibid 18, Commentary to Guiding Principle 17.
100 ibid.
101 ibid 19, Guiding Principle 18.
102 ibid.
103 Global Unions (n 85) 2.
104 See eg Tara J Melish and Errol Meidinger, 'Protect, Respect, Remedy and Participate: "New Governance" Lessons for the Ruggie Framework' in Mares, *The UN Guiding Principles on Business and Human Rights* (n 61).

A similar approach is taken to the issue of corporate disclosure of HRDD processes. The UNGPs promote transparency by stating that 'business enterprises should be prepared to communicate [on how they address their human rights impacts] externally' and that information provided should be 'sufficient to evaluate the adequacy of an enterprise's response to the particular human rights impact involved'.[105] However, formal reporting is only 'expected' when there are risks of 'severe human rights impacts'.[106]

The third principal area of strategic ambiguity concerns the relationship between human rights due diligence and the state. The characterisation by the UNGPs of the corporate responsibility to respect human rights (and to engage in HRDD) as a societal expectation rather than a legal obligation was warmly welcomed by the business community. Yet, in drafting the Guiding Principles, the SRSG was careful not to antagonise other stakeholders by excluding the possibility of the concept being further embedded in national and international legal frameworks.

First, the SRSG was consistently vague as to whether HRDD should be conceptualised as a business tool or a legal standard. On the one hand, the SRSG frequently referred to HRDD as a tool that could be usefully integrated into company risk management systems. This notion of HRDD as offering a workable and practical solution for companies was enhanced by the SRSG's strategy of encouraging business involvement in the process of developing the concept and trialling its 'workability' with a small number of companies.[107] The SRSG was also careful to emphasise that the consequences for a company failing to undertake HRDD are largely reputational rather than legal.

Yet, the SRSG did not foreclose the possibility of HRDD being used as a legal standard of conduct against which company actions can be assessed and fault assigned. Early on in his mandate, he criticised the 'spheres-of-influence' concept in the draft Norms for its lack of 'legal pedigree'.[108] In introducing HRDD to the HRC in his 2008 report, the SRSG footnoted a 'traditional definition' of due diligence from *Black's Law Dictionary*: 'the diligence reasonably expected from, and ordinarily exercised by, a person who seeks to satisfy a legal requirement or discharge an obligation'.[109] He emphasised that HRDD had been 'the subject of detailed discussions with corporate law professionals'.[110]

Second, the UNGPs are ambiguous as to the extent to which states should supervise, or even mandate, corporate HRDD. The Commentary to Guiding Principle 1 recognises that states have discretion in deciding upon the appropriate steps taken to prevent, investigate, punish, and redress private actors' abuse of human

[105] UNGPs (n 1) 23–24, Guiding Principle 21.
[106] ibid 24, Commentary to Guiding Principle 21.
[107] 'Business and Human Rights: Together at Last?' (n 88) 121–22.
[108] 2006 Interim Report (n 53) [67].
[109] Protect, Respect and Remedy Framework (n 55) 9.
[110] UNGPs (n 1) 7, [6].

rights but urges states to 'consider the full range of permissible preventative and remedial measures, including policies, legislation, regulations and adjudication'.[111] The UNGPs also recommend that home states clearly convey the expectation that companies domiciled in their territory and/or jurisdiction respect human rights and provide guidance on how to do so, including through encouraging them to engage in HRDD.[112] States should take 'additional steps' to protect against human rights abuses by business enterprises that are linked to the state (owned, controlled, or that receive substantial support or services), including, 'where appropriate', through requiring businesses to engage in HRDD.[113] The Commentary enumerates 'strong policy reasons for home states to do so and a number of approaches states have adopted in this regard, including domestic measures with extraterritorial implications'.[114]

The SRSG was equally careful not to close off the possibility of further legalisation of the concept at the international level. In presenting the UNGPs to the HRC in 2011, Ruggie emphasised that the document marked only 'the end of the beginning' 'by establishing a common global platform for action, on which cumulative progress can be built, step-by-step, without foreclosing any other promising longer-term developments'.[115]

V. Conclusion

The landscape of transnational labour governance in which the concept of HRDD has been introduced was a crowded and contested one in which many actors and regulatory initiatives jostled for influence. The diversity of initiatives reflected ongoing disagreements and associated uncertainty regarding the nature and scope of a company's responsibility with respect to workers in their supply chains, as well as the relative legitimacy and adequacy of specific approaches. The UNGPs presented a conceptual framework which held out the potential to resolve these disagreements. However, as shown in this chapter, this framework did not push aside, or even challenge, the diversity of approaches with respect to how labour rights issues in transnational supply chains should be managed. Nor did it authoritatively resolve any of the fundamental differences of opinion as to the respective legitimacy of different approaches. Moreover, it introduced into the field a new concept—HRDD—that was deeply ambiguous, both with respect to what it required of business and its connection to the state. Chapter 3 further explores this ambiguity by engaging in a conceptual analysis of HRDD on three distinct levels.

[111] ibid 3, Commentary to Guiding Principle 1.
[112] ibid 7–8, Guiding Principles 2 and 3.
[113] ibid 9, Guiding Principle 4.
[114] ibid 4, Commentary to Guiding Principle 2.
[115] Guiding Principles (n 63) [13].

3

Unpacking HRDD

Risk Management, Business Regulation, Transnational Norm

I. Introduction

This chapter unpacks human rights due diligence (HRDD) as a concept. To understand subsequent contests, it is necessary to conceive the concept at three levels: as risk management, as business regulation, and as an emerging transnational norm. At the *micro* level, the level of the business enterprise, HRDD calls for business professionals to engage in a familiar process of risk identification, assessment, prioritisation, and mitigation. At the *meso* level, HRDD is a novel approach to business regulation that is disputed with respect to its legal form, structure, and meaning. Finally, at the *macro* level, HRDD is an emerging and contested transnational norm. Each of these conceptualisations is distinct and brings its own set of complexities. But these three different levels do not operate in isolation. Rather, this book contends that these three conceptualisations of HRDD are intertwined and interact with each other in complex and problematic ways. The conceptual interrogation of HRDD undertaken in this chapter lays the foundation for the analysis in subsequent chapters by helping to explain how different actors have received and interpreted the concept (Chapter 4), and the nature and dynamics of the contests underway with respect to legalisation of the concept at the international (Chapter 5) and national levels (Chapter 6). It also provides the basis for understanding important shifts that are underway in the field of transnational labour governance as a result of the concept's ascendance. These shifts are examined in Chapter 7.

Following this Introduction, section II of this chapter examines HRDD as a form of enterprise-based risk management. It begins by locating the concept within the context of the steady expansion of risk discourse to new fields since the 1990s.[1] Drawing on the critical risk literature, I identify a number of implications of the shift to addressing problems of poor working conditions in transnational supply chains through a risk-based approach. Section III discusses HRDD as business regulation. This entails directing attention to HRDD's legal form, structure, and

[1] Michael Power, 'The Risk Management of Everything' (2004) 5 Journal of Risk Finance 58.

Human Rights Due Diligence and Labour Governance. Ingrid Landau, Oxford University Press. © Ingrid Landau 2023.
DOI: 10.1093/oso/9780198876069.003.0003

meaning. Conceptualising HRDD as business regulation also facilitates insight into how the concept is being shaped and by whom. Section IV considers HRDD as an emerging transnational norm.

II. HRDD as Risk Management

Though HRDD expands the scope of labour market governance, this expansion takes place through a risk management rather than a labour law approach. The concept is not underpinned by the values or approaches that we traditionally identify with labour regulation.[2] It does not add any novel democratic configurations to enhance corporate accountability,[3] promote shared responsibility for working conditions in global supply chains,[4] or even encourage or create mechanisms through which to pursue transnational social dialogue in the way that, for example, international framework agreements purport to do.[5]

The genealogy of HRDD in risk management helps us to understand how the concept has subsequently been interpreted and operationalised by business actors and the potential hazards implicit in the approach as a mechanism of labour governance. Risk management is directed at managing the borders between the corporation and its environment by bringing risk under control through systems, procedures, and training.[6] While originally the preserve of scientists and engineers, the concept of risk has become ubiquitous in business management and public policy. Today, risk management is seen as an essential aspect of good governance.[7]

Viewing issues of labour governance through a risk management lens brings potential benefits. It can help a business adopt a systematic approach to identifying and addressing labour rights issues in its own operations and supply chains. It can enable businesses to anticipate and avoid risks rather than dealing with them as and when they arise. If properly implemented, it can also go some way towards

[2] See Chapter 1.

[3] Ronen Shamir, 'Capitalism, Governance, and Authority: The Case of Corporate Social Responsibility' (2010) 6 Annual Review of Law and Society 531, 546.

[4] Mark Anner, Jennifer Bair, and Jeremy Blasi, 'Toward Joint Liability in Global Supply Chains: Addressing the Root Causes of Labor Violations in International Subcontracting Networks' (2013) 35 Comparative Labor Law & Policy Journal 1; Yossi Dahan, Hanna Lerner, and Faina Milman-Sivan, 'The International Labour Organization, Multinational Enterprises, and Shifting Conceptions of Responsibility in the Global Economy' in Axel Marx and others (eds), *Global Governance of Labour Rights: Assessing the Effectiveness of Transnational Public and Private Regulatory Initiatives* (Edward Elgar 2015).

[5] Christina Niforou, 'International Framework Agreements and Industrial Relations Governance: Global Rhetoric versus Local Realities' (2012) 50 British Journal of Industrial Relations 352.

[6] Robert Eli Rosen, 'Risk Management and Corporate Governance: The Case of Enron' (2003) 35 Connecticut Law Review 1157, 1170.

[7] Michael Power, *Organized Uncertainty: Designing a World of Risk Management* (Oxford University Press 2007).

ensuring that companies internalise or institutionalise social values and perceptions.[8] It can help to guide business prioritisation of activities and the deployment of resources according to an assessment of identified risks.[9]

Conceptualising HRDD as a form of enterprise-based risk management also hints at some of the limitations and hazards of the concept as a tool of transnational labour governance. Drawing on critical risk management literature, I identify three issues below: risk management as risk tolerance; risk management as a technical exercise shielded from politics and political actors; and risk management as a tool for managing, rather than meeting, public expectations.[10]

By its very nature, risk management is not about eliminating risk but about reducing risk to 'acceptable' or 'tolerable' levels.[11] Introducing the concept to transnational labour governance thus (implicitly or otherwise) acknowledges that corporate failure to respect workers' human rights in their own operations and supply chains is an acceptable option. As Julia Black explains, enterprise risk management processes generally ask business practitioners to go further and assess the costs and benefits associated with failure to address certain risks:

> compliance personnel have to accept that there is a risk of non-compliance. Someone within the firm then has to assess whether the level of risk in any particular instance is one the firm is prepared to run. Indeed, performing risk/cost trade-offs with respect to compliance is advocated by leading consulting firms as a key stage in the compliance risk management process. Firms are told to decide on the regulatory outcomes they wish to deliver, and the risk/cost trade-off of doing so.[12]

While recognition that some form of risk is acceptable, if not inevitable, may seem entirely reasonable, this position raises the possibility that non-compliance with labour standards will be rendered defensible and capable of being 'explained away'. HRDD may thus legitimise existing practices and facilitate a type of 'planned immunity' in which risks become calculable, manageable, and ultimately acceptable.[13] Problematically, what constitutes an acceptable level of risk is rarely defined, let alone publicly articulated, and tends to vary according to an entity's

8 Power, 'The Risk Management of Everything' (n 1) 59.

9 Julia Black, 'The Role of Risk in Regulatory Processes' in Robert Baldwin, Martin Cave, and Martin Lodge (eds), *The Oxford Handbook of Regulation* (OUP 2010).

10 For an alternative critique of HRDD as risk management, see Björn Fasterling, 'Human Rights Due Diligence as Risk Management: Social Risk versus Human Rights Risk' (2017) 2 Business and Human Rights Journal 1.

11 Bridget M Hutter, *Regulation and Risk: Occupational Health and Safety on the Railways* (OUP 2001) 10.

12 Julia Black, 'Forms and Paradoxes of Principles-Based Regulation' (2008) 3 Capital Markets Law Journal 425, 454.

13 Grietje Baars, '"It's Not Me, It's the Corporation": The Value of Corporate Accountability in the Global Political Economy' (2016) 4 London Review of International Law 127.

'risk tolerance' or 'risk appetite'.[14] There may be large gaps between external expectations of what constitutes an acceptable level of risk and the organisation's belief in what is reasonable.[15]

Reflecting its origins in technical risk, the language of risk management suggests objective measurement, quantification, and assessment.[16] It marks out certain issues as technical areas of expertise and inside knowledge. This is despite the fact that risk management processes, particularly when applied in a management and governance context, are rarely clear-cut, incontestable, or value neutral. As Michael Power observes, in many areas of organisational governance, the technical ideal of risk lies at the centre of the 'risk management collective imagination'.[17] Nevertheless, the façade of objectivity often means that a decision based on risk assessment is regarded as more legitimate than one that is not.[18]

By framing actual and potential labour rights violations as risks, HRDD may narrow and deflect rather than open space for workers or their representatives (or other stakeholders) to challenge company practices. When raising concerns or grievances, these actors may find themselves confronted by a bewildering and highly technical managerial discourse and by risk scores and matrices. As Christian Scheper has argued, framing human rights as risk management means that 'simple but fundamental criticism based on the idea of dignity and rights—blaming the brand firm for the inhumane conditions of its operations—is confronted with a complex system of new industries and actors', a 'realm of expertise and inside knowledge' and 'of dispersed responsibility and complex processes' that may have the effect of shielding a business from political demands.[19]

By way of simple example, the UN Guiding Principles on Business and Human Rights (UNGPs) make clear that while a company is responsible for avoiding all actual and potential adverse human rights impacts it may be involved with, it may not always be possible for a business to take action to address all such impacts simultaneously.[20] This recognition, combined with the political realities that tend, inevitably,

[14] Black, 'The Role of Risk in Regulatory Processes' (n 9) 328–29. As Black notes, there may be a significant gap between public expectations of an organisation's risk tolerance (which may be one of 'notional zero-failure') and what the organisation believes 'reasonable' expectations should be.

[15] ibid.

[16] Elizabeth Fisher, 'Risk and Governance' in David Levi-Faur (ed), *Oxford Handbook of Governance* (OUP 2012) 417, 419–20.

[17] Power, *Organized Uncertainty* (n 7) 70.

[18] Fisher, 'Risk and Governance' (n 16) 420.

[19] Christian Scheper '"From Naming and Shaming to Knowing and Showing": Human Rights and the Power of Corporate Practice' (2015) 19 International Journal of Human Rights 737, 750–52.

[20] The UNGPs make clear that, where prioritisation is necessary, the business should first seek to prevent and mitigate those risks that are most severe or where delayed response would make them irremediable. Severity is to be determined by the three factors of scale, scope, and irremediable character. UN OHCHR (United Nations Office of the High Commissioner for Human Rights), 'Guiding Principles on Business and Human Rights: Implementing the United Nations 'Protect, Respect, and Remedy' Framework' (2011) 26, Commentary on Guiding Principle 24 (hereafter UNGPs).

to guide prioritisation processes,[21] may lead a company to focus on certain risks (such as modern slavery or child labour) over others (such as freedom of association). The process of risk prioritisation may then provide a company with a seemingly rational and objective basis upon which to defend its decision not to devote resources to preventing anti-union behaviour among its suppliers. The prioritisation process may render it more difficult for outsiders to challenge company inaction in this area as the company may assure them that these less salient risks will be addressed by the company through its due diligence processes at some point in the future.

By demanding specific and extensive knowledge and expertise, the expansion of risk management into new fields tends to be accompanied (and, indeed, driven) by a corresponding expansion into the new field of the 'risk industry'.[22] As Power and others have pointed out, professions such as auditors, management consultants, and legal advisors have proven remarkably adept at using the incursion of risk management into new fields as opportunities to extend their risk management and mitigation advisory practices into new territory.[23] This expansion may come at the expense of other actors and approaches in the field.

Finally, while corporate risk management is about managing internal risk, it is also deployed as an organisational strategy to manage public expectations.[24] HRDD has the potential to be used by corporate actors to consolidate and legitimise existing approaches. Critical risk management scholars have demonstrated how, through risk management processes, organisations seek to manage, or even define and control, the terms on which they should be measured and held accountable.[25] Rather than being held to account by external actors for impacts of their activities, organisations are able to control accountability demands by delineating those risks that are manageable and those that are beyond their scope of responsibility. Sociologists and regulatory scholars studying corporate risk management processes have drawn attention to the way in which organisations' understanding and management of risk tends to 'slip' almost imperceptibly from managing *primary risk* to managing *secondary risk*.[26] Primary risk is the risk (to the company or the public interest) that is the formal focus of the risk management process. Secondary risk is the reputational (and potentially financial and legal) risk to the organisation from being seen to fail to effectively manage primary risk. Slippage between the two types of risk may be understandable and rational at the level of the individual firm or organisation.[27] There may also be synergies between the two

[21] Robert Baldwin and Julia Black, 'Driving Priorities in Risk-Based Regulation: What's the Problem?' (2016) 43 Journal of Law and Society 565.

[22] Power, *Organized Uncertainty* (n 7) 18.

[23] ibid 50; Bridget M Hutter and Clive J Jones, 'From Government to Governance: External Influences on Business Risk Management' (2007) 1 Regulation & Governance 27, 34.

[24] Black, 'The Role of Risk in Regulatory Processes' (n 9) 337.

[25] ibid.

[26] Power, 'The Risk Management of Everything' (n 1).

[27] ibid 60.

categories of risk in that secondary risk provides an incentive to properly manage primary risk. However, this 'blurring' can be problematic where the attention and efforts of organisations given responsibility to address primary risks increasingly focus on managing risks to themselves, with a view to managing external expectations and evading responsibility.[28] In this sense, risk management processes become a form of anticipatory defence, enabling entities to pre-empt accusations of blame by shaping expectations of which risks are capable of being addressed and which are not.[29]

In summary, conceptualising HRDD as risk management improves understanding of how the concept may be being interpreted by business. Critical risk management scholarship hints at both potential benefits and hazards implicit in the approach. Understanding HRDD as risk management alone, however, is insufficient as it fails to acknowledge the concept's regulatory function.

III. HRDD as Business Regulation

At the meso level, HRDD is business regulation. It constitutes a 'sustained and focused attempt to alter the behaviour of others according to defined standards and purposes with the intention of producing a broadly identified outcome or outcomes'.[30] Understanding HRDD as business regulation brings to light the many regulatory forms and structures that HRDD could take as the concept is further legalised. As explained in Chapter 2, the UNGPs are ambiguous on this question. It is also helpful for appreciating how subsequent contests (as elaborated upon in Chapters 5 and 6) have settled on some regulatory approaches and foreclosed others.[31] Conceptualising HRDD as business regulation also enables me to draw on socio-legal theories concerning the processes by which gaps within ambiguous and indeterminate business regulation are shaped and by whom.

A. HRDD's Form and Structure

This study is concerned with understanding contests over HRDD following the adoption of the UNGPs in 2011 and the implications of these contests for transnational labour governance. As elaborated upon in later chapters, much of this contestation relates to the nature of HRDD as a regulatory standard. To better understand these

[28] Power, *Organized Uncertainty* (n 7).
[29] ibid 18.
[30] Julia Black, 'Critical Reflections on Regulation' (2002) 27 Australian Journal of Legal Philosophy 1, 25.
[31] Tim Bartley, 'Certifying Forests and Factories: States, Social Movements, and the Rise of Private Regulation in the Apparel and Forest Products Fields' (2003) 31 Politics & Society 433.

contests, it is useful to offer a framework through which HRDD as business regulation can be understood. Below, I draw on a basic configuration offered by Colin Scott to understand a regulatory standard. For Scott, regulatory standards can be examined by reference to their *regulatory form* and *regulatory structure*.[32]

Regulatory form refers to the type of instrument through which the regulatory standard is set. A basic distinction can be made between 'hard law' and 'soft law' instruments. The term 'hard law' refers to legally binding obligations that are precise (or that can be made precise through adjudication or the issuance of detailed regulations) and that delegate authority for interpreting and implementing the law.[33] 'Soft law' refers to normative measures that have authority but which are not legally binding but intended to have normative effect, that is, to change behaviour.[34] In the UNGPs, HRDD is soft law. The intention is to guide corporate behaviour and encourage respect for human rights but not to bind companies in a legal sense. Corporate failure to live up to their responsibility to respect human rights will be judged not in the law courts but in the 'courts of public opinion'.[35] This feature of HRDD (and the corporate responsibility to respect human rights more broadly) has been the subject of strong criticism, particularly by human rights scholars.[36] However, as foreshadowed in Chapter 1 and discussed in Chapter 6, HRDD's legal form has been subject to contest, and the approach is finding its way into 'harder' forms of law at the national level.

The second way a regulatory standard can be characterised is by reference to its structure. Regulatory structure refers to the way the regulatory standard is expressed and the linkage between such expression and the achievement of the objectives sought.[37] While there is no generally accepted framework for categorising the structure of regulatory instruments,[38] regulatory governance scholarship commonly distinguishes between four broad regulatory approaches: prescriptive regulation,[39] self-regulation, outcome-orientated regulation, and process-orientated

[32] Colin Scott, 'Standard-Setting in Regulatory Regimes' in Baldwin, Cave, and Lodge (n 9) 105.

[33] Kenneth W Abbott and Duncan Snidal, 'Hard and Soft Law in International Governance' (2000) 54 International Organization 421, 421.

[34] Francis Snyder, 'The Effectiveness of European Community Law: Institutions, Processes, Tools and Techniques' (1993) 56(1) Modern Law Review 19.

[35] UNGPs (n 20).

[36] See eg David Bilchitz, 'A Chasm between "Is" and "Ought"? A Critique of the Normative Foundations of the SRSG's Framework and the Guiding Principles' in Surya Deva and David Bilchitz (eds), *Human Rights Obligations of Business: Beyond the Corporate Responsibility to Respect?* (CUP 2013); Surya Deva, 'Treating Human Rights Lightly: A Critique of the Consensus Rhetoric and the Language Employed by the Guiding Principles' in Surya Deva and David Bilchitz (eds), *Human Rights Obligations of Business: Beyond the Responsibility to Respect* (CUP 2012); Sally Wheeler, 'Corporate Respect for Human Rights: As Good As It Gets?' in Amanda Perry-Kessaris (ed), *Socio-Legal Approaches to International Economic Law: Text, Context Subtext* (Routledge 2013).

[37] Scott, 'Standard-Setting' (n 32) 105.

[38] Cary Coglianese and Evan Mendelson, 'Meta-Regulation and Self-Regulation' in Baldwin, Cave, and Lodge (n 9) 148.

[39] This is also often referred to as 'command-and-control'-type regulation. It entails the creation, monitoring, and enforcement of prescriptive standards by the state through orders and

regulation.[40] HRDD has the potential to be legalised as any of the latter three types of regulation.

Self-regulation is a form of regulation in which the regulated entity imposes commands and consequences upon itself.[41] As noted in Chapter 2, private labour governance overwhelmingly takes this form, and public soft law instruments such as the Organisation for Economic Co-operation and Development (OECD) Guidelines for Multinational Enterprises also encourage corporate self-regulation. As presented in the UNGPs, HRDD also takes this form. However, as also discussed in Chapter 2, the UNGPs are ambiguous as to the role of the state in steering or mandating the practice. This leads us to examine other regulatory structures—outcome-orientated and process-orientated regulation—which assign a more active role to the state in shaping corporate conduct.

Both outcome and process-orientated regulation involve 'outside regulators deliberately … seek[ing] to induce targets to develop their own internal, self-regulatory responses to public problems'.[42] These types of regulation are 'intended to alleviate regulators' limited access to information and expertise, enlist corporate commitment, enhance firms' self-regulatory capacity, and overcome the inherent limitations of prescriptive rules'.[43] *Outcome-orientated regulation* involves 'regulatory specification of outcomes' or 'goals-oriented duties of care'.[44] It is left to the organisation to determine what actions are appropriate in the circumstances, and regulators analyse the congruence between the regulated actor's outputs and regulatory objectives. As its name indicates, the regulatory focus is on *outcomes*. According to Gilad, this type of regulation is valuable where industries are heterogeneous or rapidly changing, or both, and the outputs that regulators can observe and assess are valid measures of firms' regulatory performance.[45]

In contrast, *process-orientated regulation* focuses on systems design. It requires firms to engage in a process of self-evaluation, design, and management of their operations and their internal governance and controls. Firms are required to devise compliance systems that embody regulatory goals and objectives in ways that are

sanctions: Robert Baldwin, 'Regulation: After "Command and Control"' in Keith Hawkins (ed), *The Human Face of Law: Essays in Honour of Donald Harris* (OUP 1997).

40 While these are identified as distinct regulatory approaches in the literature, in practice, regulatory regimes are unlikely to conform precisely to one of these but rather to combine different features of several approaches: Sharon Gilad, 'It Runs in the Family: Meta-Regulation and Its Siblings' (2010) 4 Regulation & Governance 485, 489.

41 Coglianese and Mendelson (n 38) 150. As Coglianese and Mendelson note, an action can be considered self-regulatory where it is motivated by implicit threats from outside regulators such as civil society, investors, or the state.

42 ibid.

43 Gilad, 'It Runs in the Family' (n 40) 486.

44 ibid.

45 ibid 487.

relevant to their individual contexts.[46] This type of regulation requires businesses to engage in planning and other management processes to address a given problem, with firms being held to account for the adequacy and efficacy of their self-regulatory systems. Broadly speaking, process-orientated regulation seeks to mandate and monitor both organisations' first-tier operations and their second-tier governance and controls. It involves a deliberate process by which, as described by Power, internal management systems become the 'critical interface between regulatory and business values, and hence between society and organizational operations'.[47]

Process-orientated regulation is common in advanced industrialised economies and found in public policy areas such as occupational health and safety, employment discrimination, and food safety. It offers several benefits to regulators. It capitalises on a company's inherent capacity to regulate itself and its superior access to company-specific information. It is considered particularly useful in contexts where more prescriptive or outcome-based forms of regulation are unlikely to be successful. This includes where industries are heterogeneous and complex, where there is a lack of commitment or capacity for compliance among large parts of the business community, and/or where regulators and regulated organisations have limited understanding of what outcomes they are seeking or what a good self-regulatory system looks like.[48] Regulatory scholarship has identified a range of conditions under which process and outcome-orientated regulation are likely to succeed in securing regulatory objectives. In a broad-ranging review of outcome and process-orientated strategies, for example, Sharon Gilad concludes that their effective use 'requires a rare combination of high regulatory capacity, a stable regulatory agenda, and a supportive political environment'.[49]

B. Shaping Ambiguous Business Regulation

Conceptualising HRDD as business regulation enables me to draw on new institutionalist theories of how the meanings of ambiguous and/or open-ended regulatory terms are shaped and by whom. As Lauren Edelman and Shauhin Talesh note, much of the socio-legal and regulatory governance literature presumes that contests over norms are fought out prior to the norm's adoption or through questions of compliance or non-compliance.[50] Yet, many rules are drafted in such a

[46] Sharon Gilad, 'Institutionalizing Fairness in Financial Markets: Mission Impossible?' (2011) 5 Regulation & Governance 309, 309–10.

[47] Power, *Organized Uncertainty* (n 7) 41–42.

[48] Gilad, 'It Runs in the Family' (n 40) 486–87.

[49] ibid 485.

[50] Lauren B Edelman and Shauhin A Talesh, 'To Comply or Not to Comply—That Isn't the Question: How Organizations Construct the Meaning of Compliance' in Christine Parker and Vibeke Lehmann Nielsen (eds), *Explaining Compliance: Business Responses to Regulation* (Edward Elgar 2011) 103.

way as to be open to alternative interpretations. It is also increasingly common for regulatory approaches to shift the responsibility for interpreting what constitutes compliance onto the regulated entity, for example, through forms of outcome and process-orientated regulation described above.[51] As Gilad emphasises, this underscores the importance of understanding '*who* constructs the meaning of compliance with regulation and *how*'.[52]

Legal endogeneity theory helps to explain how meaning of ambiguous law is shaped.[53] Legal endogeneity theorists posit that ambiguous rules leave spaces and political opportunities for public and private actors to interpret and apply rules in ways that are consistent with their frames, values, and interests. These interpretations are then fed back into public norms through judicial interpretation, legislation, or regulatory interpretation and application.[54] This process may be understood as a form of norm 'renegotiation during the implementation and enforcement phases of governance'.[55] Certain features render some norms more amenable to this process of renegotiation than others. This includes where norms use vague and ambiguous language, where they shift the responsibility for interpreting what compliance means to regulated entities, where they are politically contested, and where they provide for weak enforcement mechanisms.[56]

Edelman poses a basic and idealised sequence by which this process of endogeneity occurs. First, in response to uncertainties allowed by ambiguous laws, organisations undergo a process of *legalisation*, in which they adopt formal structures which may be decoupled from their actual practices to symbolise compliance. Second, the meaning of the law and of compliance is *managerialised* as organisations attribute managerial and business goals and values to their compliance structures. Third, through processes of isomorphism, these formal compliance structures, and business goals and values attached to them, diffuse to other business entities. Finally, public legal institutions *defer* to these business understandings of compliance by way of judicial rulings, legislation, and/or regulation.[57]

Subsequent elaborations on legal endogeneity theory have shown that it is not just the regulated actors that shape the meaning of compliance with specific norms. Business professionals—acting as intermediaries—may also play key roles in co-constructing and mediating understandings of compliance. Again, a stylised

[51] Sharon Gilad, 'Beyond Endogeneity: How Firms and Regulators Co-Construct the Meaning of Regulation' (2014) 36 Law & Policy 134, 135.

[52] ibid.

[53] For a brief discussion of other approaches to this question, including the theory of incomplete contracts, see Kimberley D Krawiec, 'Cosmetic Compliance and the Failure of Negotiated Governance' (2003) 81 Washington University Law Quarterly 487.

[54] Edelman and Talesh (n 50).

[55] Krawiec (n 53) 495.

[56] Lauren Edelman, 'Legal Ambiguity and Symbolic Structures: Organizational Mediation of Civil Rights Law' (1992) 97 American Journal of Sociology 1531.

[57] Lauren Edelman, *Working Law: Courts, Corporations, and Symbolic Civil Rights* (Chicago UP 2016) 27–41.

sequential process for this phenomenon is put forward. First, business professionals induce business to legalise by amplifying the risk of non-compliance with ambiguous laws. Second, business professionals contribute to the managerialisation of law by constructing the meaning of compliance in ways that match their professional identities and enhance corporate demand for their services. Third, as participants in business and legal networks, professionals play an active part in the process of endogeneity by transmitting institutionalised business practices into legal jurisdictions.[58]

To date, legal endogeneity studies have largely focused on the interpretation of business laws at the national level.[59] However, there is recognition in socio-legal and regulatory governance literatures of the influential roles that businesses play in shaping transnational law. Intermediaries such as lawyers, auditors, and other practitioners mediate between the global and local through translating, advising, and implementing global norms.[60] It is also recognised that these roles are often not neutral and that further research is necessary to show who these intermediaries are and 'what price they exact in their mediation of norms that are globally authorized and locally enacted or implemented'.[61]

While conceiving of HRDD as business regulation is important, it is of limited heuristic value in understanding the multiple levels at which HRDD is currently being contested and shaped. For this reason, it is also necessary to consider HRDD as an emerging transnational norm.

IV. HRDD as an Emerging Transnational Norm

The final level at which this book conceptualises and examines HRDD is as an emerging transnational norm. Understanding HRDD in this way directs attention to the specific sites and dynamics through which struggles over the concept are taking place. However, it adds another layer of complexity as it requires theorisation of the way in which contests over the meaning of transnational norms are fought and, potentially, resolved. This section begins by briefly explaining the emergent nature of HRDD as a transnational norm, drawing on Martha Finnemore and Kathryn Sikkink's theory on norm dynamics.[62] Using scholarship on global

[58] Gilad, 'Beyond Endogeneity' (n 51) 137–38.

[59] See eg Shauhin Talesh, 'Rule-Intermediaries in Action: How State and Business Stakeholders Influence the Meaning of Consumer Rights in Regulatory Governance Arrangements' (2015) 37 Law & Policy 1.

[60] Terence C Halliday, 'Recursivity of Global Normmaking: A Sociolegal Agenda' (2009) 5 Annual Review of Law and Society 263, 285–86; Kenneth W Abbott, David Levi-Faur, and Duncan Snidal, 'Theorizing Regulatory Intermediaries: The RIT Model' (2017) 670 Annals of the American Academy of Political and Social Sciences 14.

[61] Halliday (n 60) 286.

[62] Martha Finnemore and Kathryn Sikkink, 'International Norm Dynamics and Political Change' (1998) 52 International Organization 887.

norm-making, it then addresses three relevant issues. These are *how* rules are interpreted and elaborated upon in transnational regulatory governance, *by whom*, and with what *authority*.

A. Transnational Norm Dynamics

Many theories on transnational norm-making emphasise that norm development goes through various processes, cycles, rounds, or episodes. Prominent among these is Finnemore and Sikkink's theory of the norm 'life cycle'.[63] There are three stages to this cycle: norm acceptance, norm cascade, and internalisation. In the initial stage of norm acceptance, norm entrepreneurs persuade a critical mass of states (norm leaders) to embrace a new norm. Support for the norm by a critical mass of actors creates a tipping point, leading to the second stage. In this second stage of norm cascade, norm leaders (largely states, intergovernmental organisations (IGOs) and networks) employ methods such as institutionalisation and demonstration to socialise others to become norm followers. In the final stage, norms are 'internalised' as they acquire a 'taken-for-granted' quality and are no longer a matter of broad public debate. This final stage of internalisation entails the increased involvement of actors such as lawyers, other professions, and bureaucracies in establishing norms as prevailing practice. As Finnemore and Sikkink explain, each of these three stages is led by different actors and has different mechanisms of diffusion.[64] Completion of this life cycle is not inevitable, with numerous examples in history of norms failing to proceed from the first to the second stage.

Finnemore and Sikkink's life cycle framework of norms is useful for understanding the status of HRDD in transnational governance. HRDD can be characterised as being broadly located in the second stage of the three stages. Acting as a 'norm entrepreneur' and through the United Nations, the United Nations Special Representative of the Secretary-General on the Issue of Human Rights and Transnational Corporations and Other Business Enterprises (SRSG) has successfully generated a new norm through reframing corporate responsibility for human rights in terms of due diligence, a frame that has resonated and become a new way of talking about and understanding the issues (see further Chapter 4). This norm is now 'cascading', by way of adoption by international organisations and states, among other actors (see Chapters 5 and 6, respectively).

While theories such as that of Finnemore and Sikkink help to elucidate the extent to which HRDD, as an emergent norm, is diffused within transnational governance, they are not intended to, nor do they adequately explicate *transnational legal processes*, that is, the processes through which norms are constructed, carried,

[63] ibid 895–905.
[64] ibid 898.

and diffused across national borders.[65] Moreover, their theory conceptualises norms rather narrowly in a way that fails to recognise either that behavioural prescriptions may not be binding law, but nonetheless codified and accepted as legitimate and authoritative, or that transnational norms may emanate from non-state bodies.[66]

The theory of legal recursivity, developed by socio-legal scholars Terence Halliday and Bruce Carruthers, offers an account of transnational legal processes which more adequately elucidates the actors and processes involved in norm elaboration.[67] Legal recursivity theory recognises that global norm-making is a more complex process than simply states, acting collectively, formulating norms which are then imposed on individual states or on private organisations. Building on insights from transnational regulatory studies, including on the multilayered and polycentric nature of transnational regulation, Halliday and Carruthers theorise that transnational norm elaboration occurs in an iterative, dynamic, and recursive manner. Like legal endogeneity theory, legal recursivity emphasises that the formal adoption of a norm at an IGO is often the beginning of a transnational norm-making process. As Halliday explains, 'to reach consensus or agreement among strongly contending actors, a global institution ... may forge an agreement that appears to be a settlement but in fact merely places in juxtaposition quite divergent diagnoses and prescriptions for action'.[68] There may be years and numerous processes of clarification between the time a new concept or norm is introduced into transnational governance and the time it 'settles', that is, obtains a stable meaning.[69] Norms may change in form (eg from soft to hard forms of law), may be embraced by various types of actors (eg they may begin as management ideas or industry self-regulation but later be adopted by states or IGOs),[70] and may be shaped by various cycles of lawmaking at different levels (national, regional, and global) that engage and interact with each other.[71] At each point in its transposition, a norm is reinterpreted and 'translated'. These processes of interpretation and translation may take place by way of formal dispute resolution but also by way of quasi-judicial and non-judicial guidance from state and non-state regulators, as well as local interpretations and codes by private actors, individual firms, and intermediaries.[72]

65 Gregory Shaffer, 'Transnational Legal Process and State Change' (2021) 37 Law & Social Inquiry 229, 233.

66 Halliday (n 60) 268.

67 Terence C Halliday and Bruce G Carruthers, 'The Recusivity of Law: Global Norm Making and National Lawmaking in the Globalization of Corporate Insolvency Regimes' (2007) American Journal of Sociology 1135.

68 Halliday (n 60) 280.

69 See also Terence C Halliday and Gregory Shaffer, *Transnational Legal Orders* (CUP 2015) 42–44.

70 John Braithwaite and Peter Drahos, *Global Business Regulation* (CUP 2000) 481. See also Marie-Laure Djelic and Kerstin Sahlin-Andersson, 'Reordering the World: Transnational Regulatory Governance and Its Challenges' in Levi-Faur (n 16) 752–53.

71 Halliday (n 60); Braithwaite and Drahos (n 70).

72 Julia Black, '"Says Who?" Liquid Authority and Interpretive Control in Transnational Regulatory Regimes' (2017) 9 International Theory 286, 290.

B. Interpretive Authority in Transnational Governance

The discussion above has established that transnational norms may be ambiguous, that there may be multiple and potentially conflicting interpretation of a norm, and that norm elaboration is recursive and iterative. How, if at all, does one interpretation emerge as authoritative? Resolving conflicting interpretations of rules is more complex in the transnational sphere than in the domestic one. In the latter, interpretive authority tends to be exercised by a regulator in accordance with its legal mandate. In the international context, there are examples of international institutions with the power to issue and enforce binding interpretations of rules (eg the World Trade Organisation's Dispute Settlement Body and the International Criminal Court), but these are relatively rare. In the 'thin' institutional context of international relations, judicial and quasi-judicial institutions are less developed and infrequently used. This is the case with HRDD: there is no one institution with the power to issue an authoritative interpretation of the concept, 'no constitutionalized place for the final decision'.[73]

Scholars in regulatory studies, political science, and law tend to link the question of interpretive control over the meaning of a rule or standard to the issue of *authority* and, more specifically, *epistemic authority* (the authority to provide interpretations).[74] Here, we come across another important distinction between domestic and transnational regulatory spheres. In the domestic arena, authority tends to be 'solid' in that it is expressed through rules issued by a governing institution and binding on those to whom it is addressed.[75] In the transnational setting, however, as already noted, there is rarely a single institution capable of providing an authoritative interpretation of a rule or standard. This does not mean that authority is not exercised in transnational regulatory governance.[76] But authority tends to operate differently.

It is useful to conceptualise authority in global governance not as the power to issue commands but to induce deference in others.[77] Here, scholars have used the metaphor of liquidity to describe authority in the transnational sphere because it draws attention to the notion of authority as dynamic, contested, and dispersed unevenly over multiple actors.[78] As Julia Black summarises,

> [A]uthority in the transnational context is informal, based on social and political acceptance not formal legal rules; it is ideational, based on ideas of what is the appropriate thing to do (though often articulated in technocratic terms and based

[73] Nico Krisch 'Liquid Authority in Global Governance' (2017) 9 International Theory 237, 238.
[74] ibid 269.
[75] ibid 238.
[76] ibid.
[77] ibid 239–43.
[78] ibid 243.

> on epistemic claim to expert knowledge); it is necessarily exercised through non-legal or 'soft' law norms and 'enforced' through social or community practices.[79]

The notion of liquid authority clarifies a range of dynamics in transnational regulatory regimes, including, as Black points out, in the 'little explored' aspect of how interpretive control over written norms is exercised.[80] The diffusion of a norm into different instruments and settings means that there are multiple entities or regulators purporting to interpret what the concept means.

Where authority is liquid, the extent to which an organisation (and, by extension, that organisation's interpretation of a rule) will be regarded as authoritative depends upon perceptions of its legitimacy. In a transnational context, unable to rely on state-based constitutional settlements as the source of their legitimacy, actors must rely on social acceptance.[81] Legitimacy can be defined as

> a generalized perception or assumption that the actions of an entity are desirable, proper, or appropriate within some socially constructed set of norms, values, beliefs and definitions.[82]

In a regulatory context, legitimacy rests on the acceptability and credibility of the organisation to those it seeks to govern.[83] In seeking to understand how legitimacy works in a transnational context, a number of scholars have drawn upon sociologist Mark Suchman's categorisation of different types of legitimacy that external audiences can grant to an organisation.[84] Legitimacy can be *pragmatically based*, meaning that it is rooted in a person or organisation's own calculation of their self-interest—where the person or social group perceives that the organisation will pursue their interests directly or indirectly. It may be *normatively based*, by which the person or social group perceives the goals and/or procedures of the organisation to be normatively or morally appropriate. Finally, it may be *cognitively based*,

79 Black, '"Says Who?"' (n 72) 287.

80 ibid 292. As Black emphasises, it is important to recognise that interpretation is distinct from dispute resolution: the question is not 'Who can impose sanctions on another?' but 'How, if at all, are interpretations stabilized through the exercise of interpretive control and/or interpretive authority within the regulatory regime?': 291.

81 ibid 293.

82 Mark C Suchman, 'Managing Legitimacy: Strategic and Institutional Approaches' (1995) 20 Academy of Management Review 571, 574.

83 Julia Black, 'Constructing and Contesting Legitimacy and Accountability in Polycentric Regulatory Regimes' (2008) 2 Regulation & Governance 137, 144; Deborah D Avant, Martha Finnemore, and Susan K Sell, 'Conclusion: Authority, Legitimacy, and Accountability in Global Politics' in Deborah D Avant, Martha Finnemore, and Susan K Sell (eds), *Who Governs the Globe?* (CUP 2012) 360.

84 Suchman (n 82). See eg Sigrid Quack, 'Law, Expertise and Legitimacy in Transnational Economic Governance: An Introduction' (2010) 8 Socio-Economic Review 3; Benjamin Cashore, 'Legitimacy and the Privatization of Environmental Governance: How Non-State Market-Driven (NSMD) Governance Systems Gain Rule-Making Authority' (2002) 15 Governance 503; Black, 'Constructing and Contesting Legitimacy' (n 83).

where the organisation is accepted as necessary or inevitable.[85] Black further divides normative-based legitimacy into four sub-types or 'claims': constitutional, justice, functional or performance, and democratic.[86] Constitutional claims focus on the extent to which an organisation conforms with written norms and broader legal values of procedural justice, consistency, and so on. Justice claims emphasise values or ends which the organisation is pursuing. Functional claims focus on the outcomes and consequences of the organisation, such as efficiency, expertise or effectiveness, and the extent to which the organisation conforms to professional norms. Finally, democratic claims concern the extent to which the organisation or regime is seen as operating in accordance with particular models of democratic governance, whether representative, participatory, or deliberative.[87] Legitimacy may depend on the function being performed: a non-governmental organisation (NGO), for example, may be perceived by some as legitimate in performing an advocacy role but less so in an advisory role.[88] Legitimacy is strategically constructed by transnational actors, often alongside rule-making activities.[89]

V. Conclusion

This chapter has proposed that HRDD needs to be conceptualised at three distinct levels if we are to understand subsequent contests that have taken place with respect to its meaning and elaboration at international, regional, and national levels. HRDD can be approached and understood as a practical business tool of *risk management*, as a novel *regulatory approach* to securing greater business accountability, and as an *emerging transnational norm*. At the micro level, HRDD's embodiment of a risk management approach has implications for how corporate actors approach and respond to issues and how these processes and their legitimacy are framed and understood. Risk management is intimately bound up with notions of technical data collection, quantification, and objectivity. In addition, as critical risk scholars remind us, risk management carries its own hazards. These include the tendency for risk management language to mask subjectivity and political judgement and to shield actors from external critique. There is also the probability of slippage or elision occurring whereby focus shifts from primary to secondary risk.

HRDD is not just an internal process of risk management. As articulated in the UNGPs, it is also a form of business regulation. Conceptualising HRDD at this meso level illuminates the many regulatory forms and structures that HRDD may take as the concept is subject to further legalisation. Legal endogeneity theory

85 Suchman (n 82).
86 Black, 'Constructing and Contesting Legitimacy' (n 83) 145–46.
87 ibid 146.
88 Black, '"Says Who?"' (n 72).
89 Quack (n 84) 8.

hints at the broad scope for contestation over rules subsequent to formal adoption and the range of actors involved in these processes of norm translation and implementation.

Finally, this chapter has emphasised that HRDD is an emerging transnational norm. Legal recursivity theory directs attention to the multiple levels and sites at which HRDD is being contested and interpreted (Chapters 5 and 6). Transnational regulatory theory suggests that while there may be no single global institution with the capacity to fix the meaning of HRDD, this does not mean that the transnational space is devoid of interpretative authority or that a meaning will not solidify. Different actors enjoy different types and degrees of interpretive authority, and this dynamic may influence the extent to which, and how, one actor's interpretation emerges as dominant. Actors and organisations may also compete for interpretive authority. However, before considering how and by whom interpretive authority is being exercised with respect to HRDD, it is necessary to examine divergent understandings of the concept. This task is taken up in Chapter 4.

4

HRDD and Divergent Logics in Transnational Labour Governance

I. Introduction

In Chapter 2, I demonstrated that the United Nations Special Representative of the Secretary-General on the Issue of Human Rights and Transnational Corporations and Other Business Enterprises (SRSG), was able to garner broad-based support for the concept of human rights due diligence (HRDD) by reframing human rights as risk management and by the use of strategic ambiguity. I intimated that both these devices had implications for subsequent elaboration and contestation over the concept. This chapter empirically explores how key stakeholder groups in transnational labour governance interpreted the concept as presented in the UN Guiding Principles on Business and Human Rights (UNGPs).[1] This exercise helps reveal the extent that a shared understanding of the concept has emerged within transnational labour governance. Elucidating different interpretations of the concept is also a precursor to examining contests to further institutionalise the due diligence approach at different levels, as examined in Chapters 5 and 6.

Drawing on in-depth interviews conducted between 2015 and 2017 and document analysis,[2] I show, in this chapter, that HRDD has enabled a shared language among actors with formerly very diverse frames and approaches. However, actors interpreted HRDD in different ways. These divergences in interpretation of HRDD have arisen largely from the fact that actors are filtering the meaning of the concept through divergent logics.[3] I identify two stylised logics in the field. The first of these is a transnational labour rights logic, which emphasises labour and human rights; empowerment of workers and unions; and principles of transparency, participation, and accountability. The second is a managerialist logic that emphasises risk

[1] UN OHCHR (United Nations Office of the High Commissioner for Human Rights), 'Guiding Principles on Business and Human Rights: Implementing the United Nations 'Protect, Respect, and Remedy' Framework' (2011) (hereafter UNGPs).

[2] See Chapter 1 for discussion of method.

[3] Drawing on Talesh, the term 'logic' is used here to refer 'to the way in which individuals organise their thoughts and assumptions about meaning, values, schemas, and culture': Shauhin Talesh, 'How Dispute Resolution System Design Matters: An Organizational Analysis of Dispute Resolution Structures and Consumer Lemon Laws' (2012) 46 Law & Society Review 463, 470. See further Roger Friedland and Robert R Alford, 'Bringing Society Back In: Symbols, Practices, and Institutional Contradictions' in Walter Powell and Paul J DiMaggio (eds), *The New Institutionalism in Organizational Analysis* (University of Chicago Press 1991).

Human Rights Due Diligence and Labour Governance. Ingrid Landau, Oxford University Press. © Ingrid Landau 2023.
DOI: 10.1093/oso/9780198876069.003.0004

management; managerial discretion; and control, flexibility, and efficiency. When mediated through these competing logics, HRDD assumes different purposes and implications. The former conceptualises HRDD largely as *business regulation*, whereas the latter conceptualises HRDD as *risk management*.[4] While a transnational labour rights logic leads to a robust interpretation that challenges extant business models and activities, a managerialist logic leads to an interpretation of HRDD that is discretionary, process-orientated, and constrained. This latter logic ultimately presents much less of a challenge to existing corporate practice.

Following this Introduction, section II elaborates on the notion of the transnational labour governance field and identifies two dominating and competing field logics. Section III examines how, when filtered through these two logics, understandings of HRDD diverge. I show how the two logics lead to divergent understandings of HRDD with respect to its scope and breadth and to divergent approaches to risk tolerance, stakeholder engagement, transparency, and accountability. Section IV offers concluding observations.

II. Transnational Labour Governance and Competing Logics

This chapter explores areas of convergence and divergence in field actors' understandings of HRDD. In doing so, it follows a similar structure and approach to that adopted by legal endogeneity scholars in other policy domains to understand how various actors give different meanings to substantially similar laws.[5] I begin by delineating the field before using empirical data to inductively explore different field logics. I identify areas of consensus and cohesion among actors in the field with respect to HRDD before turning to consider significant divergences in how actors understand the concept and its purpose. The extent to which regulatory bodies at the international and national level are deferring to either interpretation is addressed in Chapters 5 and 6.

A. Delineating the Field

As explained in Chapter 1, this project conceives of transnational labour governance as a semi-autonomous space where various actors are shaping and contesting state and non-state efforts to regulate transnational business conduct with respect to labour rights. The field is multi-organisational and is a socially constructed arena of 'organizations that, in the aggregate, constitute a recognized area of

[4] See Chapter 3.

[5] See eg Talesh (n 3); Lauren B Edelman, *Working Law: Courts, Corporations, and Symbolic Civil Rights* (University of Chicago Press 2016).

institutional life',[6] which 'brings together a number of different actors (often with different interests, ideologies, and organizational forms) into routine contact with one another, under a common frame of reference, in pursuit of an at least partially shared project'.[7] The transnational labour governance field is issue-specific, but it overlaps (conceptually and in practice) with other fields such as business and human rights. While 'loosely networked', the field 'consists of several centres of activity that monitor each other'.[8] These centres are geographic (North America and Western Europe) and institutional (located within the United Nations (UN), Organisation for Economic Co-operation and Development (OECD), and International Labour Organization (ILO)). The field is populated by many actors, including intergovernmental organisations (IGOs), states, business representative organisations, non-governmental organisations (NGOs), and trade unions, as well as law firms and other types of organisations offering advisory and consultancy services.

B. A Common Language But Not a Common Understanding

Interviews and documentary analysis confirmed that HRDD has enjoyed a swift and broad ascension in transnational labour governance. A wide range of actors have quickly become familiar with the concept and begun to draw on it in their work. In the transnational labour governance field, HRDD has played an important and welcome function as a bridge between long-established and formerly disparate actors in relation to the standard of responsible business conduct in a global economy. According to one interviewee, for example, HRDD offers 'a framework around which we can have a conversation' and a 'sort of scaffolding around which all these different actors are able to build'.[9] Whereas before,

> everyone talked about human rights but no-one really had a concept of how it applied in business or the relationship between business and NGOs. It was all very loose ... now there's an actual structure around which to have these discussions.[10]

The concept has enabled 'a shared language' and 'a way of talking about ... core concepts and debating how this plays out in this particular case'.[11] For business, the

[6] Paul J DiMaggio and Walter W Powell, 'The Iron Cage Revisited: Institutional Isomorphism and Collective Rationality in Organizational Fields' in Powell and DiMaggio (n 3) 63, 64.

[7] Tim Bartley, 'How Foundations Shape Social Movements: The Construction of an Organizational Field and the Rise of Forest Certification' (2007) 54(3) Social Problems 233.

[8] ibid 235.

[9] Interviewee 9E.

[10] ibid.

[11] Interviewee 6E.

concept offers an attractive and familiar framework through which to recast and augment their corporate social responsibility efforts and to respond to stakeholder demands in a way that is likely to be seen by such actors as legitimate and desirable. For international labour rights advocates, the concept is largely used in an instrumental fashion. As one interviewee succinctly explained, 'you get more out of them by talking about risk'.[12]

While HRDD is facilitating a shared discourse, actors have not understood the concept in the same way. Documentary analysis and interviews revealed significant divergences between key actors in the field with respect to what HRDD entails. These divergences embrace the purposes of HRDD as well as what it requires a business to do. I elaborate on these divergences below.

C. The Transnational Labour Rights Logic and the Business Logic

Based on interview and documentary analysis, I argue that there are two distinct logics at play with respect to the interpretation of HRDD: a transnational labour rights logic and a business logic. It is important to recognise that these are stylised logics, which different actors may embrace to varying degrees. It is also the case that certain businesses may undertake HRDD in a way that is broadly consistent with a transnational labour-orientated logic. Nonetheless, it is the contention of this book that these logics coexist in the transnational labour governance field and have implications for how HRDD has been interpreted and legalised.

The first distinct logic I describe as a transnational labour rights logic. It is adopted by what I term for shorthand below 'labour actors'. These include the International Trade Union Council (ITUC) and the Trade Union Advisory Committee to the OECD (TUAC), workers' rights advocacy organisations such as the Clean Clothes Campaign (CCC), certain multi-stakeholder initiatives such as the Ethical Trading Initiative (ETI), and global human rights organisations such as Human Rights Watch (HRW) and Oxfam International. These organisations see the goals and purposes of HRDD through a logic tied to labour and human rights, accountability, and social justice.

The second distinct logic is a business one. Business actors (which, for the purposes of this chapter, include corporations, business representative organisations, industry groups, and a significant segment of the business advisory services market) regard HRDD, including as it relates to labour rights, as a valuable process for managing risk not only to rights holders but also to the business. In approaching HRDD, the business-orientated logic emphasises managerial discretion, flexibility,

[12] Interviewee 27E.

and efficiency. Business actors emphasise the need for expectations relating to the scope and nature of HRDD to be 'reasonable' and to acknowledge resource constraints and the complexity of business models, arrangements, and relationships. Most actors adopting a business-orientated logic see HRDD as a practical tool and resist the notion that the concept should be used as a standard to which legal liability should be attached. When mediated through these distinct logics, HRDD takes on different purposes and meanings.

III. Key Areas of Divergence

Interviews and documentary analysis revealed significant divergences between labour and business actors in five areas: the purpose of HRDD, its scope, risk tolerance, stakeholder engagement, and transparency and accountability. These differences are summarised in Table 1.

A. HRDD's Purpose

Viewed through a transnational labour rights logic, the purpose of HRDD was to enable a company to meet its corporate responsibility to respect human rights. As one labour actor explained, 'The purpose [of HRDD] is for the company to discharge its responsibility relating to actual and potential harm to society.'[13] Another put it simply as 'there is a responsibility of companies to respect human rights and due diligence is the way you get there'.[14] It was this broader responsibility to avoid actual or potential adverse human rights impacts that was seen as paramount. As one interviewee from the international trade union movement explained, the fact that the SRSG had 'got it right' concerning the respective responsibilities of states and private actors with respect to human rights meant that the unions 'were not bothered by the due diligence'.[15] Interviewees adopting a transnational labour rights logic also tended to strongly emphasise the innovative nature of HRDD in terms of shifting corporate focus away from risks to the company to an exclusive focus on risks to *rights holders*.

Business actors were much more likely to position HRDD as the ultimate measure of responsible business conduct and to downplay, or even omit, discussion of the broader corporate responsibility to respect human rights. Business actors also often articulated that the purpose of HRDD was to help a company identify and prevent adverse human rights risks to rights holders. However,

[13] Interviewee 30B.
[14] Interviewee 29A.
[15] Interviewee 30B.

Table 1 Summary of differences between two competing logics

Human rights due diligence	Transnational labour rights logic	Business logic
Purpose	To discharge responsibility to respect human rights To protect rights holders	To demonstrate corporate responsibility To protect rights holders *and* minimise risks to company (eg reputational risk)
Scope	Extensive: labour rights, human rights, and social justice	Limited: theoretically all rights but subject to prioritisation and resources the company is willing to commit
Risk tolerance	Zero tolerance of rights violations	Some level of rights violations inevitable and acceptable
Stakeholder engagement	Workers, unions, and NGOs as partners, collaborators, and critics	Workers, unions, and NGOs predominantly viewed as informational resources, particularly in relation to risk identification
Transparency and accountability	Transparency of process central to legitimacy Evolving public standard of corporate conduct Outcome-focused	Transparency subject to discretion, including in prioritising risks for prevention and mitigation Tool for internal risk management Limited accountability to other actors Process-focused

Source: author.

they also tended to frame the purpose and value of HRDD in terms of business value. Interviewees often moved swiftly from discussing HRDD's purpose in identifying and managing risks to rights holders to its purposes in identifying and managing corporate reputational, and potentially financial and legal, risks.[16]

Divergent understandings of the purpose of HRDD were further reflected in the relative emphasis placed on the various stages of the due diligence process. Consistent with an understanding of HRDD as a process directed at ensuring respect for human rights, labour actors emphasised the equal importance of all four stages of HRDD (assessing actual and potential adverse human rights impacts, integrating and acting on the findings, tracking responses, and communicating about how impacts are addressed). HRDD involves the 'full circle ...: you assess

[16] In doing so, they displayed slippage between primary and secondary risk, a hazard associated with risk management as discussed in Chapter 4.

your risks, you understand what's wrong and then you try to change it, and then you monitor if that worked, then you assess the risk again'.[17]

In contrast, business actors placed paramount emphasis on the initial stages of risk identification and assessment as the stages that were most valuable in identifying and assessing risks to the company arising from a failure to manage adverse human rights impacts. As one business actor explained, '[companies] probably wouldn't say this out loud—but [HRDD is] more a matter of getting a sense of the risks—a risk assessment process'.[18] The interviewee explained:

> a lot of people will then say ok, we'll do an assessment of which countries we have problems in, of our hotspots and so on. And then they may do something like an audit to learn more. And then most companies stop there. They may try to tinker around some remedial actions ... They are sort of stopping a quarter of the way around the circle in terms of just getting a better sense of the risks.[19]

A business consultant similarly observed: 'when I talk to clients about it, the main thing that I'm talking about when I use human rights due diligence is the identification of impacts that are human rights impacts, and the segregation of those impacts by severity and by involvement'. The interviewee went on to emphasise, 'I treat integration and response as different from due diligence. So in a global sense, I use due diligence as the impact assessment.'[20]

The business logic's framing of HRDD as having the dual purpose of protecting rights holders and the company itself also led to differing interpretations of the prioritisation process. While the UNGPs recognise that large companies may need to prioritise certain risks of adverse human rights impacts for remediation over others, they emphasise that any such prioritisation is only to take place 'where necessary' and should be determined by the severity of the risk of harm.[21] Yet, for business actors, the prioritisation process was informed by both primary risk (risk to rights holders) and secondary risk, that is, potential risk to the company. As one consultant explained,

> the prioritisation still comes from what the outside world is telling them is the priority, which depends on where their hotspots are and the media is driving things or advocates or activists are driving things. Which may or may not be their most risky areas and may not be where they have the most leverage.[22]

[17] Interviewee 28B.
[18] Interviewee 16E.
[19] ibid.
[20] Interviewee 21E.
[21] UNGPs (n 1) 26, commentary to Guiding Principle 24.
[22] Interviewee 16B.

Another interviewee noted the persistence of the broader risk management context, explaining that the prioritisation process was necessarily governed by corporate risk frames,

> even if you do identify a priority human rights risk in the right way—I mean it's not a science ... People can go different ways on any given set of rights. But that's still just going to feed into a broader risk management program decision making process. And I don't think that's going to go away.[23]

As a further example, when explaining how certain rights were prioritised for action in a specific company's HRDD, a business actor explained that the business had engaged an external consultant with expertise in HRDD as a first step in the process. This consultant had applied a matrix to score risks by factors such as severity, scale, and irremediability (consistent with the UNGPs' recommendations on prioritisation). The business then combined this analysis with a materiality analysis and engagement of another consultancy to go out and speak with NGOs about what they thought the issue to the company was.[24] Based on these three data sources (the second and third of which go to secondary rather than primary risk), the company prioritised certain impacts for preventative action.

This slippage between primary and secondary risk is also found in literature prepared by industry actors. A guide co-authored by the UN Global Compact and a business advisory firm on managing risks in supply chains, for example, recommends that companies should first assess where the biggest risks to human rights lie in their supply chain. It proceeds to note that other criteria can also be considered in the prioritisation process, including risks that could impact the company's ability to do business, that is, business risk.[25]

In summary, labour and business actors tended to see the purposes and value of HRDD differently. The former emphasised the overriding objective of the process in terms of protecting rights holders and placed equal emphasis on all four stages of the HRDD process. The latter tended to reposition HRDD as a process directed at protecting rights holders and corporate interests. In this regard, the business logic demonstrates the tendency, identified by critical risk scholarship, and discussed in Chapter 3, for understandings of risk to slip from managing primary to managing secondary risk. With respect to HRDD, this slippage appears to be having two important effects. First, business actors tend to interpret HRDD as *risk identification* and *assessment* rather than as a process demanding equal attention to the subsequent stages of integration and action on the findings, the tracking of responses,

[23] Interviewee 21E.
[24] Interviewee 27E.
[25] United Nations Global Compact and Business for Social Responsibility, 'Supply Chain Sustainability: A Practical Guide for Continuous Improvement' (2nd edn, United Nations 2015) 32 <www.unglobalcompact.org/library/205> accessed 20 September 2021.

and communication. Second, business actors appear to be operationalising the prioritisation process in a way that is inconsistent with the formulation in the UNGPs. In both respects, business actors appear to be narrowing HRDD in ways that may undermine its original elaboration in the UNGPs.

B. HRDD's Scope

While labour and business actors interviewed both recognised that, in principle, HRDD required a business to identify and address potential and adverse impacts on *all* internationally recognised human rights, interviews revealed conflicting views as to what this demanded of business in practice. Labour actors tended to take a very broad and comprehensive view of the rights to be addressed through HRDD. In contrast, business actors tended to significantly narrow the concept through focusing on the process of prioritisation according to available business resources.

For labour actors, HRDD was seen as capable of redressing the longstanding neglect in corporate practice of rights to freedom of association and collective bargaining.[26] As the ITUC emphasised in 2012, HRDD's 'focus is on the adverse impacts on others that business must address. There is no "picking and choosing" of what rights must be respected.'[27] For labour actors, HRDD offered the potential to overcome the selectivity of standards exhibited by many private labour governance initiatives.[28] This included, importantly for trade unions, rights to freedom of association and collective bargaining. As the ITUC, IndustriALL, CCC, and Uni Global Union emphasised in a co-produced publication on the UNGPs, '[t]he right to join or form a trade union and the right to bargain collectively are established human rights falling within the scope of almost every business enterprise in almost every situation or context'.[29] The organisations proceed to note:

> we expect business enterprises to apply the Guiding Principles, putting in place policies and due diligence processes that facilitate the avoidance of any adverse human rights impacts which their decisions and activities may have on workers

[26] Interviewee 12B. See also ETI (Ethical Trading Initiative), 'Freedom of Association in Company Supply Chains: A Practical Guide' (2013) <www.ethicaltrade.org/sites/default/files/shared_resources/foa_in_company_supply_chains.pdf> accessed 25 September 2022.

[27] ITUC (International Trade Union Confederation), 'The United Nations "Protect, Respect, Remedy" Framework for Business and Human Rights and the United Nations Guiding Principles for Business and Human Rights: A Guide for Trade Unionists' (May 2012) 12 <www.ituc-csi.org/IMG/pdf/12-04-23_ruggie_background_fd.pdf> accessed 5 October 2022.

[28] See Chapter 2.

[29] ITUC, IndustriALL, CCC, and Uni Global Union, 'The UN Guiding Principles on Business and Human Rights and the Human Rights of Workers to Form or Join Trade Unions and to Bargain Collectively' (November 2012) 28 <www.ituc-csi.org/IMG/pdf/12-11-22_ituc-industriall-ccc-uni_paper_on_due_diligence_and_foa.pdf> accessed 20 September 2021.

> seeking to form or join trade unions or to bargain collectively. We also expect that business enterprises remediate their adverse impacts on these human rights.[30]

Similarly, in another publication, the CCC has described freedom of association and collective bargaining as 'central elements of any human rights due diligence process'.[31] While labour actors recognised that prioritisation of rights may be necessary, they stressed that any such prioritisation process should be sequenced and time-bound.[32]

While business actors also recognised that HRDD requires a business to initially consider its actual and potential adverse impacts on *all* internationally recognised human rights, they emphasised the critical role played by the prioritisation process in rendering HRDD manageable and affordable. A business interviewee explained:

> from a human rights perspective, one human rights violation is too many and there's a focus on preventing human rights impacts before they happen. Once you discover them, you have to cease immediately any connection to them and seek to mitigate and mediate. From the business side, like all business functions, there are no infinite resources to put behind an issue. So … it's acknowledged that companies will not be able to address everything simultaneously so, to that degree, issues have to be prioritised.[33]

Another example from a large business with transnational operations:

> you know I think you have so many different concepts associated with [HRDD]. I mean you can investigate an issue until the ends of the earth, you know, a discrete issue but I think that realistically you have to take a practical approach and figure out what are the things that we should be looking at, in what depth, how much, and that's why we use the term 'reasonable'.[34]

Business actors also emphasised the discretionary nature of HRDD and the need for expectations to reflect a company's willingness to devote resources to addressing its actual and potential adverse human rights impacts. One interviewee laid stress on the importance of

> the discretion and the flexibility that exists in the Guiding Principles to make that severity-based assessment because the company … and those people responsible

30 ibid 3.

31 CCC, 'Position Paper on Human Rights Due Diligence' (2016) 5 <https://archive.cleanclothes.org/resources/publications/position-paper-on-human-rightsdue-diligence/view> accessed 7 October 2022.

32 Interviewee 16B.

33 Interviewee 13E.

34 Interviewee 5A.

> do not have infinite resources. They can't just say 'oh, we'll just double our budget and in addition to addressing our sweatshop impacts, we'll address our conflict mineral impacts'. It doesn't work that way.[35]

This emphasis on what can realistically be expected and on prioritisation also manifests in the guidance produced by business representative organisations. The Business and Industry Advisory Council to the OECD (BIAC) has emphasised that

> companies cannot be realistically expected to address all risks in the supply chain ... there are practical limitations to address all the risks arising from the activity of a company's suppliers and contractors, and that the focus should be on the ones with manifestly more critical profiles which companies are capable of influencing effectively.[36]

The International Organisation of Employers (IOE) guide to the UNGPs also noted the importance of prioritisation, going so far as to identify it as an integral step in the HRDD process.[37]

The stress on prioritisation appears to be reinforced through the work of business advisory services that have focused significant efforts on developing products and services in this area. While the reasons for this are not clear from the interview and documentary data, it appears that the early stages of the due diligence process (identification and assessment) and the prioritisation process are more feasible based on desk-based analysis. These service providers are also less likely to run into commercially sensitive issues such as the extent to which certain business practices may need to be reconsidered to prevent or avoid identified adverse human rights impacts.

While business actors' emphasis on the prioritisation of risks for subsequent due diligence measures (such as prevention and mitigation) may be understandable from a business perspective, it would appear to significantly broaden the role for prioritisation, as established in the UNGPs. It would also seem to have the effect of narrowing the scale and scope of HRDD. As one interviewee observed, through their prioritisation processes, companies may, in effect, be 'choosing [what] to have

[35] Interviewee 15A.

[36] OECD, 'Public Consultation on the Due Diligence Guidance for Responsible Business Conduct: Compilation of Responses' (2017) 20 <https://mneguidelines.oecd.org/OECD-Due-Diligence-Guidance-for-RBC-Public-Consultation-Responses.pdf>> accessed 5 October 2022.

[37] IOE (International Organisation of Employers), 'UN Guiding Principles on Business and Human Rights: Employers' Guide' (February 2012) 5 <www.ioe-emp.org/fileadmin/ioe_documents/publications/Policy%20Areas/business_and_human_rights/EN/_2012-02__UN_Guiding_Principles_on_Business_and_Human_Rights_-_Employers__Guide.pdf> accessed 5 October 2022 (hereafter IOE, 'Employers' Guide').

responsibility over'.[38] In effect, the prioritisation process appears to run the risk of reintroducing precisely the selectivity of standards it was intended to redress.

C. Risk Tolerance

A further key divergence between the transnational labour rights and business logics lies in the question of what level of risk of adverse human rights impacts, if any, a business may legitimately tolerate. Labour actors presumed that, done properly, HRDD will compel businesses to address *all* identified risks of actual and potential adverse human rights impacts that they may be causing, contributing to, or to which they are directly linked. The ITUC, for example, has emphasised that responsibility of a business does not stop at the first tier of its supply chain. According to the ITUC, HRDD

> should lead to profound changes in both the 'business led' and the 'multi-stakeholder' initiatives that deal with supply chain labour practices. The concept of 'business relationships' is broader than 'supply chain' and can encompass the indirect work relationships (for instance agency work and dependent contractors) that are having adverse impacts on increasing numbers of workers and that are imposing obstacles to workers for organising and for collective bargaining.[39]

Importantly, labour actors also evinced a presumption that, where a company engages in HRDD and discovers that their purchasing practices or business models are causing, or contributing to, human rights harms, the company is obliged to adjust their practices to the extent necessary to cease causing or contributing to the adverse human rights impacts. As the UK Trade Union Congress (TUC) explained in 2012, the UNGPs require

> businesses to prevent their negative human rights impacts wherever they occur, even beyond the direct employment relationship. This could include workers in jobs that business outsourcing has made insecure, low paid, and dangerous.[40]

The TUC goes on to provide an example of a UK supermarket with purchasing practices that are denying an agricultural worker her legal wage or resulting in unsafe working conditions. In this scenario, the TUC suggests, HRDD would require

[38] Interviewee 11B.
[39] ITUC, 'The United Nations "Protect, Respect, Remedy" Framework' (n 27) 3.
[40] TUC (Trade Union Congress), 'Implementing the UN Guiding Principles on Business and Human Rights' (24 October 2012) <www.tuc.org.uk/research-analysis/reports/implementing-un-guiding-principles-business-and-human-rights> accessed 20 September 2020.

the company to act to prevent that, irrespective of whether or not the worker is directly employed by them.[41]

Labour actors also presumed that, where a company found it impossible to undertake HRDD because of complex and obscure supply chains, the company would be obliged to consider how to overcome these systemic barriers to enable HRDD. As the CCC emphasised,

> Meaningful human rights due diligence [is about] acknowledging corporate responsibility . . . which will often mean in practice that business operations need to be adapted.[42]

Similarly, Oxfam explains:

> If you really want to respect human rights, you need to be willing to give up some power or financial benefit. It could mean choosing not to move forward with a project because it has too many negative impacts or choosing lower margins to ensure a living wage is paid and the financial benefits are spread.[43]

For business actors, however, the very nature of HRDD as a process of risk management meant an implicit endorsement of the existence of some level of acceptable risk.[44] This level appears to be determined by the company, according to corporate objectives and available resources. As one consultant observed,

> I think right now there's great dissonance between how particularly certain industries understand 'cause, contribute and directly linked' and the way civil society understands it . . . And that's one of the things we found with leading companies in the supply chain context. Because there are no definitions or fixed approaches to identifying the scope, they use an arbitrary concept of relevance. They sort of think 'this kind of matters to my business, this doesn't'.[45]

For business actors, the acknowledgement of risk is often framed in terms of the need for expectations of HRDD to be 'reasonable' and for 'excessively broad interpretations' to be avoided.[46]

[41] ibid.

[42] CCC (n 31) 5–6.

[43] Chloe Poynton, 'Five Questions for Business and Human Rights Leaders: Irit Tamir, Oxfam America' (*Article One*, 6 June 2016) <https://articleone.squarespace.com/insights/2016/6/2/irittamir> accessed 9 September 2023.

[44] See Chapter 3.

[45] Interviewee 21A.

[46] BIAC, 'Responsible Business Conduct: The OECD Guidelines for Multinational Enterprises' (*BIAC*, June 2015) 15.

D. Stakeholder Engagement

Labour and business actors diverged significantly on the question of what degree and nature of consultation with stakeholders is required by HRDD. Transnational labour rights activists viewed genuine and meaningful consultation as key to a credible HRDD process. They saw—and valued—HRDD largely for its capacity to open new spaces for engagement and negotiation with businesses. In contrast, business actors regarded consultation with stakeholders as another aspect of HRDD subject to managerial discretion and authority. They also tended to emphasise the role of stakeholder consultation primarily in relation to the identification of potential and actual adverse human rights impacts, at the expense of stakeholder views on the legitimacy of various mitigation efforts and their effectiveness.

Filtered through a transnational labour logic, consultation with workers and trade unions is an essential element of a credible corporate HRDD process. As one interviewee from the labour movement emphasised,

> when it concerns workers' rights, it is very clear that one of the, if not the most important, stakeholder are the unions. The word 'unions' is not in the Guiding Principles ... But it is clear that when you talk about workers' rights that you cannot do your due diligence without involving the unions and consider them—not just involving them—but consider them as your key partner.[47]

Engagement with workers and their representatives was seen as necessary not only with respect to the early stages of the process (identifying and assessing risks) but also with respect to mitigation measures and assessing the efficacy of measures adopted. For the ETI, for example, stakeholder engagement and partnership are central to HRDD, 'including with other companies, suppliers, sub-contractors, agents, trade unions, government agencies, civil society organisations, experts and multi-stakeholder organisations'.[48] The ETI emphasises:

> effective detailed inquiry for human rights due diligence requires ... consultations and engagement with trade unions or independently elected worker representatives. Where this is not possible some other way of accessing workers and enabling them to share their perspectives is vital.[49]

In a similar vein, the CCC has emphasised that '[c]ompany engagement with stakeholders (including workers and unions) should go beyond risk assessment: it must

[47] Interviewee 20C.

[48] ETI, 'Human Rights Due Diligence Framework' (19 May 2016) 9 <www.ethicaltrade.org/sites/default/files/shared_resources/eti_human_rights_due_diligence_framework.pdf> accessed 5 October 2022.

[49] ibid 19.

also be a key part of mitigating and monitoring risks and assessing the adequacy of responses taken'.[50]

Labour actors regarded unilateral, rather than collaborative, approaches to HRDD as flawed and illegitimate. Unilateral efforts by business to identify and manage adverse impacts on labour rights, including through outsourcing the due diligence process to external consultancies, 'weakens the relationship of companies with their suppliers and can reduce their sense of ownership of and responsibility for the potential human rights risks'.[51] From a transnational labour perspective, HRDD demands that a company goes beyond a reliance on social auditing as a means of identifying and managing human rights risks.[52] Efforts by business to repackage pre-existing approaches such as the audit as human rights due diligence are considered to 'fall short' of meaningful HRDD.[53] As the American Federation of Labor–Congress of Industrial Organizations has emphasised, '[a]ny serious commitment to the [UNGPs] requires reforms to workplace audits for business enterprises to exercise the due diligence they require'.[54]

For trade unions and others, HRDD is seen as opening up new avenues for negotiation between trade unions and companies. This includes, for example, global framework agreements.[55] Labour actors have presumed that HRDD will compel companies to engage more frequently and substantively with trade unions as a key stakeholder group.

For business actors, external stakeholders such as NGOs were recognised to have a role in corporate due diligence processes. But it was seen as the company's prerogative to determine who is consulted and at what stage(s) of the process. The IOE, for example, recognises that any actions taken by a business to give effect to its responsibility to respect human rights can only be credible if the business has considered stakeholders 'in terms of assessing the relevance of certain rights vis-à-vis business operations and to explore through dialogue how the activities of the company may impact them now or in the future'. However, the IOE goes on to emphasise that '[w]ho these stakeholders are and which ones fall into that category is a matter for each business to determine, as too is the means adopted to engage with them'.[56]

Interviews and documentary analysis also revealed a tendency for business actors, including consultants, to regard workers, trade unions, and NGOs principally as important sources of information on actual and potential risks. As a

[50] CCC (n 31) 5.

[51] ETI, 'Human Rights Due Diligence Framework' (n 48) 4.

[52] The limitations of social audits are discussed in Chapter 2.

[53] See eg CCC (n 31) 2.

[54] Brian Finnegan, 'Responsibility Outsourced: Social Audits, Workplace Certification and Twenty Years of Failure to Protect Workers Rights' (2013) American Federation of Labor–Congress of Industrial Organizations Research Report 11.

[55] ibid 6.

[56] IOE, 'Employers' Guide' (n 37) 6.

business consultant explains, many companies' approach to HRDD is 'just to engage with stakeholders and find out what their concerns are'.[57] Business actors interviewed were much less likely to refer to stakeholders when discussing mitigation or efforts to track the effectiveness of any measures taken.

E. Transparency and Accountability

A final area of divergence between labour and business actors relates to transparency and accountability. For transnational labour rights actors, transparency and accountability are key factors of a legitimate HRDD process. It is considerations of transparency and accountability that render HRDD distinct and valuable in comparison to other unilateral private labour governance approaches. Transnational labour rights actors regarded accountability in terms of both accountability to other private actors (such as unions and civil society) and legal accountability. The CCC, for example, emphasises that companies 'should, in cooperation with trade unions and other stakeholders, develop action plans that include clear commitments of the brand, time-bound milestones, and that are made public'.[58]

Those adopting a transnational labour rights logic viewed accountability for HRDD largely in terms of accountability for *outcomes*. As one interviewee explained,

> let's suppose you had a company, and it performed some form of due diligence and yet there was some adverse impacts caused by that company that later came out. We would argue that the due diligence was actually not conducted because it wasn't commensurate with the risk ... Therefore, the outcome would actually be important. The business perspective is 'no, we did some kind of activity that we called due diligence and that's enough'. If the outcome isn't right, then well, it just isn't right.[59]

A number of transnational labour rights actors interviewed voiced concern over the tendency for business to interpret HRDD as a process-orientated obligation. One interviewee expressed concern over the fact that 'business is focusing on a process that is separate from outcomes'. The interviewee explained:

> business wants something very finite and very easy to do. They want to be able to say 'well look, we performed our due diligence and that's all we have to do and that

[57] Interviewee 21E.
[58] CCC (n 31) 6.
[59] Interviewee 30B.

> absolves us of responsibility and we can show you our auditor's report and that's that'. They are looking at due diligence that way.[60]

The concept of HRDD was valued by many labour actors principally because of its potential to act as a standard against which to measure, and hold companies to account for, their performance with respect to human rights. Accordingly, some level of company accountability for corporate HRDD is regarded as essential for legitimacy. This is exemplified by one interviewee's description of a specific company's HRDD process:

> it almost has no legitimacy because the company never gave up any control. They held the cards throughout that process. There was never any outside accountability. Or kind of independence in the process ... at the end of the day I think it's about 'were they willing to give up any measure of control?' And the answer was 'No'.[61]

HRDD held out the promise of crystallising into a 'harder' form of legal accountability, with which compliance can be assessed by judicial and regulatory bodies. As one interviewee explained why their organisation had supported HRDD,

> I think that the kind of due diligence in the Guiding Principles and the way it could be interpreted would allow for a fairly easy introduction of due diligence—this version of it—in national law. I don't think it's that big a stretch.[62]

Another transnational labour rights actor also expressed the view that HRDD would inevitably be further legalised:

> You're seeing extraterritorial laws on reporting. But that's just the first part on this. If you can report on it, the next step is that you can be held accountable for the quality of your reporting and your standards, and the next step after that is you can be held accountable for something going wrong. So if you look at it as an evolution, that I think is where the world is going.[63]

In contrast, for those adopting a business logic, HRDD was seen not as a standard of accountability but as 'a practical and manageable tool'[64] for business and as a framework that can be departed from where it is considered appropriate or necessary to do so.[65] Where public actors play a regulatory role, this was largely limited

60 ibid.
61 Interviewee 8F.
62 Interviewee 30B.
63 Interviewee 1B.
64 BIAC (n 46) 15.
65 Interviewee 5A.

to the promotion and diffusion of best practice and guidance with respect to the undertaking of human rights due diligence.

IV. Conclusion

Drawing on legal endogeneity theory and on in-depth interviews and document analysis, this chapter has shown that HRDD has played an important function in enabling a shared language between diverse stakeholders. Close analysis, however, suggests that while actors in the transnational labour governance field began to use the same terminology, this does not mean that understandings of the concept became uniform or settled. When filtered through different logics, HRDD takes on two quite different meanings. Despite the fact that HRDD as articulated in the UNGPs does not centre or empower workers or their representatives in any explicit way (see Chapter 2), many labour actors have seized upon the concept as capable of challenging dominant corporate-led approaches to labour rights issues in corporate supply chains. In contrast, a business orientation emphasises the dual purpose of HRDD as protecting rights holders and business interests. Business actors regard HRDD overwhelmingly as a tool for internal risk management rather than as a public standard for corporate accountability for human rights harms.

Of course, the existence of multiple interpretations of HRDD among stakeholders in transnational labour governance is not, of itself, remarkable. Indeed, given the novelty of the concept and its strategic ambiguities, it is perhaps to be expected. More important is the question of which of these two approaches is emerging as dominant and being institutionalised at the international and national levels. Chapter 5 focuses on developments at two principal sites of global norm-making in the field of labour standards: the OECD and the ILO. These institutions have overlapping mandates with respect to transnational enterprises and labour standards. Both offer the potential for further elaboration of HRDD as it relates to labour rights. However, they have very different institutional features, including with respect to normative orientation, membership, and decision-making rules and procedures. As will be demonstrated, these different characteristics have had, and continue to have, significant implications for how HRDD is being understood and promoted today.

5
HRDD at the Organisation for Economic Co-operation and Development and the International Labour Organization

I. Introduction

This chapter examines how human rights due diligence (HRDD) has been elaborated upon and contested at the international level. It focuses on developments at two prominent intergovernmental organisations (IGOs) in transnational labour governance: the Organisation for Economic Co-operation and Development (OECD) and the International Labour Organization (ILO). In the wake of the UN Human Rights Council's adoption of the UN Guiding Principles on Business and Human Rights (UNGPs) in 2011,[1] both organisations have emerged as key sites at which actors have contested the meaning and positioning of HRDD in relation specifically to labour rights.

This chapter shows that HRDD has been interpreted at the international level in a way that is broadly consistent with a managerial logic, as elaborated upon in Chapter 4. As explained below, the most authoritative and influential elaborations of the concept have emanated from the OECD. This organisation has interpreted the concept in a way that privileges managerial prerogative, flexibility, and risk tolerance. The OECD has also been careful to avoid politically sensitive questions around the extent to which stakeholders should have enforceable rights to be consulted in HRDD or the concept should be mandated in law. Efforts by the international labour movement and human rights non-governmental organisations (NGOs) to use the ILO as an alternative forum through which to develop a robust interpretation of HRDD closely aligned with a transnational labour logic have been unsuccessful. This chapter also reveals how HRDD, through its reframing of labour rights issues as risk management, has facilitated a subtle but important shift in the configuration of international organisations in transnational labour governance. The OECD's perceived high level of technical competency, along with its

[1] UN OHCHR (United Nations Office of the High Commissioner for Human Rights), 'Guiding Principles on Business and Human Rights: Implementing the United Nations 'Protect, Respect, and Remedy' Framework' (2011) (hereafter UNGPs).

Human Rights Due Diligence and Labour Governance. Ingrid Landau, Oxford University Press. © Ingrid Landau 2023.
DOI: 10.1093/oso/9780198876069.003.0005

smaller constituency and more flexible, committee-based structure, has enabled the organisation to pursue an active and broad-ranging agenda on HRDD. In contrast, the ILO's broader constituency, comparatively deliberative and democratic structures, and rights-based orientation have all rendered engagement with the concept highly problematic.

Following this Introduction, section II identifies insights from the regulatory governance and political science literatures that help elucidate the dynamics underpinning the analysis in this chapter. Section III focuses on the OECD. It begins with an overview of the background, composition, and working style of the organisation. I then outline the mechanisms through which the OECD has engaged with, and sought to shape, the HRDD concept. Section IV focuses on the ILO and follows a similar structure. Section V compares and contrasts the divergent approaches and outcomes with respect to HRDD in the two organisations. Concluding observations are offered in Section VI.

Before proceeding, it is important to acknowledge and justify the limited focus of this chapter. Thus far, this book has argued that HRDD is an ambiguous transnational labour norm and that its meaning is contested by state, non-state, and hybrid actors and institutions at multiple levels. It is impossible, within the scope of this project, to exhaustively examine all sites at which, and mechanisms through which, these contests are taking place. The focus of this chapter on the OECD and the ILO is based on the recognition that, despite the increasing presence of private actors, IGOs continue to play a significant role in norm diffusion and elaboration in transnational governance.[2] Their global scale and their multilateral state membership give them a degree of authority that may be absent from other transnational regulatory arrangements.[3] With this authority and their considerable organisational resources, these organisations perform critical roles in 'fixing meaning' to global norms[4] and bringing 'order to the unruly world of private standards'.[5] They can also help to facilitate cooperation between public and private actors and 'orchestrate' transnational governance in the pursuit of public goals.[6] The OECD and the ILO have been selected because they are the two IGOs that have been the most prominent and active sites with respect to contests over labour rights due diligence in the years following the adoption of the UNGPs in 2011.

[2] Michael N Barnett and Martha Finnemore, 'The Politics, Power, and Pathologies of International Organizations' (1999) 53 International Organization 699, 713–15.

[3] Kenneth W Abbott and Duncan Snidal, 'Taking Responsive Regulation Transnational: Strategies for International Organizations' (2013) 7 Regulation & Governance 95, 97.

[4] Barnett and Finnemore (n 2) 711.

[5] Lucio Baccaro and Valentina Mele, 'For Lack of Anything Better? International Organizations and Global Corporate Codes' (2011) 89 Public Administration 451, 453.

[6] Abbott and Snidal (n 3).

II. Intergovernmental Organisations and Norm Elaboration in Transnational Governance

In seeking to understand the divergent fates of HRDD at the OECD and the ILO, this chapter draws on transnational governance and political science literature. Three insights from these bodies of scholarship are particularly helpful in elucidating the nature and dynamics of the contests over HRDD at the two organisations. The first of these is concerned with how interpretive authority is exercised transnationally. The second and third insights relate specifically to the roles and functioning of intergovernmental organisations.

A. Interpretive Authority and Legitimacy

The first insight, as discussed in Chapter 3, is that elaboration of HRDD transnationally necessarily involves dynamic, multi-actor interpretation contingent on attendant authority and legitimacy. Unlike in domestic jurisdictions, there is no overarching body in the international sphere capable of issuing authoritative interpretations of ambiguous rules. Epistemic authority in this context tends to be (but is not always) fluid and dynamic and exercised through soft law mechanisms. The extent to which an actor's interpretation of a rule will be regarded as authoritative is determined by the organisation's perceived legitimacy. Organisational legitimacy rests, in turn, on the acceptability and credibility of the organisation to those it seeks to influence.[7]

Chapter 3 identified and briefly explained three broad types of legitimacy. Pragmatic legitimacy is tied to an organisation's own calculation of its self-interest, normative legitimacy refers to the extent that a person or organisation perceives the goals and/or procedures of the organisation to be normatively or morally appropriate, and cognitive legitimacy refers to the idea that it is not possible to think how things could be done otherwise.[8] Black further divides normative-based legitimacy into four subtypes or 'claims': constitutional, justice, functional or performance, and democratic.[9] Constitutional claims focus on the extent to which an organisation conforms with written norms and broader legal values of procedural justice, consistency, and so on. Justice claims emphasise values or ends which the organisation is pursuing. Functional or performance claims focus on the outcomes and consequences of the organisation and the extent to which the organisation conforms to professional norms. Finally, democratic claims concern the extent

[7] Julia Black, 'Constructing and Contesting Legitimacy and Accountability in Polycentric Regulatory Regimes' (2008) 2 Regulation & Governance 137, 144.
[8] Julia Black, '"Says Who?" Liquid Authority and Interpretive Control in Transnational Regulatory Regimes' (2017) 9 International Theory 286, 292.
[9] Black, 'Constructing and Contesting Legitimacy' (n 7) 145–46.

to which the organisation or regime is seen as operating in accordance with particular models of democratic governance, whether representative, participatory, or deliberative.[10]

B. IGOs as Motivated Interpreters

Second, while the agendas and activities of IGOs are shaped by their constituents, these organisations are also entrepreneurial actors themselves. International organisations pursue their own institutional interests and work to secure a leadership position in policy fields relevant to their sustainability.[11] In this process of carving out an influential position with respect to a specific policy issue, how an organisation frames a problem ('diagnostic framing') is particularly important. IGOs may increase their influence by diagnosing a problem in a particular way and enrolling other actors as allies to promote that diagnosis. The diagnostic framing, in turn, influences the solutions proposed.[12]

As regulators, IGOs create and manage their legitimacy in various ways. They can *conform* to the claims of all or a selective group of legitimacy communities or they can *manipulate* others' perception of their legitimacy by attempting to create new legitimacy beliefs and new legitimacy communities.[13] These processes of legitimacy-building often unfold in tandem with the rule-setting activities of transnational governance bodies.[14]

C. Forum Shifting

The third relevant insight relates to how other actors in transnational governance approach and use IGOs to pursue their agendas. Transnational governance is a 'messy' affair.[15] Many policy issues that require international cooperation are debated in multiple fora. While the mandates of these various international organisations may overlap, the organisations differ in their institutional characteristics, that is, with respect to membership, mandates, decision-making processes, and enforcement capabilities.[16] The existence of several possible arenas in which a policy

[10] ibid 146.

[11] Jorg Michael Dostal, 'Campaigning on Expertise: How the OECD Framed EU Welfare and Labour Market Policies—and Why Success Could Trigger Failure' (2004) 11 Journal of European Public Policy 440, 443.

[12] Terence C Halliday and Gregory Shaffer, *Transnational Legal Orders* (CUP 2015) 38.

[13] Black, 'Constructing and Contesting Legitimacy' (n 7) 146–48.

[14] Sigrid Quack, 'Law, Expertise and Legitimacy in Transnational Economic Governance: An Introduction' (2010) 8 Socio-Economic Review 3, 8.

[15] John Braithwaite and Peter Drahos, *Global Business Regulation* (CUP 2000) 23.

[16] Hannah Murphy and Aynsley Kellow, 'Forum Shopping in Global Governance: Understanding States, Business and NGOs in Multiple Arenas' (2013) 4 Global Policy 139.

issue may be pursued and elaborated upon raises the possibility of actors engaging in forum shifting. A widely recognised phenomenon in transnational governance, forum shifting is a strategy used by state and non-state actors that involves the strategic selection and use of certain fora over others on the basis of the extent to which that forum's institutional characteristics will enable them to realise their agendas and policy preferences. Actors may move a regulatory agenda from one forum to another, abandon a forum, pursue an agenda in multiple forums, or block a forum from acting.[17]

III. The OECD

The OECD has not traditionally been viewed as a key intergovernmental organisation with respect to labour standards. However, the organisation has enthusiastically embraced the concept of HRDD and successfully used the new framework as a means through which to consolidate its authority and legitimacy in transnational labour governance. In turn, the organisation has elaborated upon HRDD in a manner that has served to consolidate, rather than challenge, managerial interpretations of the concept. This section begins with an outline of the OECD's background, composition, and working style. It then traces the reception of HRDD within the organisation. Finally, it examines how the OECD has interpreted the concept.

A. Background, Composition, and Working Style

The OECD was formed in 1961 by twenty-one member states from Europe and North America to promote the liberalisation of world trade on a multilateral, non-discriminatory basis, with a view to achieving sustainable economic growth and rising standards of living.[18] The organisation's founding convention also recognises that member states may contribute to sound economic expansion in non-member countries in the process of economic development.[19] Over the years, OECD membership has expanded significantly, to a current thirty-eight. Outside Europe and North America, these include Australia, Chile, Colombia, Israel, Japan, New Zealand, South Korea, and Turkey. Brazil, China, India, Indonesia, and South Africa are 'OECD Key Partners' that 'participate in the OECD's daily work, bringing useful perspectives and increasing the relevance of policy debates'.[20]

[17] Braithwaite and Drahos (n 15) 29, 564.

[18] Convention on the Organisation for Economic Co-operation and Development (opened for signature 14 December 1960, entered into force 30 September 1961) UNTS 888 art 1.

[19] ibid.

[20] OECD, 'Our Global Reach' <http://oecd.org/about/members-and-partners> accessed 20 October 2022.

The organisation has an intergovernmental structure, with a Ministerial Council as its peak decision-making body. The bulk of OECD work is carried out by the Secretariat (led by the OECD Secretary-General and comprising specialised directorates and divisions) and various committees, working groups, and expert groups that develop ideas and review progress. Each of the Directorates is governed by a committee comprising representatives from Member countries that determine the directorate's work programme and priorities. These committees generate the outputs of the organisation: policy advice, guidelines, principles, and best practice. Along with subcommittees, working groups, and other subsidiary bodies, they are 'the beating heart' of the organisation.[21] OECD committees adopt a closed working style and decision-making is by way of consensus. No OECD document may be released publicly without approval by all Member countries, and internal documents are not publicly available. As James Salzman observes, the practice of closing meetings to the public and the consensus requirement 'eliminates much of the acrimony and political grandstanding in other IGOs such as the UN's General Assembly'.[22]

Formal participation of business and labour interests in the OECD is facilitated through the Business and Industry Advisory Council (BIAC) and the Trade Union Advisory Committee to the OECD (TUAC). BIAC is the official link between the OECD and employers, business, and industry interests. It claims a membership of 45 national business and employers' federations, representing over 7 million companies.[23] TUAC is the formal representative of labour organisations at the OECD, claiming 59 member organisations and 4 affiliates representing over 66 million workers.[24] Both BIAC and TUAC perform dual roles in policy advocacy, seeking to both influence OECD policy initiatives and communicate OECD developments to their members.

From its inception, it was envisaged that the OECD would achieve its objectives mainly through the methods of discussion, consultation, consensus, and instruments of persuasion.[25] The organisation can, and does, pass international agreements that are binding on its members. It also produces standards by way of policy principles and guidelines developed within the OECD framework. All standards are adopted by way of consensus, which, according to the organisation, means that there is a strong engagement throughout the process and a heightened

[21] Peter Carroll and Aynsley Kellow, *The OECD: A Study of Organisational Adaptation* (Edward Elgar 2011) 18.

[22] James Salzman, 'Labor Rights, Globalization and Institutions: The Role and Influence of the Organization for Economic Cooperation and Development' (21) Michigan Journal of International Law 769, 778.

[23] BIAC, 'Business at OECD (BIAC) in Brief' (2022) <https://25159535.fs1.hubspotusercontent-eu1.net/hubfs/25159535/website/documents/pdf/Business%20at%20OECD%20(BIAC)%20in%20Brief%2009%202022.pdf> accessed 20 October 2022.

[24] TUAC, 'About TUAC' (2022) <https://tuac.org/about> accessed 20 October 2022.

[25] Richard Eccleston, 'The OECD and Global Economic Governance' (2011) 65 Australian Journal of International Affairs 243, 243.

commitment by each Member to implement the standard.[26] One of the consequences of the organisation's preference for persuasion over binding law is that it has needed to rely on alternative forms of authority to influence its members and other state and non-state actors. The organisation enjoys delegated authority from member states and moral authority deriving from its commitment to sustainable economic growth. However, the principal source of its authority has long been its established reputation for technical expertise.[27] As Mahon and McBride observe, this reputation has facilitated the adoption of its policy prescriptions within member states as policymakers can claim that its policy advice represents 'an unproblematic, apolitical and relatively routine way of doing things based on evidence and policy expertise'.[28] The capacity of the OECD to present solutions as technical rather than political, in conjunction with its consensual manner of working and relatively narrow membership, has enabled the organisation, on numerous occasions, to step in to fill the gap where political differences prevent nation-states from acting decisively on an issue in other international organisations. This is particularly the case where the issue exclusively or disproportionately involves OECD member states and the organisation has acknowledged expertise in the area.[29] Indeed, it was in the wake of the failed attempts to promulgate binding standards on multinational enterprises at the United Nations (UN) in the 1970s that the OECD adopted the OECD Guidelines for Multinational Enterprises (OECD Guidelines for MNEs) in 1976.[30]

B. The OECD Guidelines for Multinational Enterprises

The OECD Guidelines for MNEs have proven to be the main vehicle through which the OECD has directly engaged with labour rights and, more recently, with HRDD. This instrument was originally intended to facilitate international investment by way of encouraging 'the positive contribution which multinational enterprises can make to economic and social progress and minimising and resolving difficulties to which their various operations may give rise'.[31] The OECD Guidelines for MNEs set out standards of responsible business conduct in a broad range of areas, including information disclosure, employment and industrial relations, taxation, and science and technology. The Guidelines are non-binding for multinational enterprises. However, they are binding on governments that adhere to them. Governments are

[26] OECD, 'Standard-Setting Review: Five Year Report (2016–2021)' (21 May 2021) C/MIN(2021)9, 4.
[27] Eccleston (n 25) 246.
[28] Rianne Mahon and Stephen McBride, 'Conclusion' in Rianne Mahon and Stephen McBride (eds), *The OECD and Transnational Governance* (University of British Columbia Press 2008) 280.
[29] Richard Woodward, *The Organisation for Economic Cooperation and Development* (OUP 2009) 79.
[30] Baccaro and Mele, 'For Lack of Anything Better?' (n 5) 454.
[31] OECD, *OECD Guidelines for Multinational Enterprises* (OECD Publishing 2011) (hereafter *OECD Guidelines*) 13.

obliged to implement and promote the instrument to multinational enterprises (MNEs) operating in or from their territories. Since 1984, the OECD Guidelines for MNEs have been accompanied by an implementation procedure, under which adhering states are obliged to establish a National Contact Point (NCP) to promote the Guidelines. In 2000, these NCPs were given a dispute resolution function. This complaints or 'specific-instance' mechanism is discussed further below and in Chapter 8. The Guidelines are open to adherence by OECD and non-OECD members. As of April 2021, there were fifty countries adhering to the Guidelines.[32]

The OECD Guidelines for MNEs are overseen by the OECD's Investment Committee. Membership of this committee is open to all OECD member states, and BIAC and TUAC act as official advisory bodies. In addition, since 2003, the views of NGOs have been represented to the Committee through the work of OECD Watch. An international network of over 130 NGOs in 55 countries, OECD Watch focuses primarily on empowering communities, individuals, and workers to use the *OECD Guidelines* and NCP system to achieve remedy for corporate misconduct.[33] The OECD Investment Committee has the discretion to periodically invite other NGOs to express their views on matters covered by the Guidelines. The Committee also maintains working relationships with 'partner organisations', including the ILO, the International Organization for Standardization, the World Bank, the UN Working Group on Business and Human Rights, the UN Global Compact, the UN Finance Initiative, the Global Reporting Initiative, and the International Coordinating Committee of Human Rights Institutions.[34]

A substantial revision to the OECD Guidelines for MNEs in 2000 positioned the instrument optimally in terms of subsequent integration of HRDD. The instrument's focus was shifted from an emphasis on MNE compliance with national law to compliance with international standards.[35] The 2000 revision recognised, for the first time, the rising prominence of global supply chains, with MNEs advised to 'encourage, where practicable, business partners, including suppliers and subcontractors, to apply principles of corporate conduct compatible with the Guidelines'.[36] According to Jill Murray, the 2000 revision also saw the adoption, for the first time within the Guidelines, of 'the jargon of modern management theory

[32] OECD, 'Stocktaking Report on the OECD Guidelines for Multinational Enterprises' (2022) 10 <https://mneguidelines.oecd.org/stocktaking-exercise-on-the-oecd-guidelines-for-multinational-enterprises.htm> accessed 20 October 2022.

[33] OECD Watch, 'Advisory Groups' <www.oecdwatch.org/oecd-ncps/stakeholders> accessed 10 October 2022.

[34] OECD, 'Partners and Stakeholders' <http://mneguidelines.oecd.org/workingwithstakeholdersandpartners.htm> accessed 10 October 2022.

[35] The 2000 Guidelines made explicit reference to a number of international instruments, including the 1948 Universal Declaration of Human Rights and the 1998 ILO Declaration on Fundamental Principles and Rights at Work for the first time: Jill Murray, 'A New Phase in the Regulation of Multinational Enterprises: The Role of the OECD' (2001) 30 Industrial Law Journal 255, 262.

[36] OECD, *OECD Guidelines for Multinational Enterprises* (2000) ch II.A.10 (hereafter '*2000 OECD Guidelines*').

to make explicit their principle of self-regulation'.[37] The revised Guidelines recommended that MNEs 'develop and apply effective self-regulatory practices and management systems that foster a relationship of confidence and mutual trust between enterprises and the societies in which they operate'.[38] MNEs were also 'encouraged' to disclose 'value statements or statements of business conduct intended for public disclosure, including information on social, ethical and environmental policies of the enterprises and other codes of conduct to which the company subscribes'.[39]

The OECD Guidelines for MNEs were revised again in 2011 to ensure their ongoing relevance as an instrument for the promotion of responsible business conduct. This revision sought, among other objectives, to bring the instrument in line with the UN Protect, Respect, and Remedy Framework.[40] The United Nations Special Representative of the Secretary-General on the Issue of Human Rights and Transnational Corporations and Other Business Enterprises (SRSG) liaised with the Investment Committee throughout this revision process, assuring the Committee that it need not wait until he had completed his mandate for them to update the Guidelines.[41] This revision process involved a series of discussions and round tables with stakeholders and other multilateral institutions (including the ILO).[42] An Advisory Group to the Chair of the Working Group responsible for revision of the Guidelines, which included interested governments as well as BIAC, TUAC, and NGOs, provided confidential feedback on draft texts and other expert advice. According to the Chair, the revision negotiations were 'very inclusive'.[43] However, some NGOs were highly critical of the nature and extent of the OECD's consultations undertaken during the 2011 review. The International Federation for Human Rights, for example, published a letter deploring the lack of transparency of the review process. The NGO emphasised that 'at no stage have the negotiated drafts been made available online nor made accessible otherwise in the public domain for stakeholders within and outside adhering countries'.[44] Public consultations on the drafts were held in Paris but could only be attended in person.

[37] Murray (n 35) 265.

[38] '*2000 OECD Guidelines*' (n 36) ch II.A.7.

[39] ibid III.A.5(a).

[40] OECD, 'Terms of Reference for an Update of the OECD Guidelines for Multinational Enterprises' (*OECD*, 4 May 2020) Investment Division, Directorate for Financial and Enterprise Affairs, 3–4.

[41] John G Ruggie, Special Representative of the UN Secretary-General for Business and Human Rights, 'Remarks at OECD Investment Committee' (*OECD Investment Committee* 4 October 2010) <https://media.business-humanrights.org/media/documents/files/reports-and-materials/Ruggie-remarks-to-OECD-Investment-Committee-4-Oct-2010.pdf> last accessed 10 October 2022.

[42] OECD, 'Annual Report on the OECD Guidelines for Multinational Enterprises 2010: Corporate Responsibility: Reinforcing a Unique Instrument' (*OECD*, 3 December 2010) 10–11.

[43] Roel Nieuwenkamp, 'The OECD Guidelines for Multinational Enterprises on Responsible Business Conduct: Soft Law with Hard Consequences' (2013) 4 Dovenschmidt Quarterly 171, 172.

[44] FIDH (International Federation for Human Rights), 'Open Letter to OECD Investment Committee on the Review Process of the OECD Guidelines for Multinational Enterprises' (28 April 2011) <www.fidh.org/en/issues/globalisation-human-rights/Open-Letter-to-OECD-Investment> accessed 20 October 2022.

The 2011 revisions made four relevant amendments to the OECD Guidelines for MNEs. First, the scope of corporate responsibility was brought into line with the UNGPs. Companies should 'avoid causing or contributing to adverse impacts on matters covered by the Guidelines, through their own activities, and address such impacts when they occur'.[45] They should also 'seek to prevent or mitigate adverse impacts where they have not contributed to that impact, when the impact is nevertheless directly linked to their operations, products or services by a business relationship'.[46] This revision was particularly significant as it extended the scope of the Guidelines from an 'investment nexus' (which had previously been the main condition for the Guidelines' applicability) to supply chains.[47]

Second, the concept of due diligence was integrated throughout the instrument. A new provision in 'Chapter II: General Policies' states that multinational enterprises should undertake 'risk-based due diligence' on all matters covered by the Guidelines (with the exception of the chapters on Science and Technology, Competition, and Tax) to identify, prevent, and mitigate actual impacts and to account for how these impacts are addressed.[48] In promoting a risk-based due diligence approach to most chapters in the Guidelines, the OECD significantly broadened the concept of corporate rights-based due diligence to encompass actual or potential adverse impacts to not only human rights but also other workers' rights and industrial relations.

Third, the 2011 revision introduced a new 'Chapter IV: Human Rights' into the OECD Guidelines for MNEs. This chapter aligns with the UNGPs, reproducing its formulation of what it means for business to respect human rights as well as stipulating the due diligence systems that companies need to put in place to meet their responsibility to respect human rights. Finally, the revision saw strengthening of the implementation (specific-instance) procedures through stronger, clearer, and more predictable rules for the handling of complaints by the NCPs and a stronger emphasis on problem-solving.[49]

C. The OECD's Proactive Agenda

Following the 2011 revisions, the OECD significantly intensified its efforts to promote the OECD Guidelines for MNEs both within its membership and more broadly. These efforts included a new annual Global Forum on Responsible

[45] *OECD Guidelines* (n 31) ch II.A.10.

[46] ibid ch 11. A.12.

[47] John Gerard Ruggie and Tamaryn Nelson, 'Human Rights and the OECD Guidelines for Multinational Enterprises: Normative Innovations and Implementation Challenges' (2015) 22 Brown Journal of World *Affairs* 99,117–20.

[48] *OECD Guidelines* (n 31) II.A.10.

[49] Nieuwenkamp (n 43).

Business Conduct, the adoption of a 'proactive agenda' to elaborate upon the Guidelines in specific sectors, and the establishment of a Working Party on Responsible Business Conduct (WPRBC).

In 2013, the OECD upgraded its long-running Annual Corporate Responsibility Roundtable to an OECD Global Forum on Responsible Business Conduct. This annual multi-stakeholder event aims to strengthen the international dialogue on responsible business conduct and contribute to the effective implementation of the Guidelines. The forum has since brought together, in Paris, hundreds of participants representing government, business, trade unions, civil society, and international organisations. These changes were accompanied by a new communications strategy and outreach activities to non-member states.

During the update to the OECD Guidelines for MNEs in 2011, the multi-stakeholder approach of the OECD's minerals implementation programme inspired the inclusion of a specific mandate for the Investment Committee to pursue a 'proactive agenda' to support responsible business conduct on a sectoral basis.[50] This proactive agenda has been central to the expansion of the OECD's work on labour rights due diligence. The initiative 'adds a new prospective dimension' to the implementation of the OECD Guidelines for MNEs through 'problem solving, as well as the avoidance of problems, in a broader context than the specific instance procedures' and complements those procedures 'by helping enterprises identify and respond to risks of adverse impacts associated with particular products, regions, sectors or industries'.[51] It aims to identify 'emerging challenges' and to 'leverage an inclusive multi-stakeholder process' to develop broadly-supported solutions to the complex challenges for implementing responsible business conduct'.[52]

In 2012, the Investment Committee created the WPRBC to enhance the effectiveness of the Guidelines, overseeing projects implemented under the proactive agenda and engaging with non-adhering countries on matters covered by the Guidelines.[53] The WPRBC has the authority to create multi-stakeholder advisory/consultative groups to facilitate collaboration with advisory bodies, international partners, business, and other affected stakeholders on specific projects. The composition and organisation of these groups are determined on an ad hoc basis. However, they 'should be comprised of sufficient members to adequately

[50] This work began in 2009 with respect to responsible mineral supply chains following calls from the G8 and the International Conference in the Great Lakes Region to help develop a framework to enable responsible sourcing of minerals from conflict-affected and high-risk areas. A multi-stakeholder collaboration, involving OECD countries, non-OECD countries, the private sector, and civil society led to the development of OECD Guidance. See OECD, *OECD Due Diligence Guidance for Responsible Supply Chains of Minerals from Conflict-Affected and High-Risk Areas* (3rd edn, OECD Publishing 2016).

[51] OECD, 'Annual Report on the OECD Guidelines for Multinational Enterprises 2013: Responsible Business Conduct in Action' (*OECD* 4 December 2013) 107 (hereafter OECD, 'Annual Report 2013').

[52] ibid 108.

[53] OECD, 'Establishment of a Working Party on Responsible Business Conduct' (15 February 2013) CE (2013) 5.

represent relevant interests and afford credibility to their recommendations, while mindful of the need to operate efficiently' as well as governments adhering to the Declaration on International Investment and Multinational Enterprises and the advisory bodies (BIAC, TUAC, and OECD Watch). Non-adhering governments with a particular interest in the project and 'other business organisations, enterprises, non-governmental organisations, experts and representatives from international partners and other stakeholders with a particular interest and expertise relevant to the project should also be considered'.[54] The composition of these multi-stakeholder advisory groups is not made public.[55]

Principles for the proactive agenda, approved by WPRBC in December 2012, call for projects under the agenda to be demand-driven and broadly supported. Projects should address issues where there may be risks of significant adverse impacts on matters covered by the OECD Guidelines for MNEs that are sufficiently important and in need of attention to justify the time, energy, and resources entailed in a broad and inclusive multi-stakeholder process. Such projects should add value in terms of contributing to the effective implementation by enterprises of the principles and standards contained in the OECD Guidelines for MNEs and avoid duplication with other efforts. Finally, projects should have a reasonable expectation of success in reaching an outcome that will be supported by adherents to the OECD Declaration on International Investment and Multinational Enterprises as well as affected stakeholders.[56]

Under the auspices of the proactive agenda, the OECD has developed sector-specific due diligence guidance to foster responsible supply chains in minerals, garment and footwear,[57] agriculture,[58] extractives,[59] and finance.[60] The OECD has also adopted implementation programmes to support its sectoral guidance in minerals, garment and footwear, and agriculture. These programmes seek to increase uptake and develop mutual understanding of due diligence among stakeholders. In April 2018, the Investment Committee also adopted, and agreed to support and monitor, implementation of a general OECD Due Diligence Guidance for Responsible Business Conduct (OECD Due Diligence Guidance).[61] As with the revision to the OECD Guidelines for MNEs in 2011, draft forms of these guidance

[54] OECD, 'Annual Report 2013' (n 51) 119.

[55] In 2019, 244 companies directly participated as members of these multi-stakeholder advisory groups. The numbers of member states and other representatives do not appear to be publicly available. OECD, 'Annual Report on the OECD Guidelines for Multinational Enterprises 2019' (2020) 15.

[56] ibid annex 2.A1.

[57] OECD, *OECD Due Diligence Guidance for Responsible Supply Chains in the Garment and Footwear Sector* (OECD Publishing 2017).

[58] OECD/FAO, *OECD–FAO Guidance for Responsible Agricultural Supply Chains* (OECD Publishing 2016).

[59] OECD, *OECD Due Diligence Guidance for Meaningful Stakeholder Engagement in the Extractives Sector* (OECD Publishing 2017).

[60] OECD, *Responsible Business Conduct for Institutional Investors* (OECD Publishing 2017).

[61] OECD, *OECD Due Diligence Guidance for Responsible Business Conduct* (OECD Publishing 2018).

documents were subject to consultation, but NGOs have expressed concern over the inclusiveness of this process.[62]

The OECD's sectoral and general due diligence guidance documents are lengthy and technical. The general OECD Due Diligence Guidance, for example, runs to nearly 100 pages, and the OECD Due Diligence Guidance for Responsible Supply Chains in the Garment and Footwear Sector to nearly 200 pages (including the modules on sector risks). These documents do not specify minimum standards for corporate decision-making or objective benchmarks against which corporate conduct can be evaluated. Rather, consistent with the managerial logic elaborated upon in Chapter 4, these documents position HRDD as a tool of business risk management, not as a standard against which businesses may be held accountable.

The OECD's due diligence guidance documents provide practical support to enterprises on the implementation of the OECD Guidelines for MNEs, with the intended audiences being primarily practitioners tasked with implementing due diligence within an enterprise.[63] While providing clarification of key concepts and practical tips, the documents give business enterprises broad discretion to define their level of responsibility, based on factors such as the enterprise's leverage over the entity concerned, how crucial the relationship is to the enterprise, the severity of the impact, and whether terminating the relationship with the entity itself would have adverse human rights impacts. They also give business wide discretion with respect to prioritising risks and appropriate steps to be taken to manage identified risks. The guidance documents have been criticised by NGOs such as OECD Watch for being too process-orientated (at the expense of outcomes), failing to adequately emphasise the importance of consultation with affected stakeholders during all stages of the due diligence process, and failing to promote a sufficient level of transparency with respect to corporate supply chains and due diligence processes.[64] NGOs have also observed that these documents contain very little guidance on how states or other actors should monitor and measure implementation.[65]

The OECD has been careful to emphasise that the due diligence guidance documents are intended to provide practical support to enterprises on the implementation of the Guidelines rather than impose new obligations.[66] This line has been strongly supported by BIAC, which has consistently emphasised that the guidance documents should be 'in line with, but not go beyond' the OECD Guidelines for

[62] See eg OECD Watch, 'OECD Watch Comments on the OECD Due Diligence Guidance for Responsible Business Conduct and the Due Diligence Companion' (2017) <www.oecdwatch.org/wp-content/uploads/sites/8/2017/02/OECD-Watch-comments-on-the-OECD-Due-Diligence-Guidance-for-Responsible-Business-Conduct-and-Due-Dilligence-Companion.pdf> accessed 10 October 2022.

[63] OECD, *OECD Due Diligence Guidance* (n 61) 3.

[64] OECD Watch, 'OECD Watch Comments' (n 62).

[65] HRW (Human Rights Watch), 'Submission to the OECD on the Draft Due Diligence Guidance for Responsible Business Conduct' (2017) <www.hrw.org/news/2017/02/09/submission-oecd-draft-due-diligence-guidance-responsible-business-conduct> accessed 25 September 2021.

[66] OECD, *OECD Due Diligence Guidance* (n 61) 3.

MNEs and that their primary purpose is to provide 'non-prescriptive practical guidance' for companies.[67] Nonetheless, such a description belies their emerging role in transnational governance. As Ruggie and Tamaryn Nelson observe, the forerunner of these guidance documents, the OECD Due Diligence Guidance for Responsible Supply Chains of Minerals from Conflict Affected and High-Risk Areas, has become 'a de facto international standard'.[68] Each of the subsequent due diligence guidance documents has been the subject of an OECD recommendation adopted by the OECD Council. While not legally binding on members, OECD recommendations are taken as political commitment to the principles they contain, and there is an expectation that adherents will do their best to implement them. The recommendations themselves call on adhering states and NCPs to actively promote, and support, the use of the guidance by enterprises operating in, or from, their territories. Following its adoption, TUAC observed that it anticipates the OECD Due Diligence Guidance for Responsible Business Conduct becoming '*the* authoritative international reference on due diligence'.[69] In a similar vein, writing in 2018, Catie Shavin observed that the OECD intended for the OECD Due Diligence Guidance to 'become the primary reference point' for companies under the OECD Guidelines for MNEs, the UNGPs, and the ILO's Tripartite Declaration of Principles Concerning Multinational Enterprises and Social Policy (ILO Tripartite Declaration).[70] She also foreshadowed that the OECD Due Diligence Guidance would be drawn on by governments considering mandatory HRDD initiatives.[71] Other transnational labour governance instruments and initiatives are already beginning to make reference to the document.[72]

In addition to stepping up its standard-setting activities on HRDD, the OECD has adopted a range of measures directed at promoting the uptake of its approach to HRDD in transnational labour governance. It has, for example, instigated a process of 'alignment assessments' of industry or multi-stakeholder certifications, frameworks, and initiatives with the OECD Guidelines for MNEs and related guidance. These assessments evaluate the extent to which OECD standards on due diligence have been incorporated into the written standards and implementation of private/

[67] BIAC, 'OECD Due Diligence Guidance for Responsible Business Conduct: BIAC Contribution' (2018) <https://mneguidelines.oecd.org/BIAC-Due-Diligence-Guidance-Contribution-2018.pdf> accessed 20 October 2022.

[68] Ruggie and Nelson (n 47) 121.

[69] TUAC, 'Implementing the OECD Due Diligence Guidance' (2018) 2 (emphasis in original) <https://tuac.org/wp-content/uploads/2018/05/140PS_E_10_duediligence.pdf> accessed 10 October 2022.

[70] Catie Shavin, 'Unlocking the Potential of the New OECD Due Diligence Guidance on Responsible Business Conduct' (2018) 4 Business and Human Rights Journal 1, 1–2.

[71] ibid 4.

[72] The ASOS/ IndustriALL International Framework Agreement, for example, identifies the OECD Guidance on Due Diligence in the Garment and Footwear Sector as a relevant standard: IndustriALL Global Union, 'IndustriALL Signs Global Framework Agreement with ASOS' (2 October 2017) Annex 1 <www.industriall-union.org/industriall-signs-global-framework-agreement-with-asos> accessed 27 April 2023.

multi-stakeholder initiatives and the extent to which the initiatives' requirements for companies and the activities undertaken are aligned with the specific recommendations of the OECD due diligence framework. According to the OECD, these assessments help to promote concrete implementation of the Guidelines and help to support the comparability and quality of these initiatives in order to reduce inefficiencies and costs and strengthen positive outcomes.[73]

The OECD has also begun to more actively engage with states to encourage 'policy coherence' through the implementation of OECD responsible business conduct standards in related policy areas, including corporate governance, state-owned enterprises, export credits, and public procurement.[74] It has launched a Due Diligence Policy Hub directed at enabling information sharing between policymakers and instigated regular meetings of policymakers as part of its Annual Forum on Responsible Business Conduct (RBC). Reflecting the expansion of its work in this area, in 2019, the OECD launched a dedicated Centre for Responsible Business Conduct to give the organisation's work in this area more visibility within and outside the organisation.[75] In 2021, the OECD released a draft OECD Recommendation on the Role of Government in Promoting RBC for consultation.[76]

D. The OECD National Contact Points

The influence of the OECD with respect to HRDD has been further consolidated by the activities of the OECD National Contact Points. As explained earlier, each member state adhering to the OECD Guidelines for MNEs is required to establish an NCP. NCPs are tasked with furthering the effectiveness of the OECD Guidelines for MNEs by undertaking two key functions: providing information on the Guidelines and engaging in related promotional activities; and handling complaints (termed 'specific instances') concerning alleged non-observance of the Guidelines. States are given significant flexibility as to the form and structure of their NCP; however, they are required to ensure that the office has the financial and human resources to function and that it does so in a visible, accessible, transparent, and accountable manner.[77]

The OECD NCP system has broad rules of standing: any individual, organisation, or community with an interest in the matter may bring an issue concerning

73 OECD, 'Stocktaking Report' (n 32).

74 OECD, 'Annual Report on the OECD Guidelines for Multinational Enterprises 2019' (n 55) 67–68.

75 OECD, 'Stocktaking Report' (n 32) 22.

76 OECD, 'Driving, Supporting and Promoting Responsible Business Practices through Government Policies' (2022) <https://mneguidelines.oecd.org/public-consultation-draft-oecd-recommendation-on-the-role-of-government-in-promoting-responsible-business-conduct.htm> accessed 20 October 2022.

77 *OECD Guidelines* (n 31), Part II, Procedural Guidance.

non-compliance with the Guidelines to an NCP where an enterprise is operating or based regarding the enterprise's operations anywhere in the world. The Guidelines make clear that, in handling complaints, NCPs should offer their 'good offices' to help parties resolve the dispute.[78] This entails NCPs facilitating access to consensual and non-adversarial procedures, such as conciliation or mediation. NCPs are required to follow a three-stage process to resolution of the dispute. An NCP must conduct an initial assessment to evaluate whether the issue raised merits further examination. It either accepts the case or publishes a statement explaining why the case was not accepted. If the case is accepted, the NCP assists the parties in reaching an understanding and possibly entering into an agreement. An agreement may include a restitution of the harm incurred and/or steps to be taken by the company to avoid similar issues arising in the future. At the end of the process, the NCP either issues a report (where an agreement has been reached) or a final statement (regarding the issues raised in the case, the support offered by the NCP, and the outcomes). Both a report and a final statement may contain recommendations to the parties. As an optional fourth step, the NCP may choose to follow up on implementation of any agreement reached or any recommendation made.

Largely in response to ongoing pressure from TUAC, OECD Watch, and other civil society groups, successive rounds of reform to the OECD Guidelines for MNEs have led to progressive strengthening of the rules governing the establishment and functioning of NCPs (found in the form of Procedural Guidance attached to the Guidelines).[79] Under the proactive agenda, the OECD has also made sustained efforts to improve the quality and visibility of NCPs, including by way of adopting a system of voluntary peer review.[80]

Since the revision of the OECD Guidelines for MNEs in 2011, there has been a significant increase in complaints relating to Chapter 1 (Concepts and Principles) of the Guidelines as well as Chapter IV (Human Rights). Chapter 1—which includes the recommendation that businesses carry out due diligence and engage in meaningful consultations with stakeholders—has been raised in 53 per cent of all cases submitted to NCPs since 2011.[81] Chapter IV, which establishes that companies should conduct HRDD, has been cited by over half (55 per cent) of all cases received by NCPs. This makes the human rights chapter the most cited chapter in specific instances.[82] Chapter V (Employment and Industrial Relations)—which makes clear that businesses are expected to exercise due diligence to identify,

[78] ibid I.C.2.

[79] Nieuwenkamp (n 43) 171. See also OECD, 'National Contact Points for Responsible Business Conduct: Providing Access to Remedy—20 Years and the Road Ahead' (2020) <https://mneguidelines.oecd.org/NCPs-for-RBC-providing-access-to-remedy-20-years-and-the-road-ahead.pdf> accessed 20 October 2022.

[80] OECD, 'National Contact Points for Responsible Business Conduct' (n 79) 11.

[81] OECD, 'Stocktaking Report' (n 32) 33.

[82] ibid 45.

prevent, and mitigate actual or potential adverse impacts, including in relation to employment and industrial relations—has been cited in 39 per cent of all cases submitted to NCPs since 2011. As the OECD notes, this chapter has constituted a lower proportion of cases than prior to 2011 (where it constituted 70 per cent of all NCP submissions). The OECD tentatively attributes this decline in cases concerning the Employment and Industrial Relations chapter to the facts that some cases that would have been filed under Chapter V previously are now filed under Chapter IV and trade unions' diminishing interest in using NCPs.[83]

Identifying and examining all cases in which NCPs have clarified or elaborated upon HRDD in a manner relevant to the protection and promotion of labour rights is beyond the scope of this study.[84] However, scholars have observed that NCPs are playing a significant role in elaborating, explaining, and constructing the meaning of HRDD in the OECD Guidelines for MNEs and due diligence guidance within the context of specific disputes.[85] The OECD NCP system is discussed further in Chapter 8.

IV. The ILO

While the OECD has embraced HRDD and adopted a broad and ambitious related work programme, the ILO has struggled to find its bearings with respect to its own role in interpreting the concept. This section begins by briefly describing the ILO's background, composition, and working style. It then traces the reception of HRDD within the organisation. I show how the international union movement and labour and human rights NGOs have sought to use the ILO as an alternative forum in which to secure a more robust interpretation of HRDD. However, these efforts have been met with fierce resistance from the ILO's employer constituency, who have sought to position the ILO as a source of information and advice for businesses undertaking HRDD rather than as an IGO with the authority to elaborate on due diligence-related standards.

A. Background, Composition, and Working Style

Created in 1919 as part of the Versailles Peace Accord, the ILO was founded to arrest the progress of Bolshevism by regulating the excesses of industrial labour

[83] ibid 50. See further Chapter 8.

[84] For doctrinal analysis of NCP decisions on HRDD generally, see Karin Buhmann, 'Analysing OECD National Contact Point Statements for Guidance on Human Rights Due Diligence: Method, Findings and Outlook' (2018) 36 *Nordic Journal of Human Rights* 390 ; Sander van 't Foort, 'Due Diligence and Supply Chain Responsibilities in Specific Instances' (2019) 4 Erasmus Law Review 61.

[85] See eg Buhmann (n 84).

markets. The organisation's constitutional objectives include full employment, the raising of living standards, and the improvement of working conditions.[86] The Philadelphia Declaration, which refined the organisation's mission in the aftermath of the Second World War, recognised that 'labour is not a commodity' and placed the promotion of social dialogue at the heart of the organisation's mandate.[87] Today, the ILO presents itself as the agency with the capacity to embed globalisation within an institutional framework that reconciles economic progress with social justice.[88] According to Guy Standing, the organisation has sought to maintain its role as the 'world's labour standards setter' while also endeavouring to become a leading development and knowledge agency.[89]

The ILO has a tripartite structure, reflecting the post-Second World War Western European consensus on tripartite industrial relations and rendering it unique among international governmental organisations. The key decision-making bodies of the organisation—the International Labour Conference (ILC) and the Governing Body—have a tripartite constituency. Representatives of workers and employers each hold a quarter of the seats in these bodies, while government representatives hold the remaining half.[90] ILO activities are supported by a large secretariat, the International Labour Office, headquartered in Geneva. The Workers' and Employers' Groups both have their own organisational structures within this Office.

Like other intergovernmental organisations, the ILO's regulatory focus has traditionally been on the nation-state. ILO conventions, recommendations, and declarations, now numbering in the hundreds, are ratified by and/or directed at states. These commitments and standards are given effect at the national level through labour laws, policies, and programmes.[91] The ILO's system of supervising member-state compliance with these obligations is recognised as among the most sophisticated dialogic mechanisms for securing compliance of international organisations.[92] In recent years, however, the organisation's traditional standard-setting function has floundered. The organisation has found it increasingly difficult both to generate the consensus necessary to adopt new conventions and to achieve high levels of state ratifications of conventions once adopted.[93] Its tripartite structure has also been criticised as anachronistic in a transnational environment in

[86] Constitution of the International Labour Organization (opened for signature 28 June 1919, entered into force 10 January 1920) 15 UNTS 35 (entered into force 10 January 1920) Preamble and Annex (hereafter ILO Constitution).

[87] ibid Annex.

[88] Guy Standing, 'The ILO: An Agency for Globalization' (2008) 39 Development and Change 355.

[89] ibid 355.

[90] ILO Constitution (n 86) arts 3, 7.

[91] Janelle M Diller, 'Pluralism and Privatization in Transnational Labour Regulation: Experience of the International Labour Organization' in Adelle Blackett and Anne Trebilcock (eds), *Research Handbook on Transnational Labour Law* (Edward Elgar 2015) 330.

[92] Braithwaite and Drahos (n 15) 239.

[93] Standing (n 88) 355.

which trade union membership has significantly declined and civil society plays an increasingly important role in labour rights advocacy and regulation.[94]

Since the mid-1990s, and in response to these concerns regarding its relevance and effectiveness, the organisation has engaged in various efforts to bolster its credibility in transnational governance. These have included a shift from detailed legal norms, in the form of binding international instruments, to non-binding declarations of principles and attempts to more actively involve NGOs in its work.[95] The extent to which these reforms have successfully reinvigorated the organisation is a subject of ongoing debate.[96]

Unlike the OECD, the ILO has longstanding ambivalence towards private labour governance.[97] Historically, it has had little direct involvement in such initiatives, despite the fact that many reference ILO standards.[98] As Standing observes, the organisation has 'slipped into endorsing them by association rather than through constructive debate and formal decisions'.[99] The organisation's antipathy has been based on a number of grounds, including the arbitrary focus of these initiatives on some standards (such as child labour) over others (such as freedom of association), the narrow reach of such initiatives, inadequate monitoring, and questions over the legitimacy of such initiatives.[100]

In 2013, however, the ILO Director-General, Juan Somavia, identified the rise of MNEs and their operations via international supply chains as 'one particular area worth examining'.[101] In his report to the ILC, the Director-General noted that the adoption in 2011 of the UNGPs 'opened up' an important new area of work for their implementation, with clear responsibilities for the ILO in respect of labour standards.[102] The report went on to suggest that, as a minimum, the ILO needed to engage in in-depth discussion of its own stance and responsibilities in respect to private initiatives, with a 'wide range of options open to it, either in support of the initiatives of others or to promote its own'.[103] Notably, however, in receiving

[94] Lucio Baccaro and Valentina Mele, 'Pathology of Path Dependency? The ILO and the Challenge of New Governance' (2012) 65 Industrial and Labour Relations Review 195; Sean Cooney, 'Testing Times for the ILO: Institutional Reform for the New International Political Economy' (1999) 20 Comparative Labor Law & Policy Journal 365.

[95] Baccaro and Mele, 'Pathology of Path Dependency?' (n 94); Velibor Jakovleski, Scott Jerbi, and Thomas Biersteker, 'The ILO's Role in Global Governance: Limits and Potential' (2019) 11 International Development Policy 82.

[96] Baccaro and Mele, 'Pathology of Path Dependency?' (n 94).

[97] Yossi Dahan, Hanna Lerner, and Faina Milman-Sivan, 'The International Labour Organization, Multinational Enterprises, and Shifting Conceptions of Responsibility in the Global Economy' in Axel Marx and others (eds), *Global Governance of Labour Rights: Assessing the Effectiveness of Transnational Public and Private Regulatory Initiatives* (Edward Elgar 2015).

[98] ILO, 'Towards the ILO Centenary: Realities, Renewal and Tripartite Commitment—Report of the Director-General' (2013) ILC.102/DG/1A [138].

[99] Standing (n 88) 68.

[100] Baccaro and Mele, 'Pathology of Path Dependency?' (n 94) 206.

[101] ILO, 'Towards the ILO Centenary' (n 98) [141].

[102] ibid [138].

[103] ibid [139].

the Director-General's report, the ILO's Governing Body appeared to disregard the suggestion in the Report to the effect that the ILO assist in the implementation of the UNGPs.[104]

B. Due Diligence Enters ILO Parlance

Despite the International Labour Office's engagement in an advisory capacity to the SRSG during the drafting of the UNGPs and to the OECD during the 2011 revisions to the OECD Guidelines for MNEs, and the Director-General's 2013 call for greater consideration of the UNGPs, it took several years for the concept to make its way into the ILO's own standard-setting activities. In 2014, the ILC adopted a Protocol to Supplement the Forced Labour Convention, 1930 (No 29).[105] This Protocol sought to provide specific guidance on effective measures to be taken to eliminate all forms of forced labour. Article 2 sets out measures that should be taken by states to prevent, protect, and compensate victims of forced or compulsory labour and to intensify efforts to eliminate contemporary forms of slavery to this end, including 'supporting due diligence by both the public and private sectors to prevent and respond to risks of forced or compulsory labour'.[106] However, the term 'due diligence' is not elaborated upon in the instrument, and it appears that the term was only included as an afterthought during drafting on the suggestion of the Workers' Group.[107] A further instrument adopted in 2017, the Recommendation Concerning Employment and Decent Work for Peace and Resilience, 2017, also referenced due diligence. This recommendation calls on member states to create incentives for MNEs to cooperate with national enterprises in order to 'undertake human rights due diligence with a view to ensuring respect for human and labour rights'.[108] Again, however, this recommendation did not elaborate on what constitutes adequate due diligence in the context of the particular instrument.

C. The 2016 International Labour Conference

It was not until five years after the adoption of the UNGPs that the ILO was compelled to directly engage in a substantive way with HRDD. This engagement came

[104] Dahan, Lerner, and Milman-Sivan (n 97) 281.

[105] Protocol of 2014 to the Forced Labour Convention, 1930 (103rd Session Geneva 11 June 2014) (hereafter Protocol of 2014) . This Protocol supplements the Forced Labour Convention, 1930 (No 29) (opened for signatures 28 June 1930, entered into force 1 May 1932) 39 UNTS 55.

[106] Protocol of 2014 (n 105) art 2(e).

[107] Anne Trebilcock, 'Due Diligence on Labour Issues: Opportunities and Limits of the UN Guiding Principles on Business and Human Rights' in Blackett and Trebilcock (n 91) 96.

[108] Recommendation Concerning Employment and Decent Work for Peace and Resilience, 2017 (No 205) (106th Session Geneva 16 June 2017) art 11(h).

by way of the 2016 ILC.[109] Following sustained lobbying by the Workers' Group over a seven-year period,[110] the agenda for this ILC included a 'general discussion' to consider the opportunities and challenges for the realisation of decent work and inclusive development emerging from global supply chains. For the international labour movement and labour and human rights NGOs, this conference discussion represented an important opportunity to move towards an institutional and enforcement framework to accompany labour rights due diligence. It was also seen as a way for the ILO to reposition itself at the centre of the global governance of supply chains.[111]

In the lead-up to the 2016 ILC, the international labour movement and labour and human rights NGOs called publicly for a binding international instrument on decent work in global supply chains.[112] Such a convention, it was argued, should mandate HRDD and so move the UNGPs from simply 'a new generation of voluntary programs' to 'minimum performance requirements' or 'regulatory standards'.[113] The convention should require member states to regulate their multinational enterprises to undertake due diligence to identify labour rights risks in their supply chains. The instrument should also impose transparency obligations so as to enable firms and workers to know who forms part of the supply chain, which would, in turn, allow for greater oversight and, ultimately, accountability.[114] It was also suggested that the ILO instrument should create a permanent dispute settlement facility, housed at the ILO, where MNEs could be called to account for breaches of existing standards, including the UNGPs and the OECD Guidelines for MNEs.[115]

[109] The ILC convenes annually in Geneva for a three-week period. Each member state is represented by a delegation consisting of two government delegates, an employer delegate, a worker delegate, and their respective advisors.

[110] The Workers' Group in the Governing Body first raised the issue of decent work in global supply chains in March 2006. They proceeded to support the proposal for an agenda item on decent work in global supply chains at every meeting of the Governing Body until 2013, when the proposal was finally agreed to. See Huw Thomas and Peter Turnbull, 'From Horizontal to Vertical Labour Governance: The International Labour Organization (ILO) and Decent Work in Global Supply Chains' (2018) 71 Human Relations 536, 547.

[111] Sharan Burrow, 'Global Supply Chains: What Does Labour Want?' (*OpenDemocracy* 31 May 2016) <www.opendemocracy.net/en/beyond-trafficking-and-slavery/global-supply-chains-what-does-labour-want> accessed 28 September 2022.

[112] See eg CCC (Clean Clothes Campaign), 'Position Paper on Human Rights Due Diligence' (2016) 5 <https://archive.cleanclothes.org/resources/publications/position-paper-on-human-rightsdue-diligence/view> accessed 7 October 2022; HRW, 'Human Rights in Supply Chains: A Call for a Binding Global Standard on Due Diligence' (2016) <https://www.hrw.org/report/2016/05/30/human-rights-supply-chains/call-binding-global-standard-due-diligence> accessed 7 October 2022; AFWA (Asia Floor Wage Alliance) and others, 'Precarious Work in the Gap Global Value Chain' (2016) <www.globallaborjustice.org/wp-content/uploads/2018/05/Precarious-Work-in-the-GAP-Global-Value-Chain.pdf> accessed 20 September 2018.

[113] Judy Gearhart, 'Global Supply Chains: Time for a Convention on Decent Work' (*Huffpost* 2 June 2016) <www.huffpost.com/entry/global-supply-chains-time_b_10228772> accessed 20 September 2018.

[114] See eg CCC (n 112).

[115] Burrow (n 111).

The focus of the international labour and human rights movements on HRDD in the lead-up to the ILC caught the ILO's secretariat, the International Labour Office, unprepared. As noted above, there had been little prior engagement by the ILO with HRDD, and it was seen largely as being 'something that sits with other UN agencies'.[116] However, the International Labour Office also realised that the HRDD frame presented an opportunity to discuss pressing issues around labour rights and global supply chains in a way that was possibly more appealing to the Employers' Group than direct discussion of binding standards.[117]

The tripartite Conference Committee discussion held in Geneva in June 2016 proved a fraught affair. As is customary, the International Labour Office produced a background report in the lead-up to the meeting of the committee, which sought to set the scene for the meeting and identify 'suggested points' for committee discussion.[118] While recognising the benefits and opportunities global supply chains presented for economic and social development, this report observed that the expansion of global supply chains had contributed to significant governance gaps, with negative consequences for working conditions. It provided an overview of existing supply-chain governance arrangements, including public and private initiatives. It identified a number of ways in which the ILO could strengthen its efforts to promote decent work in global supply chains. These included increasing the abilities of the Office to provide capacity-building, evidence-based policy advice and advocacy; assessing whether existing ILO instruments were sufficient and/or whether new standards were needed; and consideration of the role of the ILO with regard to public, private, and social governance systems. The report also offered options concerning the ILO's role in promoting social dialogue.[119]

To the surprise of the International Labour Office, which maintained that it had consulted extensively with both the Workers and Employers' Groups in the report's drafting,[120] the background report met with fierce criticism from the employers. It was described as lacking an understanding of the dynamics of global supply chains and failing to take account of existing research.[121] Somewhat unexpectedly, given the broad support of employer organisations for the work of the SRSG, the Employers' Group also took strong issue with the proposition in the report that there were 'governance gaps' that needed to be addressed by way of standard-setting.[122] While agreeing that decent work deficits existed, the Employers' Group

[116] Interviewee 17C.
[117] ibid.
[118] International Labour Conference (105th Session), 'Decent Work in Global Supply Chains—Report' (*ILO* 2016) ILC.105/IV.
[119] ibid [196]–[208].
[120] Interviewee 17C.
[121] International Labour Conference (103rd Session), 'Reports of the Committee on Decent Work in Global Supply Chains: Summary of Proceedings' (2016) ILC105-PR14-2(Rev)[16] (hereafter ILC, 'Summary of Proceedings').
[122] ibid [18]–[19].

insisted that these were the result of poor implementation of international and national labour standards by nation-states rather than by cross-border supply chains. What was needed, according to them, was better implementation by states of their existing ILO commitments rather than any new instrument.[123] The Office's understanding of HRDD was also subject to criticism.[124] The Employers emphasised that the role of the ILO was not to set any new standard on global supply chains but to continue to promote ratification and effective implementation by states of the ILO Declaration on Fundamental Principles and Rights at Work, and to provide capacity building for states.[125] The ILO should also engage in higher-quality research so that it was better positioned to support states and enterprises in promoting respect for labour rights across supply chains. Finally, the ILO could help multinational enterprises directly by establishing 'a global supply chain knowledge centre' where companies could exchange good practices and learn about multi-stakeholder initiatives.[126]

By the end of the nine days of discussion, the Employers' Group had conceded that the expansion of global supply chains had, indeed, exacerbated governance gaps, and the tripartite Committee was able to agree on Conference Conclusions (as is common practice). These Conclusions acknowledged that decent work deficits and governance gaps should be addressed and identified roles for governments, business, and the social partners.[127] The Conclusions called on the ILO to work with international organisations and forums, including the OECD, and take into account international frameworks such as the UNGPs and the OECD Guidelines for MNEs. The ILO should, upon request, provide expertise to the NCPs on social and labour standards. It should also consider the setting up of mechanisms to address disputes.

With respect to the role of the ILO, the Conclusions emphasised the role of the organisation as a source of information and expertise on labour standards in global supply chains. The ILO should, according to the Conclusions, promote ratification and implementation of relevant ILO standards, provide technical assistance to member states on labour administration and inspection, and promote social dialogue.[128] It should 'provide leadership', help drive policy coherence among

[123] ibid [19], [63].

[124] On this claim, the Employers' Group received some support, albeit indirectly, from the SRSG himself. In a letter sent to the ILO Director-General prior to the conference, Professor Ruggie offered 'two points of clarification' with respect to the ILO's report. See John G Ruggie, 'Letter from John G Ruggie to Guy Ryder (*Business and Human Rights Centre* 30 May 2016) <www.business-humanrights.org/en/latest-news/letter-from-john-ruggie-to-guy-ryder-regarding-supply-chains-in-the-context-of-the-un-guiding-principles> accessed 18 September 2020.

[125] ILC, 'Summary of Proceedings' (n 121) [135].

[126] ibid [138].

[127] International Labour Conference (103rd Session) 'Reports of the Committee on Decent Work in Global Supply Chains: Resolution and Conclusions Submitted for Adoption by the Conference' (2016) ILC105-14-1 [6], [15]–[21].

[128] ibid [23(a)]–[23(c)].

multilateral initiatives and processes, and work in partnership with other organisations such as the OECD.[129] The ILO should strengthen its capacity to provide guidance to enterprises on the application of labour standards within their supply chains and make information available on specific country situations, laws, and regulations, including on the implementation of labour rights due diligence in coherence with already existing international frameworks.[130] It should also carry out further research and analysis to better understand how supply chains work in practice and, in general, become a knowledge centre to provide guidance and advice to stakeholders inside and outside the organisation and build the capacity of constituents.[131]

The Conference Committee's Conclusions left open the possibility of further standard-setting, with the tripartite constituents agreeing to 'consider what guidance, programmes, measures, initiatives or standards are needed to promote decent work and/or facilitate reducing decent work deficits in global supply chains'.[132] Overall, however, the Conclusions were described as 'disappointing' by the Workers' Group.[133] The Employers characterised the committee's outcomes as positive: they were, as described by one interviewee, 'much better than what we were given and the hand that we were dealt'.[134]

D. The ILO's Programme of Action on Global Supply Chains

The 2016 Committee Conclusions formed the basis of a five-year Programme of Action on Decent Work in Global Supply Chains approved by the ILO's Governing Body in 2017.[135] Five areas of action are to be pursued simultaneously: (i) knowledge generation and dissemination; (ii) capacity building of member-states, enterprises, and the social partners; (iii) advocacy for decent work through promoting ratification of international standards relevant to decent work in global supply chains; (iv) policy advice and technical assistance to member-states; and (v) partnerships and policy coherence with respect to UN agencies, multilateral institutions, and other international forums and global supply chain actors.[136] The Governing Body also decided that the Office should convene three further expert

[129] ibid [23(e)]. The Conclusions recommend that this should extend to, upon request, providing NCPs with expertise on labour standards.

[130] ibid [23(f)] and [23(h)].

[131] ibid [23(i)].

[132] ibid [25].

[133] ILC, 'Summary of Proceedings' (n 121) [200].

[134] Interviewee 15A.

[135] ILO Governing Body, 'Follow-Up to the Resolution Concerning Decent Work in Global Supply Chains: Roadmap for the Programme of Action' (*ILO* 20 February 2017) GB.329/INS/3/2.

[136] ibid.

or technical meetings to complement the programme of action.[137] Two of these meetings are discussed further below as they have proven to be sites for further contest between ILO constituents concerning the proper role of the ILO with respect to HRDD.

First, in February 2019, the ILO convened a tripartite Meeting of Experts on Cross-Border Social Dialogue. The meeting was attended by eight experts nominated by Governments, and eight experts nominated by the Employers' Group and Workers' Group, respectively. This meeting proved an additional opportunity for the Workers' Group to call on the ILO to facilitate a more substantive infrastructure for HRDD. This took two main forms. First, the Workers' Group called on the ILO to promote and facilitate transnational company agreements (TCAs) or international framework agreements (IFAs) as important vehicles for workers' involvement in corporate HRDD processes and remedy mechanisms, in particular with respect to labour rights.[138] TCAs, for this purpose, included single-issue agreements, IFAs, and transnational collective agreements. For the workers, TCAs were 'essential to secure workers' rights' and 'instrumental to addressing governance gaps in global supply chains'.[139] Second, the Workers' Group emphasised the 'need to clarify the role of trade unions in due diligence processes, including in the identification of risks, preventative measures and remedies'. The OECD Guidelines for MNEs did not cover this issue in any detail (referring only to 'meaningful engagement with stakeholders') and it was necessary for the ILO to produce guidance on what meaningful engagement of workers and trade unions in due diligence means, and how it can be structured, and to identify appropriate models where trade unions were key partners,[140] including on the role TCAs should play in these processes.[141]

Both propositions were met with hostility by the Employers' Group. The Employers' Group emphasised the diverse forms and levels of social dialogue and the need for the meeting to address all forms and levels of cross-border social dialogue in 'a balanced manner'.[142] It also emphasised cross-border social dialogue as 'one of many types of stakeholder engagement used by companies to meet their responsibility to respect human rights and conduct business responsibly'.[143] According to the Employers, TCAs were separate from, and unrelated to,

[137] ibid [7]. These meetings included a tripartite Meeting of Experts to Promote Decent Work and Protection of Fundamental Principles and Rights at Work for Workers in Export Processing Zones (Geneva 21–23 November 2017), a Meeting of Experts on Cross-Border Social Dialogue (Geneva 12–15 February 2019), and a Technical Meeting on Achieving Decent Work in Global Supply Chains (Geneva 25–28 February 2020).

[138] ILO Governance and Tripartism Department, 'Final Report: Meeting of Experts on Cross-border Social Dialogue' (*ILO* 12–15 February 2020) MECBSD/2019/5 (19 September 2019) [14], [98].

[139] ibid [11].

[140] ibid [71], [100].

[141] ibid [100].

[142] ibid [18].

[143] ibid [20].

HRDD.[144] The Employers regarded the notion that the ILO should produce additional guidance on due diligence 'with skepticism', pointing out that the OECD Guidelines for MNEs on the issue had already been drafted in consultation with the social partners.[145] Rather, the ILO should focus its efforts on helping companies to identify risks, by providing accessible, country-specific, up-to-date information on labour rights issues, and otherwise play an important role in knowledge generation and research.[146]

These disagreements culminated in heated arguments during the drafting of conclusions over the inclusion of the term 'due diligence', with the Workers' Group advocating for references to the term at various points in the conclusions and the Employers' Group steadfastly rejecting the notion that cross-border social dialogue was relevant to HRDD.[147] Finally, 'after lengthy discussion', the two parties reached agreement concerning the acceptable number of references to due diligence in the document.[148] Significantly, the Employers' Group refused to accept any concluding text which would provide a role for the ILO in providing 'guidance' on due diligence. At best, the Employers would accept the ILO producing a 'compendium of good practice'.[149] In conceding this point, the Workers Vice-Chairperson noted a 'fundamental disagreement between the Employers' and Workers' Groups about the role of trade unions in due diligence, which could not be resolved at the meeting'.[150] The relevant text in the final conclusions—which identified a role for the ILO in 'developing policy guidance on different forms of cross-border social dialogue, based on good practices, including in the area of due diligence'[151]—was accepted but regarded as disappointing by both the Workers' and Government Groups.[152]

Widely recognised as the meeting at which the role of the ILO with respect to any standard-setting on HRDD was to be further discussed, the Technical Meeting on Achieving Decent Work in Global Supply Chains (Technical Meeting) only proved even more fraught.[153] This meeting, in February 2020, was attended by government representatives of fifty member states and eight Employer and eight Worker representatives. It provided an opportunity for both the Workers' and Employers' Groups to further prosecute their positions as initially presented at the 2016 ILC. During the meeting, the Workers reiterated their views as to the inadequacy of

[144] ibid [251].
[145] ibid [93].
[146] ibid [104]–[105].
[147] ibid [185]–[198].
[148] ibid [304].
[149] ibid [381]
[150] ibid [396].
[151] ibid [15B(i)].
[152] ibid [396]–[406].
[153] ILO Governance and Tripartism Department, 'Note on the Proceedings, Technical Meeting on Achieving Decent Work in Global Supply Chains' (*ILO* 25–28 February 2020) TMDWSC/2020/7 (5 October 2020).

voluntary and non-binding measures on HRDD and the need for an ILO standard. The Employers again attacked the ILO's work with respect to global supply chains for its lack of intellectual rigour, coordination, and balance.[154] The Employers maintained that there was no need for a new ILO standard on HRDD and that the ILO should develop a coherent strategy on global supply chains before considering any additional programmes or activities in the area. While the Government representatives expressed a diversity of views, many indicated frustration at the failure of the Employers' and Workers' Groups to reach agreement. In an unusual turn of events for ILO tripartite discussions, the Technical Meeting failed to reach any mutually acceptable conclusions.[155]

E. Revision of the ILO Tripartite Declaration of Principles Concerning Multinational Enterprises and Social Policy

Finally, the ILO has engaged with HRDD through revision of its own non-binding instrument on corporate responsibility, the ILO Tripartite Declaration. Initially adopted by the ILO Governing Body in 1977, shortly after the OECD adopted its Guidelines, this Declaration was similarly directed at encouraging the positive contribution of multinational enterprises to economic and social progress while mitigating and resolving difficulties to which their operations may give rise.[156] However, it dealt with a much broader and more comprehensive range of labour rights than its OECD counterpart. It also addressed a wider audience: MNEs, governments, and employers' and workers' organisations.

Like the OECD Guidelines for MNEs, the ILO Tripartite Declaration has long contained a voluntary procedure for disputes concerning the application of the instrument.[157] A complaint may be submitted by an ILO member state (acting either on its own initiative or at the request of a national organisation of employers or workers) or by the representative national organisation of employers or workers. International organisations of employers or workers may also submit a complaint on behalf of a representative national affiliate. Complaints are received by the Office, who will bring them before Officers of the Governing Body. These Officers shall decide unanimously, after consultations with their respective groups (governments, workers, and employers), whether the request is receivable under the procedure. If they cannot reach agreement, the request shall be referred to the

[154] ibid [12].
[155] ibid [117]–[170].
[156] ILO, 'Tripartite Declaration of Principles Concerning Multinational Enterprises and Social Policy' (*ILO* 1977).
[157] ILO, *Tripartite Declaration of Principles Concerning Multinational Enterprises and Social Policy* (5th edn, International Labour Organization 2017) Annex II(3). This procedure was introduced in an earlier form in 1980, replaced in 1986, and revised in March 2017.

Governing Body for decision. This dispute resolution process has rarely been used. Up until 2016, only twenty-one requests have been received by the Office, with only five proceeding to decision by the Governing Body.[158]

In 2015, the Governing Body discussed a possible review of the ILO Tripartite Declaration. It was acknowledged that the instrument had not been updated since 2006 and that a 'forward looking MNE Declaration would allow the ILO and its Members to play a leading role in promoting respect by businesses of decent work at the global, regional and national level'.[159] In March 2016, the ILO Governing Body resolved to establish a tripartite ad hoc working group (comprising eight governments, four Worker and four Employer Members) to review the text.[160] The review was intended to take account of developments within and outside the ILO since its last revision in 2006, including the introduction of the UNGPs. The review also took into account the conclusions of the 2016 ILC Committee on Decent Work in Global Supply Chains.

The revised ILO Tripartite Declaration, approved by the Governing Body in March 2017, contains a number of changes relevant to the ILO's work on HRDD.[161] It opens with a new paragraph emphasising the organisation's 'essential role' in evolving principles for MNEs and governments, workers', and employers' organisations, given 'its unique tripartite structure, its competence and its long-standing experience in the social field'.[162] The revised Declaration includes a new paragraph 10 on HRDD. This paragraph makes clear that HRDD

> should involve meaningful consultation with potentially affected groups and other relevant stakeholders, *including workers' organisations*, as appropriate to the size of the enterprise and the nature and context of the operation. *For the purposes of achieving the aim of the MNE Declaration, this process should take account of the central role of freedom of association and collective bargaining as well as industrial relations and social dialogue as an ongoing process.*[163]

The revised text also includes a new subsection on the elimination of forced or compulsory labour, recommending, *inter alia*, that governments provide guidance and support to employers and enterprises to take effective measures to identify,

[158] ILO Governing Body, 'Proposed Modalities to Review the Tripartite Declaration of Principles Concerning Multinational Enterprises and Social Policy' (24 February 2016) GB.326/POL/8 [7].

[159] ibid [2].

[160] ILO Governing Body, 'Decision on the Eighth Item on the Agenda: Proposed Modalities to Review the Tripartite Declaration of Principles Concerning Multinational Enterprises and Social Policy' (24 March 2016).

[161] For a summary of these changes, see ILO Governing Body, 'Recommendations of the Tripartite Ad Hoc Working Group Concerning the Review of the Tripartite Declaration of Principles Concerning Multinational Enterprises and Social Policy Text, Annex and Addenda and the Interpretation Procedure' (6 March 2017) GB.329/POL/7.

[162] *ILO Tripartite Declaration* 2017 (n 157) 1.

[163] ibid [10(e)] (emphasis added).

prevent, mitigate, and account for how they address the risks of forced and compulsory labour in their operations or in products, services, or operations to which they may be directly linked.[164]

The revision to the ILO Tripartite Declaration also sought to increase the visibility of ILO efforts to promote uptake of the Declaration and its principles by including a new Annex II. The name of this Annex—'Operational Tools'—was ultimately agreed upon in the face of fierce employer opposition to the Office's original proposed 'Implementation Mechanisms'.[165] The Annex provides for regional reports (based on a four-yearly cycle) on the promotion and operation of the ILO Tripartite Declaration in ILO member states. The tripartite constituents at the national level are also 'encouraged' to appoint 'national focal points' to promote the use of the Declaration in the national context.[166] Annex II also details activities of the Office to promote the Declaration. This includes by way of technical assistance to tripartite constituents in the ILO Member states as well as the ILO Helpdesk for Business on International Labour Standards providing information and guidance. Finally, Annex II provides for a confidential company–union dialogue facilitation service. Under this process, a company and union can request ILO assistance with dialogue on the application of the principles of the ILO Tripartite Declaration.[167] The Office may assist by providing a neutral ground for the parties to engage, providing input from a technical or expert adviser, and facilitating dialogue. As of February 2019, this process had been used only once.[168]

V. The OECD Emerges as Authoritative Interpreter

The discussion above has revealed that the OECD successfully engaged in a broad-ranging and active work programme on HRDD. It has produced a raft of documents which, while non-binding, have been widely characterised as authoritative guidance on HRDD. In contrast, the ILO has struggled to engage with the concept. It has yet to elaborate upon HRDD in any meaningful way, despite being repeatedly asked to do so by its Worker constituency and many member states. Below, I contend that the OECD has emerged as dominant interpreter of HRDD

164 ibid [10], [24].

165 IOE (International Organisation of Employers), 'IOE's Main Points Following the 2nd Meeting of the Tripartite Ad-Hoc Working Group to Review the ILO MNE Declaration' (23–26 January 2017) <http://uscib.informz.net/uscib/data/images/Main%20points%20from%202nd%20meeting%20of%20WG%20review%20of%20ILO%20MNE%20Declaration_FINAL.pdf> accessed 20 September 2018.

166 Only nine ILO member states have established such national focal points: ILO, 'Promotion at the National Level/Promotion by Tripartite Appointed National Focal Points' <www.ilo.org/empent/areas/mne-declaration/WCMS_570379/lang--en/index.htm> accessed 20 October 2022.

167 *ILO Tripartite Declaration* 2017 (n 157) Annex II(2).

168 ILO, 'Cross-Border Social Dialogue: Report for discussion at the Meeting of Experts on Cross-border Social Dialogue (12–15 February 2019)' MECBSD/2019 [42].

because of the resonance of the HRDD framework with the OECD's approach to responsible business conduct, strong support by the business community, and the organisation's own successful efforts to consolidate its interpretive legitimacy in the field. These considerations of institutional approach, degree of business support, and legitimacy also help to explain why the ILO continues to struggle in its engagement with the concept.

HRDD's reframing of labour rights in terms of risk management positioned the OECD optimally to adopt a leading role in interpreting the concept. The organisation has drawn on its long-established technical expertise and formidable research capacity to expand its activities in the area of labour rights. At the same time, its approach to HRDD has garnered the support of the business community. The OECD has become the preferred interpreter of HRDD for the business community because it has cast HRDD as a technical exercise that privileges flexibility and managerial prerogative. It is also preferred because it attributes the challenge of securing responsible business conduct not to an absence of binding standards but to a lack of managerial knowledge and expertise. The solution, therefore, is detailed guidance rather than standard-setting or enforcement. The organisation's narrower constituency and flexible, committee-based structure have also facilitated its active work programme as these features have enabled the organisation to avoid politically charged questions such as the extent to which the concept should be mandated in international and/or national law.

As explained in Chapter 3, notions of legitimacy are central to the exercise of interpretive authority in transnational regulatory regimes. The OECD has been able to draw on a range of legitimacy claims. The organisation enjoys a high level of functional legitimacy deriving from its technical expertise and perceived relative insulation from 'political' interference. It has also sought to enhance its normative legitimacy through broadening the involvement of states beyond its membership and emphasising the consultative nature of its processes. At the same time, it has drawn on the moral and cognitive legitimacy of other organisations, such as the ILO, through formally inviting these organisations to contribute to its work. Finally, the OECD has enjoyed pragmatic legitimacy in its work as businesses have an interest in supporting the OECD's pragmatic and non-prescriptive approach over harder norms. As the Chair of the OECD Working Party on Responsible Business Conduct himself emphasised, while the OECD's work may have redefined the 'gold standard' for responsible business conduct in a global context, 'the business community also considers it to be a protection against unreasonable expectations'.[169]

For actors dissatisfied with the OECD's approach, the ILO has offered an alternative forum through which to secure a more robust and substantive interpretation

[169] Nieuwenkamp (n 43) 171, 174.

of HRDD and to do so in a more inclusive, transparent, and deliberative setting. Its tripartite structure and inclusive membership and working style have traditionally lent the organisation a relatively high degree of cognitive and normative (democratic) legitimacy.[170] However, these features also render the organisation cumbersome[171] and have prevented it from side-stepping politically sensitive questions as the OECD has been able to do. Moreover, the ILO's longstanding antipathy to private governance initiatives has rendered the task of engaging with HRDD challenging. The International Labour Office itself has been wary of HRDD as a private governance initiative, without adequate safeguards around transparency and accountability.

At first glance, the ILO would appear to enjoy significant interpretive legitimacy when it comes to elaborating upon what HRDD means in the labour rights context. The organisation enjoys a high level of moral legitimacy (ie the goals and/or procedures are seen as morally appropriate) when it comes to the world of work. It has pragmatic legitimacy, at least among international labour and human rights NGOs, who favour the organisation's commitment to a rights-based approach and social justice. However, the managerial risk-based frame of HRDD has proven unfamiliar to the organisation and many of its constituents. Furthermore, unlike at the OECD, key ILO constituents (most notably the Workers' Group and some states) have been unwilling to accept that the problem of poor working conditions in global supply chains can be addressed solely by way of additional guidance. Stronger regulatory frameworks are seen as essential.

The ILO's authority to interpret HRDD, even as regards solely to labour rights, has been undermined by the organisation's employer constituency. The Employers' Group has essentially challenged the functional legitimacy of the organisation. At the 2016 ILC, and subsequently, the employers have repeatedly questioned the International Labour Office's understanding of the UNGPs and HRDD. They have also challenged its research capacity and technical expertise with respect to global supply chain dynamics. This attitude is epitomised by the words of an employer representative interviewee, who described the Office's background report to the tripartite Conference Committee discussion in June 2016 as 'an embarrassment for an international organisation', with the Office ignoring 'a huge array of empirical literature ... It confirmed to us what we've been saying for a long time—that the organisation is not well-balanced in terms of its approach.'[172] Another interviewee, however, saw it differently, expressing the view that the Employers' Group

[170] Braithwaite and Drahos (n 15) 248. In recent years, the ILO's membership structure has been criticised for failing to adapt to developments, including drastic declines in trade union membership and the rise of non-governmental organisations at all levels of governance. See further Jannelle M Diller, 'International Labour Law and the Challenge of Pluralism in the International Order' (2013) 10 Manchester Journal of International Economic Law 128.

[171] Diller, 'International Labour Law and the Challenge of Pluralism' (n 170).

[172] Interviewee 15A.

had decided, for strategic reasons, prior to the ILC, to avoid engagement on this issue and stall debate, including with respect to the nature or detail of any potential due diligence instrument.[173]

VI. Conclusion

Both the OECD and the ILO have sought to interpret what HRDD means when it comes to labour rights. With its technical expertise and flexible, committee-based structure, the OECD has been well positioned to explicate HRDD. It has done so in a way that is broadly consistent with a managerial logic. Despite the volume of work on labour rights due diligence emanating from the OECD, the organisation has not directly engaged in standard-setting in a way that resolves any of the concept's ambiguities. First and foremost, the OECD Guidelines for MNEs and due diligence documents provide only voluntary standards for responsible business conduct. They do not establish, or require, minimum standards of due diligence. They do not confer any substantive rights on workers or representative organisations in business supply chains. Nor do they impose any minimum requirements for the transparency or accountability of due diligence processes. Recognising the limitations of the OECD's approach to HRDD, the international labour movement and human rights NGOs have pursued an alternative approach at the ILO. However, the nature of HRDD, along with successful blocking efforts by the Employers' Group, have greatly circumscribed the ILO's role.

The framing of labour rights as a technical matter of corporate risk management, along with the outcome of political contests over the appropriate forum in which to interpret the concept, has enabled the OECD to emerge as the dominant authority on HRDD. This is the case even when it concerns labour rights, the traditional bailiwick of the ILO. The implications of the OECD's ascendancy in transnational labour governance are examined further in Chapter 7. Chapter 6 moves the level of analysis from the global to the national and regional, examining how HRDD is being received and interpreted in regulatory frameworks at the state and European Union level.

[173] Interviewee 17C.

6
Paths Diverge
The Interpolation of HRDD in National and Regional Law

I. Introduction

This chapter looks at how the concept of human rights due diligence (HRDD) is being translated into national and regional legal frameworks. This examination is necessary to understand how the meaning of HRDD is being shaped, by whom, and with what implications because of the recursive nature of transnational norm elaboration. As explained in Chapter 3, legal recursivity theory emphasises the multilayered and iterative nature of transnational norm elaboration. Norms evolve recursively, through iterations between global and national and public and private actors. In these complex and dynamic processes, nation-states and regional organisations play an important role in shaping and reshaping global norms. States 'promote, appropriate, resist, hybridize, and transform' norms, which then recursively feed back into subsequent interpretations of the norm at the international level.[1] This is particularly the case with ambiguous norms, where legalisation at national and regional levels provides opportunity for further contestation over the norm's shape and content. The 'filtering' of international norms through domestic structures and domestic norms can produce major variations in compliance and interpretation.[2] Examining the rapid reception and interpolation of HRDD at these levels sheds further light on how the concept is being contested and institutionalised in transnational labour governance.

Recent years have seen a 'wave of new public governance designed to strengthen corporate accountability'[3] in a number of developed states. Influenced by normative developments at the global level, including the United Nations Guiding Principles on Business and Human Rights (UNGPs), many of these national initiatives draw on the due diligence approach to promote greater corporate awareness and action on labour standards in global supply chains.[4] In doing so, they play an

[1] Gregory Shaffer, 'How the World Trade Organization Shapes Regulatory Governance' (2015) 9 Regulation & Governance 1, 12.

[2] Martha Finnemore and Kathryn Sikkink, 'International Norm Dynamics and Political Change' (1998) 52 International Organization 887, 893.

[3] Genevieve LeBaron and Andreas Rühmkorf, 'Steering CSR through Home State Regulation: A Comparison of the Impact of the UK Bribery Act and Modern Slavery Act on Global Supply Chain Governance' (2017) 8 Global Policy 15, 15.

[4] See further Nicola Phillips, Genevieve LeBaron, and Sara Wallin, 'Mapping and Measuring the Effectiveness of Labour-Related Disclosure Requirements for Global Supply Chains' (2018) Working

Human Rights Due Diligence and Labour Governance. Ingrid Landau, Oxford University Press. © Ingrid Landau 2023.
DOI: 10.1093/oso/9780198876069.003.0006

important role in clarifying what the approach demands of businesses with respect to the prevention and/or mitigation of adverse human rights impacts.[5] Today, such laws are found in the United States, the United Kingdom, Australia, Germany, the Netherlands, France, and Norway. This legislative trend is likely to continue. At the time of writing this book, the European Union (EU) Commission has released a proposal for an EU-wide Directive on Corporate Sustainability Due Diligence (EU Proposed Directive)[6] and political processes and/or civil society campaigns for mandatory HRDD are underway in Austria, Belgium, Canada, Denmark, Finland, Ireland, Luxembourg, the Netherlands, Poland, Spain, Switzerland, Sweden, and the United Kingdom.[7]

In this chapter, I show that as the emerging transnational norm of HRDD has influenced the development of domestic law in a number of jurisdictions, two distinct approaches are emerging. I term these approaches *statutory deference* and *statutory elaboration*. Legislatures in the Anglo-Saxon economies such as the United States, the United Kingdom, and Australia have adopted a deferential approach to managerial interpretations of HRDD. In these countries, the rise of HRDD as a transnational norm has overlapped and intersected with modern slavery abolition movements. The legislative initiatives in these jurisdictions are limited to the most egregious forms of labour exploitation, impose reporting duties only, and do not hold businesses accountable for the quality of their due diligence processes. The laws have enjoyed the support of key sections of the business community. In contrast, European legislatures are adopting a statutory elaboration approach. An example of this approach to date is the French *Loi 2017-399 du 27 Mars 2017 Relative au Devoir de Vigilance des Sociétés Mères et des Enterprises Donneuses D'ordre* (Duty of Vigilance Law). In France, despite strong business opposition, civil society campaigners and politicians have secured legislation that reflects a more robust interpretation of HRDD. Other, more recent, examples of this statutory elaboration approach are Germany's 2021 *Lieferkettensorgfaltspflichtengesetz* (Supply Chain Due Diligence Law) and the proposed EU Directive.

Paper No 32/2018, ILO Research Department; Claire Bright, 'Mapping Human Rights Due Diligence Regulations and Evaluating Their Contribution in Upholding Labour Standards in Global Supply Chains' in Guillaume Delautre, Elizabeth Echeverría Manrique, and Colin Fenwick (eds), *Decent Work in a Globalized Economy: Lesson from Public and Private Initiatives* (ILO 2021).

[5] Justine Nolan, 'Human Rights and Global Corporate Supply Chains: Is Effective Supply Chain Accountability Possible?' in Surya Deva and David Bilchitz (eds), *Building a Treaty on Business and Human Rights: Context and Contours* (CUP 2017) 238, 245–46.

[6] European Commission, 'Proposal for a Directive of the European Parliament and of the Council on Corporate Sustainability Due Diligence and Amending Directive (EU) 2019/1937' COM (2022) 71 final (hereafter EU Proposed Directive).

[7] See further ECCJ (European Coalition for Corporate Justice), 'Map: Corporate Accountability Legislative Progress in Europe' (25 January 2022) <https://corporatejustice.org/publications/map-corporate-accountability-legislative-progress-in-europe> accessed 10 September 2022.

This chapter advances the arguments in this book in two ways. First, it shows that there is little evidence to suggest that HRDD is being legalised at the national level in a way that meets the initial expectations accorded to the concept by the international labour movement and human rights activists. This is particularly the case with laws that adopt a statutory deferential approach. These laws narrow the concept and endorse an almost unfettered discretion by business to determine the extent to which, and how, they go about identifying and addressing labour rights risks in their operations and supply chains. They also defer to managerial interpretations of the concept by privileging process over outcomes and failing to institutionalise any monitoring mechanisms or rights to consultation or participation by workers, their representatives, or other affected stakeholders. This is despite intensive and sustained advocacy by domestic and international civil society networks for forms of due diligence more consistent with a transnational labour rights approach. The laws and proposed laws adopting a statutory elaboration approach also significantly defer to managerial interpretations of HRDD and recognise only limited institutional channels through which workers or their representatives may meaningfully challenge extant corporate practice. Second, this chapter lays the foundation for discussion in subsequent chapters by demonstrating the trend towards further legalisation of HRDD and the form this is taking. As elaborated in Chapter 7, the rise of 'hard law' HRDD regulatory initiatives has facilitated a significant expansion in the market for HRDD-related services and, potentially, the role of courts in transnational labour governance.

Following this introduction, section II categorises the diverse national legislative initiatives that have emerged subsequent to the adoption of the UNGPs into three groups: mandatory disclosure laws, mandatory due diligence laws, and mandatory due diligence laws with liability provisions.[8] Section III of this chapter organises the various laws into two broad approaches and reflects on the implications of these approaches for transnational labour governance. Conclusions are offered in section IV.

Before proceeding, it is important to offer several caveats concerning this chapter's scope. The analysis focuses on legislative interventions that (i) seek to incentivise companies to consider certain human rights issues in not only their own operations but also their supply chains, including where these extend transnationally and (ii) draw on and/or make reference to HRDD as articulated in the UNGPs and other international instruments. This chapter does not cover other means through which states may seek to promote or incentivise HRDD (eg by way of public procurement) or ways in which the due diligence concept may be influencing judicial or academic reasoning in areas such as tort law. While the

[8] This categorisation builds on that offered by Nicolas Bueno, 'Multinational Enterprises and Labour Rights: Concepts and Implementation' in Janice Bellace and Beryl ter Haar (eds), *Labour, Business and Human Rights Law* (Edward Elgar 2019) 430–35.

scope of this chapter is global, it does not purport to be exhaustive but rather to identify and examine legislative trends. Finally, this chapter is concerned with the extent to which, and how, HRDD has been received and interpreted at the national and EU level. I do not evaluate the effectiveness of the laws discussed from a theoretical or empirical perspective. As important as these questions are, they lie beyond the scope of this book.

II. The Diffusion of HRDD in National and Regional Law

Paralleling the recent wave of national laws promoting corporate due diligence with respect to labour rights in transnational supply chains is a growing body of scholarship identifying, describing, and evaluating these laws.[9] These laws (and proposed laws) are diverse in their objectives, scope, and approach. However, existing laws can be broadly categorised into three groups, based on the actions required by the corporation and the enforcement/incentive mechanism for compliance. These groups are (i) mandatory disclosure laws, (ii) mandatory due diligence laws, and (iii) mandatory due diligence laws with liability provisions. Each of these three categories is described in more detail below and summarised in Table 2. The first group of initiatives—found in Anglo-Saxon liberal economies such as the United States, the United Kingdom, and Australia—requires large companies to disclose information on their efforts to monitor and address certain forms of extreme labour exploitation in their operations and supply chains, triggering responses by other market actors. As Jolyon Ford and Justine Nolan point out, these laws 'implicitly assume—but do not explicitly require—HRDD adoption'.[10] The second type of initiative goes further in requiring companies to not only disclose information but also engage in a certain level of due diligence, triggering responses by market actors and regulators. The third type of initiative is broader in terms of the rights covered, imposes due diligence obligations on companies, and clarifies the legal consequences of failure to do so.

A. Mandatory Disclosure Laws

The first group of relevant laws at the national level requires companies that meet threshold criteria to disclose their due diligence efforts with respect to specified human rights risks in their operations and supply chains. These laws are often

[9] See Chapter 1.

[10] Jolyon Ford and Justine Nolan, 'Regulating Transparency on Human Rights and Modern Slavery in Corporate Supply Chains: The Discrepancy between Human Rights Due Diligence and the Social Audit' (2020) 26 Australian Journal of Human Rights 27, 28.

Table 2 Selected regional and national HRDD-related laws

Jurisdiction	Law	Scope (rights covered)	Disclosure obligation	Due diligence obligation	Clarification on civil liability for harms caused	Enforceable rights for third parties (eg to consultation, information)
Group 1: Mandatory disclosure laws						
Australia	Modern Slavery Act 2018 (Cth)	Narrow	X	–	–	–
United Kingdom	Modern Slavery Act 2015 (UK)	Narrow	X	–	–	–
United States	California Transparency in Supply Chains Act 2010	Narrow	X	–	–	–
European Union	EU Directive 2014/95 on Disclosure of Non-Financial Information	Broad	X	–	–	–
Group 2: Mandatory due diligence laws						
United States	Dodd–Frank Wall Street Reform and Consumer Protection Act, 12 USC § 1502 (2010)	Narrow	X	X	–	–
European Union	Regulation 2017/821 Laying Down Supply Chain Due Diligence Obligations for Union Importers of Tin, Tantalum and Tungsten their Ores and Gold Originating from Conflict-Affected and High-Risk Areas	Narrow	X	X	–	–

The Netherlands	Dutch Child Labour Due Diligence Law	Narrow	X	X	–	–
Norway	Act Relating to Enterprises' Transparency and Work on Fundamental Human Rights and Decent Work Conditions	Broad	X	X	–	X
Group 3: Mandatory due diligence laws with liability provisions						
France	Duty of Vigilance Law	Broad	X	X	X	X
Germany	Supply Chain Due Diligence Act	Broad	X	X	X	X
European Union	Proposed EU Directive on Corporate Sustainability Due Diligence	Broad	X	X	X	X

Source: author.

referred to as 'mandatory disclosure laws' as, while these measures may impose some form of administrative or civil liability for failure to comply with the reporting requirements, they are predicated on the assumption that transparency will empower and lead market actors to reward and sanction companies for their human rights performance.[11] Examples include the California Transparency in Supply Chains Act,[12] section 54 of the Modern Slavery Act 2015 (UK), and the Modern Slavery Act 2018 (Aust). This approach is also found in the European Union's Non-Financial Reporting Directive.[13]

Modern Slavery Reporting Requirements in the United States (California), the United Kingdom, and Australia

Passed in September 2010 and entering into force in January 2012, the California Transparency in Supply Chains Act of 2010 was the first law adopted in the United States that aims to address forced labour and human trafficking in transnational supply chains through compelling corporate disclosure to consumers.[14] The law applies to all retail sellers and manufacturers 'doing business' in California with worldwide gross receipts in excess of US$100 million.[15] Entities that fall within the scope of the law must publicly disclose the extent to which they engage in efforts to address risks of slavery and human trafficking in their supply chains. Specifically, a company must state whether it (i) engages in verification of product supply chains to evaluate and address risks of human trafficking and slavery, (ii) conducts audits of suppliers to evaluate supplier compliance with relevant company standards, (iii) requires direct suppliers to certify that materials incorporated into its products comply with laws on slavery and human trafficking, (iv) maintains internal accountability standards and procedures for employees and contractors who fail to meet relevant company standards, and (v) provides company employees and management with training on human trafficking and slavery.[16] Importantly, the law does not require companies to undertake any of these activities—only to report on whether or not they do so. A company that falls within the scope of the law but fails to comply with the reporting requirement will not face a monetary penalty; however, an action may be brought by the California Attorney-General for injunctive relief.[17]

[11] Genevieve LeBaron and Andreas Rühmkorf, 'The Domestic Politics of Corporate Accountability Legislation: Struggles over the 2015 UK Modern Slavery Act' (2019) 17 Socio-Economic Review 709.

[12] California Civil Code §1714.43 (West 2012); California Transparency in Supply Chains Act of 2010, ch 556 Cal Stat § 2641 (West 2012) (hereafter California Civil Code).

[13] Directive (EU) 2014/95 of the European Parliament and of the Council of 22 October 2014 amending Directive 2013/34/EU as Regards Disclosure of Non-Financial and Diversity Information by Certain Large Undertakings and Groups [2014] OJ L 330/1 (hereafter EU Directive 2014/95).

[14] Benjamin Thomas Greer and Jeffrey G Purvis, 'Corporate Supply Chain Transparency: California's Seminal Attempt to Discourage Forced Labour' (2016) 20 International Journal of Human Rights 55.

[15] California Civil Code 1714.43 (n 12) § 1714.43(a)(2).

[16] ibid § 1714.43(c).

[17] ibid § 1714.43(d).

Section 54 of the Modern Slavery Act 2015 (UK) (MSA UK) adopts a similar disclosure-based approach. This provision imposes a requirement on 'commercial organisations' with an annual turnover of no less than £36 million to prepare a modern slavery statement annually.[18] This statement must disclose steps the company has taken during the financial year to ensure that slavery and human trafficking is not taking place in any of its supply chains or in any part of its own business (even if this means stating that the organisation has taken no such steps).[19] The statement must be approved by the board, or its equivalent, and published on the organisation's website, including a link to the statement in a prominent position on the website's homepage.[20] There is no mandatory content to these statements, but the law offers suggestions as to information that companies 'may include'. The UK Home Office has published statutory guidance which elaborates on the detail companies may wish to include within their statement.[21] Where a business fails to produce a Modern Slavery Statement, the UK Secretary of State may seek an injunction through the High Court.[22]

Inspired by the UK model, Australia adopted its own modern slavery reporting requirement in 2018.[23] The primary purpose of Australia's Modern Slavery Act 2018 (MSA AUS) is 'to support large businesses to identify and address modern slavery risks' and 'to drive a "race to the top" as reporting entities compete for market funding and investor and consumer support'.[24] Entities based, or operating, in Australia, with an annual consolidated revenue of more than AU$100 million, are required to report annually on the risks of 'modern slavery' in their operations and supply chains and on actions to address those risks.[25] An entity's Modern Slavery Statement must be approved by the board of directors or equivalent and signed by a director.[26] All Modern Slavery Statements are to be registered on a publicly available Modern Slavery Register.[27]

18 Modern Slavery Act 2015 (UK) ss 54(1), (2).

19 ibid s 54(4).

20 ibid s 54(6).

21 UK Home Office, 'Transparency in Supply Chains: A Practical Guide' (2021) <www.gov.uk/government/publications/transparency-in-supply-chains-a-practical-guide/transparency-in-supply-chains-a-practical-guide> accessed 20 October 2022 (hereafter UK Home Office Statutory Guidance).

22 ibid s 54(11). Failure to comply with this injunction may result in a finding of contempt of court and punishable by an unlimited fine: UK Home Office, 'Transparency in Supply Chains Etc: A Practical Guide' (Statutory Guidance 29 October 2015) 6.

23 Modern Slavery Act 2015 (Cth) (hereafter MSA AUS). The Australian state of New South Wales has also passed modern slavery reporting legislation. The Modern Slavery Act 2018 (NSW) adopts a similar approach to the federal statute but imposes a lower revenue reporting threshold of $50 million and provides for penalties for businesses that do not comply of up to AU$1.1 million. It also establishes an independent Anti-Slavery Commissioner.

24 Explanatory Memorandum, Modern Slavery Bill 2018 (Cth) 7.

25 MSA AUS (n 23) ss 5, 13, 14. 'Modern slavery' is defined to include eight forms of conduct that would constitute criminal offences under Australian law: trafficking in persons, slavery, servitude, forced marriage, forced labour, debt bondage, deceptive recruiting for labour or services, and the worst forms of child labour: s 4.

26 ibid ss 13–14.

27 ibid Part 3. This register, launched in July 2020, is accessible at <https://modernslaveryregister.gov.au>.

Unlike the US (Californian) and UK models, the Australian legislation prescribes mandatory criteria against which companies must report. A Modern Slavery Statement must (i) identify the reporting entity; (ii) describe the structure, operations, and supply chains of the reporting entity; (iii) describe the risks of modern slavery practices in the operations and supply chains of the reporting entity and any entities that the reporting entity owns or controls; (iv) describe the actions taken by the reporting entity and any entity that the reporting entity owns or controls to assess and address those risks, including due diligence and remediation processes; (v) describe how the reporting entity assesses the effectiveness of such actions; (vi) describe processes of consultation with any entities that the reporting entity owns or controls; and (vii) include any other information that the reporting entity, or the entity giving the statement, considers relevant.[28]

Non-compliance with the law may result in the relevant minister writing to the non-compliant entity requesting an explanation for its failure to comply and/or that the entity undertake specific remedial action within a specified timeframe.[29] The minister may also 'name and shame' the entity by publishing certain details pertaining to the entity on the Modern Slavery Register or in any other way the minister considers appropriate.[30]

The EU Directive 2014/95 on Disclosure of Non-Financial Information

The EU Directive 2014/95 on Disclosure of Non-Financial Information has been described as 'the first step in embedding into EU law the corporate responsibility to respect human rights and the environment as it is expressed in the UN Guiding Principles and the OECD [Organisation for Economic Co-operation and Development] Guidelines for Multinational Enterprises'.[31] The Directive applies to all 'public-interest entities' with more than 500 employees.[32] Such entities are required to produce a non-financial statement containing 'information to the extent necessary for an understanding of the undertaking's development, performance, position and impact of its activity, relating to, as a minimum, environmental, social and employee matters, respect for human rights, anti-corruption and bribery matters'.[33]

[28] MSA AUS (n 23) s 16.

[29] ibid s 16A.

[30] ibid ss 16A(3) and (4).

[31] ECCJ, 'Assessment of the EU Directive on the Disclosure of Non-Financial Information by Certain Large Companies' (*ECCJ Briefing* May 2014) <https://media.business-humanrights.org/media/documents/files/media/documents/eccj-assessment-eu-non-financial-reporting-may-2104.pdf> accessed 20 June 2020. For analysis of this instrument as a tool to promote business respect for human rights, see Karin Buhmann, 'Neglecting the Proactive Aspect of Human Rights Due Diligence? A Critical Appraisal of the EU's Non-Financial Reporting Directive as a Pillar One Avenue for Promoting Pillar Two Action' (2018) 3 Business and Human Rights Journal 23.

[32] Directive (EU) 2013/34 as Regards Disclosure of Non-Financial and Diversity Information by Certain Large Undertakings and Groups [2014] OJ L 330/1. 15/11/2014 art 19a (1) (hereafter Directive 2013/34).

[33] ibid.

This information must include (i) a brief description of the undertaking's business model; (ii) a description of the policies pursued by the undertaking in relation to those matters, including due diligence processes implemented; (iii) the outcome of those policies; (iv) the principal risks related to those matters linked to the undertaking's operations, including, where relevant and proportionate, its business relationships, products, or services which are likely to cause adverse impacts in those areas and how the undertaking manages those risks; and (v) non-financial key performance indicators relevant to the particular business.[34]

Companies should report on the risks of adverse impact stemming from not only their own activities but also those linked to its operations, products, services, and business relationships (including supply and contracting chains).[35] The Directive suggests certain issues for inclusion in the report, including working conditions; social dialogue; respect for the rights of workers to be informed and consulted; respect for trade union rights; health and safety at work; protection of, and dialogue with, local communities; implementation of the ILO's fundamental conventions; actions to ensure gender equality; and the prevention of human rights abuses more generally.[36]

The Directive permits companies to choose between several reporting frameworks. These include the UNGPs, the OECD Guidelines for Multinational Enterprises (OECD Guidelines for MNEs), the ILO's Tripartite Declaration of Principles Concerning Multinational Enterprises and Social Policy (ILO Tripartite Declaration), and the Global Reporting Initiative.[37] The Directive adopts a 'comply-or-explain' approach in that it is open to a company to note that it does not adopt policies or processes relating to the specific non-financial matters enumerated, but it must explain why it has not done so.[38] The Directive does not impose any minimum performance standards on companies with respect to due diligence: rather, it focuses on the obligation to deliver a report, formal rights of access to information for stakeholders, and sanctions for non-compliance with the obligation to report.[39] EU member states are required to establish and enforce means to guarantee disclosure in compliance with the Directive.[40]

B. Mandatory Due Diligence Laws

The second group of laws are also disclosure-based; however, they differ from Group 1 laws in that they not only mandate disclosure but also that companies

[34] ibid.
[35] Directive 2014/95 (n 13) para 7.
[36] ibid.
[37] ibid para 9.
[38] Directive 2013/34 (n 32) art 19a (1).
[39] Buhmann (n 31) 30.
[40] Directive 2014/95 (n 13) para 10.

undertake due diligence in certain circumstances. These laws are accompanied by enforcement mechanisms that go beyond those in Group 1 above. Examples include section 1502 of the US Dodd–Frank Wall Street Reform and Consumer Protection Act (Dodd–Frank Act),[41] the EU's Regulation 2017/821 Laying Down Supply Chain Due Diligence Obligations for Union Importers of Tin, Tantalum and Tungsten, Their Ores, and Gold Originating from Conflict-Affected and High-Risk Areas (EU Regulation 2017/821), the Dutch *Wet Zorgplicht Kinderarbeid* (Dutch Child Labour Due Diligence Law),[42] and Norway's Transparency Act.[43]

Section 1502 of the Dodd–Frank Act

Passed in 2010, section 1502 of the Dodd–Frank Act requires companies listed on the US Securities Exchange Commission (SEC) to evaluate and disclose their use of 'conflict minerals'[44] sourced from the Democratic Republic of Congo ('DRC') and adjoining countries. In doing so, the provision seeks to help prevent funding to the region that fuels violent conflict and human rights abuses.[45] It is implemented through regulations issued by the SEC in 2012.[46]

All listed companies that file reports with the SEC are required to conduct reasonable and good-faith efforts to determine whether the specified minerals used in the manufacture of their products originated in the DRC or an adjoining country.[47] Companies that determine this in the affirmative are required to exercise due diligence on the source and chain of custody of the mineral. Neither section 1502 nor the SEC's regulations specifies the standard of supply-chain due diligence a company must adopt for their report. However, the latter states that an issuer's due diligence must follow a nationally or internationally recognised due diligence framework, such as the OECD Due Diligence Guidance for Responsible Supply

[41] Dodd–Frank Wall Street Reform and Consumer Protection Act 12 US Code §1502 (hereafter Dodd–Frank Act).

[42] *Wet van 24 oktober 2019 houdende de invoering van een zorgplicht ter voorkoming van de levering van goederen en diensten die met behulp van kinderarbeid tot stand zijn gekomen (Wet zorgplicht kinderarbeid)* [Act of 24 October 2019 Introducing a Duty of Care to Prevent the Supply of Goods and Services That Have Been Created with the Help of Child Labour (Child Labour Due Diligence Law)] (hereafter Child Labour Due Diligence Law).

[43] *Lov om virksomheters åpenhet og arbeid med grunnleggende menneskerettigheter og anstendige arbeidsforhold (åpenhetsloven)* [Act relating to Enterprises' Transparency and Work on Fundamental Human Rights and Decent Working Conditions] LOV-2021-06-18-99 (hereafter Transparency Act).

[44] These are defined as 'columbite-tantalite (coltan), cassiterite, gold, wolframite, or their derivatives' or 'any other mineral or its derivatives determined by the Secretary of State to be financing conflict in the [DRC] or an adjoining country'): Dodd–Frank Act (n 41) §1502(e)(4).

[45] For an overview of this legislation and its rationale, see Jonathan C Drimmer and Noah Joshua Phillips, 'Sunlight for the Heart of Darkness: Conflict Minerals and the First Wave of SEC Regulation of Social Issues' (2012) 6 Human Rights and International Legal Discourse 131.

[46] Conflict Minerals, 77 Fed Reg 56,274 (12 September 2012) (hereafter Final Rule).

[47] This reasonable country-of-origin inquiry 'does not require an issuer to determine to a certainty that all its conflict minerals did not originate in the Covered Countries because the standard required is a reasonable inquiry and requiring a certainty in this setting would not be reasonable and may impose undue costs': ibid 56,312–13.

Chains of Minerals from Conflict-Affected and High-Risk Areas.[48] This OECD Guidance, first published in 2011, aims to help companies involved in mining and trade in minerals to 'respect human rights and avoid contributing to conflict through their sourcing decisions, including the choice of their suppliers'.[49]

Companies that undertake due diligence must also submit a Conflict Minerals Report to the SEC and make it publicly available online.[50] This report must contain a description of the measures taken to exercise due diligence to determine the source and chain of custody of conflict minerals and a description of the products manufactured or contracted to be manufactured with conflict minerals that are not DRC-conflict free, including the facilities used to process the conflict minerals, the country of origin of the conflict minerals, and the efforts to locate the mine or origin with the greatest possible specificity.[51] Companies must also obtain an independent, private-sector audit of their Conflict Minerals Report.[52]

Section 1502 does not prohibit the use of conflict minerals and relies largely on the leveraging of consumer, non-governmental organisation (NGO), and investor pressure on companies to avoid sourcing conflict minerals.[53] Penalties may be imposed on companies for not reporting or complying in good faith.[54] Companies may also be liable under section 18 of the Securities Exchange Act of 1934 for any false or misleading statements.[55] While the task of monitoring and securing compliance with section 1502 of the Dodd–Frank Act falls to the SEC,[56] the SEC has not engaged in any enforcement actions against companies for failing to comply with the regulations, and in 2017, it announced that it was suspending enforcement of the due diligence and audit requirements of the regulation.[57]

EU Regulation 2017/821

The approach taken by the EU in EU Regulation 2017/821 is very similar to that by the United States in section 1502 of the Dodd–Frank Act.[58] Adopted by the

[48] Final Rule (n 46) 56,324.

[49] OECD, *OECD Due Diligence Guidance for Responsible Supply Chains of Minerals from Conflict-Affected and High-Risk Areas* (3rd edn, OECD Publishing 2016) 12.

[50] Dodd–Frank Act (n 41) §1502(b)(1)(A) and (E).

[51] ibid § 1502(b)(p)(1)(A), (B).

[52] Final Rule (n 46) 56,276.

[53] Galit Safarty, 'Shining Light on Global Supply Chains' (2015) 56 Harvard International Law Journal 419, 439.

[54] Final Rule (n 46) 56,280.

[55] ibid 56,280.

[56] See Karen E Woody, 'Conflict Minerals Legislation: The SEC's New Role as Diplomatic and Humanitarian Watchdog' (2012) 81 Fordham Law Review 1315.

[57] Celia R Taylor, 'The Dodd–Frank Death Knell' (2018) 49 Loyola University Chicago Law Journal 655, 659; Rachel Chambers and Anil Yilmaz Vastardis, 'Human Rights Disclosure and Due Diligence Laws: The Role of Regulatory Oversight in Ensuring Corporate Accountability' (2021) 21 Chicago Journal of International Law 323, 341.

[58] Regulation (EU) 2017/821 of the European Parliament and of the Council of 17 May 2017 Laying Down Supply Chain Due Diligence Obligations for Union Importers of Tin, Tantalum and Tungsten, Their Ores, and Gold Originating from Conflict-Affected and High-Risk Areas, OJ L 130, 1.

European Parliament and the Council in 2017, this regulation applies across the EU as of 1 January 2021. It sets out supply-chain due diligence obligations for EU importers of tin, tantalum, and tungsten, their ores, and gold originating from conflict-affected and high-risk areas. It differs from section 1502 of the Dodd–Frank Act in that it targets minerals originating from conflict-affected or high-risk areas without being limited to specific geographical locations and requires due diligence in accordance with the five steps of the OECD Due Diligence Guidance for Responsible Supply Chains of Minerals from Conflict-Affected and High-Risk Areas. The Regulation provides for EU member states to designate responsible authorities for oversight of the Regulation's implementation at the national level and for such authorities to issue companies notices of remedial action, where necessary.[59]

Dutch Child Labour Due Diligence Act

The Dutch Child Labour Due Diligence Law was adopted in May 2019 but, at the time of writing, is yet to come into effect. It is distinct from other legislative initiatives discussed in this chapter for its focus on child labour[60] and on consumer protection. The objective of the law is to ensure that goods or services entering the Dutch market are free from child labour so that consumers can purchase with 'peace of mind'.[61] Companies that fall within the scope of the law must investigate 'whether there is a reasonable suspicion that the goods or services to be supplied have been produced using child labor'.[62] If such a suspicion arises, the company must adopt and implement a plan of action.[63] Finally, all companies that fall within the scope of the law are required to issue a statement declaring that the company has exercised due diligence as set out in the legislation.[64] Declarations will be published in an online public register to be established by the public supervising authority.

The Act has broad coverage, applying to any company that sells goods or supplies services to the Dutch market twice or more a year (irrespective of where it is

[59] ibid arts 10–11.

[60] Child labour, defined in the law by reference to the ILO's Worst Forms of Child Labor Convention, 1999 (No 182) as well as the ILO's Minimum Age Convention, 1973 (No 138), includes

> (i) any form of work, whether or not under an employment contract, performed by persons who are subject to compulsory schooling or who have not yet reached the age of 15, and (ii) any form of work, whether or not under an employment contract, performed by persons who have not yet reached the age of 18, insofar as such work, by virtue of the nature of the work or the conditions under which it is performed, may endanger the health, safety or morality of young persons.

Child Labour Due Diligence Law (n 42) art 2.

[61] ibid, preamble, cited in Bright (n 4) 85. One of the implications of this focus on Dutch consumer protection is that the Act does not require Dutch companies to exercise due diligence with respect to goods or services supplied outside the country: ibid 87.

[62] Child Labour Due Diligence Law (n 42) art 5.

[63] ibid.

[64] ibid art 4.

registered).[65] However, the scope of the Act—in terms of the extent to which the due diligence obligation extends throughout the supply chain—remains somewhat unclear. Whereas some commentators have expressed the view that the due diligence obligation applies only to the first tier of the supply chain, others have maintained that due diligence efforts must cover the entire supply chain.[66]

Requirements pertaining to due diligence and the plan of action are not specified in more detail in the Act but are to be established by General Administrative Order, which will take into account the ILO–International Organisation of Employers (IOE) Child Labour Guidance Tool for Business.[67] The law makes clear, however, that the investigation (as to whether there is a reasonable presumption of child labour) is to be based on sources that can reasonably be known to, and accessed by, the company.[68] The Act also specifies that the Dutch Minister for Foreign Trade and Development Cooperation can approve a joint action plan that is concluded between one or more civil society organisations, trade unions, and/or employers' organisations and that aims to make the participating companies conduct due diligence in order to prevent the use of child labour in the production of goods and services. A company that conducts its business in accordance with such a joint action plan is presumed to conduct due diligence as required by the Act.[69]

The Dutch Child Labour Due Diligence Law provides for a public supervising authority to monitor compliance with the legislation. Enforcement may only be triggered by third-party complaints. Any person (natural or legal) whose interests are affected by the actions or omissions of a company relating to compliance with the Act may submit a complaint.[70] Where a company fails to comply with the Act, the public supervisory authority can give legally binding instructions to the company, accompanied by a time frame for execution, and the company may be subject to an administrative penalty of up to €8,200, in case of failure to submit the statement, or up to 10 per cent of its worldwide annual turnover, in case of failure

[65] ibid. This article enables the exemption of certain sectors or categories of companies in which the risk of child labour is low.

[66] See Bright (n 4) 87. Article 5(1) of the law specifies that companies may discharge their due diligence obligation by purchasing goods or services from companies that have issued a statement. According to Krajewski and Faracik, this article suggests that companies may fulfil their obligations by only considering by their direct contractual partners: Markus Krajewski and Beata Faracik. 'Substantive Elements of Potential Legislation on Human Rights Due Diligence' (*Briefing No 1, Policy Department for External Relations, European Parliament* June 2020) 10.

[67] Child Labour Due Diligence Law (n 42) art 5(3). The Child Labour Guidance Tool was created by the ILO and the IOE as a resource for companies to meet the due diligence requirements in the UNGPs as they pertain to child labour. See ILO, How to Do Business with Respect for Children's Right to Be Free from Child Labour: ILO-IOE Child Labour Guidance Tool for Business (*International Programme on the Elimination of Child Labour and International Organisation of Employers* 2015).

[68] Child Labour Due Diligence Law (n 42) art 5(1).

[69] ibid art 5(4).

[70] ibid arts 3(2). This complaint must first be submitted to the company itself, and if the company's reaction is 'inadequate' and/or the company has failed to address the complaint within 6 months, he or she can submit the complaint to the designated regulator: art 3(4).

to exercise due diligence.[71] Directors of a company who repeatedly fail to comply with the Act may also be subject to criminal sanctions.[72]

Norway's Transparency Act

Taking effect from 1 July 2022, Norway's Act relating to Enterprises' Transparency and Work on Fundamental Human Rights and Decent Work Conditions (Transparency Act) imposes both reporting and due diligence obligations on large enterprises domiciled within Norway and foreign enterprises that sell products and services in Norway and are liable to pay tax in the country. The recent nature of this law, along with the fact that many of its provisions permit elaboration by way of ministerial regulations that are yet to be produced, render it difficult to provide a detailed account of how the law will operate. However, key features of the law are outlined below.

The Transparency Act's scope is significantly broader than that adopted by many other initiatives examined in this chapter, with a large company defined as a company that meets at least two out of the three following criteria: at least fifty full-time employees during the fiscal year, an annual turnover of at least NOK70 million, and a balance sheet of at least NOK35 million.[73] Companies that fall within the scope of the Act must undertake due diligence on fundamental human rights (those rights enumerated in the International Covenant on Economic, Social and Cultural Rights (ICESCR), the International Covenant on Civil and Political Rights (ICCPR), and the ILO's Declaration on Fundamental Principles and Rights at Work), as well as 'decent working conditions', defined to include work that safeguards fundamental human rights and health, safety, and environment in the workplace and that provides a living wage.[74]

Companies that fall within the scope of the Act are required to undertake due diligence in line with the OECD Guidelines for MNEs.[75] This means that the due diligence duty extends to the operations of the enterprise, as well as its supply chain and business partners.[76] The legal commentary includes extensive references to the OECD Guidelines for MNEs and the OECD Due Diligence Guidance for Responsible Business Conduct.[77] Due diligence is required to be carried out regularly and in a manner proportionate to the enterprise's size, nature, operational context, and the severity and probability of adverse impacts on fundamental human rights and decent working conditions.[78] All companies are required to

71 ibid art 3.
72 ibid art 9.
73 Act relating to Enterprises' Transparency and Work on Fundamental Human Rights and Decent Work Conditions (2022) ss 2, s. 3(a).
74 ibid s 3(b) and (c).
75 ibid s 4(1)(a)–(f).
76 ibid s 3.
77 See Chapter 5 for a discussion of these instruments.
78 ibid s 4(2).

report an account of their due diligence annually. This account must be signed off by all Board members and made publicly available.

A distinctive feature of the Norwegian initiative is the provision of a statutory right for any person to request information from a company on how it addresses its actual and potential impacts on human rights and decent working conditions.[79] Responses to such requests must be 'adequate and comprehensible' and provided within certain time frames. The law enumerates certain grounds upon which an enterprise may deny any such request, and the minister may issue regulations providing further details as to the exercise of this right.

The Norwegian Consumer Authority is responsible for implementing the Act, including by way of publishing appropriate guidance and enforcing compliance.[80] It may issue fines for contraventions of the Act and issue prohibitions and injunction orders, accompanied by enforcement penalties. Repeated violations of the information duties may result in infringement penalties.[81] While the law imposes obligations on companies to provide or cooperate to ensure remedy for harms caused, it does not address rights of individuals harmed to seek remedy in court.

C. Mandatory Due Diligence Laws with Liability Provisions

The third group of laws is distinct with respect to its broader scope, the extent to which the laws elaborate on corporate due diligence obligations, and the mechanisms in place to promote due diligence and monitor due diligence efforts. These laws also elaborate on the nature of corporate liability for harm once it has occurred. Laws in this category include the French Duty of Vigilance Law, the German Supply Chain Due Diligence Act, and the proposed EU Directive on Corporate Sustainability Due Diligence.

Duty of Vigilance Law

Adopted in 2017, the French Duty of Vigilance Law seeks to 'encourage multinational companies to act responsibly with the aim of preventing tragic events' in France or abroad that would violate human rights and harm the environment and to 'obtain remediation for the victims' where damage is sustained.[82] It has been described as the 'first ever duty established by a law of general application requiring multinational enterprises to monitor human rights abuses in their supply chains'

[79] ibid ss 6–7.
[80] ibid ss 8–11.
[81] ibid ss 11–14.
[82] Explanatory Memorandum to the draft Law, cited in Stéphane Brabant and Elsa Savourey, 'A Closer Look at the Penalties Faced by Companies' (2017) (50) Revue Internationale de la Compliance et de l'Éthique des Affaires—Supplément à la Semaine Juridique Enterprise et Affaires 2.

and has been held up as a model for other mandatory HRDD campaigns in Europe and beyond.[83]

The law imposes a duty of vigilance (*devoir de vigilance*) on any company that employs, for a period of two consecutive financial years, at least 5,000 people itself, and in its direct or indirect subsidiaries, whose registered office is located in French territory or at least 10,000 people itself, and in its direct and indirect subsidiaries, whose registered office is located within French territory or abroad.[84] The duty of vigilance comprises three main obligations: establishing, implementing, and publishing a vigilance plan. First, companies must establish a plan (*plan de vigilance*). This plan should include

> the reasonable vigilance measures to allow for risk identification and for the prevention of severe violations of human rights and fundamental freedoms, serious bodily injury or environmental damage or health risks resulting directly or indirectly from the operations of the company and of the companies it controls ... as well as from the operations of the subcontractors or suppliers with whom it maintains an established commercial relationship.[85]

The due diligence plan itself should include five 'vigilance measures'. These are an identification, analysis, and ranking of risks; procedures to assess the situation of certain subsidiaries, subcontractors, or suppliers; actions to prevent and mitigate risks and serious harms; an 'alert mechanism' to allow for the identification of risks; and a monitoring scheme to follow up on the plan's implementation and efficacy.[86] Second, the company must 'effectively implement' the plan. Third, the company must make its plan and its report on how the plan is effectively implemented public and include them in its annual management report.[87]

Compliance with the law is secured through three mechanisms: a formal notice to comply, an injunction with periodic penalty payments, and a civil liability action in tort. Any interested party may serve a non-complying company with a formal notice (*mise de demeure*) requesting that the company comply with its obligations to publish a vigilance plan.[88] Where the company continues to fail to comply (after being given three months' official notice), the interested party may

[83] Dalia Palombo, 'The Duty of Care of the Parent Company: A Comparison between French Law, UK Precedents and the Swiss Proposals' (2019) 4 Business and Human Rights Journal 265, 275.

[84] *Loi 2017-399 du 27 Mars 2017 Relative au Devoir de Vigilance des Sociétés Mères et des Enterprises Donneuses D'ordre* art 1 (hereafter Duty of Vigilance Law).

[85] ibid. An 'established commercial relationship' is defined under French law as a stable, regular commercial relationship, taking place with or without contract, with a certain volume of business, and under a reasonable expectation that the relationship will last: Code de Commerce [Commercial Code] (France), art L. 442-6-I-5.

[86] Duty of Vigilance Law (n 84) art 1 (4)–(9).

[87] ibid art 1.

[88] Interested parties may include affected individuals or communities, employees, consumers, trade unions, and NGOs: Brabant and Savourey, 'A Closer Look at the Penalties' (n 82) 4.

seek an injunction from the relevant court to order the company to comply, with periodic penalty payments in case of continued non-compliance.[89] Finally, where a company fails to adopt and implement a vigilance plan and a risk materialises that could have been prevented by the execution of the due diligence obligations in the law, the company may be liable under French tort law for harm incurred.[90]

German Supply Chain Due Diligence Act

Adopted by the German Parliament in June 2021, Germany's Supply Chain Due Diligence Act followed undertakings by the German Government in 2016 to enact mandatory due diligence legislation if voluntary compliance proved insufficient.[91] The law commences operation on 1 January 2023, with initial application to companies that have their statutory seat, principal place of business, or branch office in Germany with 3,000 or more employees. From 1 January 2024, the threshold number of employees will be lowered to 1,000. Companies that fall within the scope of the law must undertake due diligence with respect to a list of enumerated human rights, labour rights, and environmental risks.[92] A human rights risk is defined as 'a condition in which on the basis of factual circumstances there is sufficient probability that a violation of one of the prohibitions is imminent'.[93]

Companies that fall within the scope of the Supply Chain Due Diligence Act are required to fulfil nine due diligence obligations. They must issue a due diligence policy statement; designate a responsible person (or persons) within the enterprise; establish a risk management system; conduct regular risk analyses; put in place preventative measures in their own business operations and vis-à-vis direct suppliers; take remedial action; establish a complaints procedure (which is accessible, transparent, independent, and trustworthy); implement due diligence obligations with regards to risks at indirect suppliers; and document, and report on, their due diligence efforts.[94] The law makes clear that, with respect to the standard of due diligence expected, companies are to apply the requirements in 'an appropriate manner'.[95] What determines appropriateness is subject to considerations including the nature and extent of the company's business activity; the nature and extent of its leverage over the entity which immediately caused the human rights or environmental risk; the severity, probability, and reversibility of the violation;

[89] Duty of Vigilance Law (n 84) art 1.
[90] ibid art 2.
[91] Markus Krajewski, Kristel Tonstadt, and Franziska Wohltmann, 'Mandatory Human Rights Due Diligence in Germany and Norway: Stepping, or Striding, in the Same Direction?' (2021) 6 Business and Human Rights Journal 550, 552. A government-commissioned review of voluntary corporate due diligence initiatives in 2019–20 found that only 13–17 per cent of all companies with more than 500 employees actively engaged in HRDD: ibid.
[92] *Lieferkettensorgfaltspflichtengesetz* (Germany) (hereafter Supply Chain Due Diligence Act), art 2(2)–(3).
[93] ibid art 2(2) S.1.
[94] ibid ss 4–10.
[95] ibid s 3.

and the nature of the company's causal contribution to the risk or violation.[96] In establishing and implementing due diligence measures, companies are to give due consideration to the interests of stakeholders.[97]

Companies are required to undertake proactive and systematic risk analyses with respect to their own business operations and subsidiaries, as well as direct suppliers. In the case of indirect suppliers, companies are only required to undertake risk analyses on an ad hoc basis when they gain 'substantiated knowledge' indicating the possibility of a human rights violation or environmental damage. Where this is the case, the company is required to adopt adequate preventative measures and draw upon and implement an appropriate preventative and minimisation plan. It is made clear that breach of the due diligence obligations does not give rise to civil liability; however, the law does not exclude liability claims arising from the general law of tort.[98]

The Supply Chain Due Diligence Act is monitored and enforced by the Federal Office for Economic Affairs and Export Control (BAFA). BAFA is responsible for receiving and assessing company reports and has broad powers to adopt measures necessary to detect, end, and prevent violations of the law. It may initiate such enforcement measures on its own motion or upon the request of persons with a substantiated claim that their rights have been, or are at imminent risk of being, violated by a company through non-fulfilment of its obligations under the law. BAFA may impose administrative fines of up to €500,000 or, in some cases, up to 2 per cent of the annual turnover of the company, and companies that have been subject to such fines may be excluded from public procurement opportunities for a maximum of three years.

Proposed EU Directive on Corporate Sustainability Due Diligence

In February 2022, the European Commission released its proposed EU Directive on Corporate Sustainability Due Diligence following several years of consultation at the EU level. This instrument aims to improve corporate governance practices, avoiding fragmentation of due diligence requirements in the single market and creating legal certainty for businesses and stakeholders; increase corporate accountability for adverse impacts; and enhance access to remedy.[99] If adopted, the Directive would require EU member states to transpose into national law a corporate due diligence duty to apply to EU companies with more than 500 employees and a net global turnover of more than €150 million (Very Large EU Companies) and EU companies that have more than 250 employees and a net global turnover of more than €40 million where at least 50 per cent of this net turnover has been

[96] ibid s 3(2).
[97] ibid s 4(4).
[98] ibid ss 3(3) S.1 and 2.
[99] EU Proposed Directive (n 6) explanatory memorandum.

generated in one or more 'high-impact' sectors (Large EU Companies). High-impact sectors include sectors to which there is existing sectoral OECD guidance: textiles and clothing, agriculture, and the extraction and trading in mineral resources.[100] It also applies to non-EU companies that are active in the EU and generate turnover in the EU exceeding the above-mentioned thresholds.

Companies that fall within the scope of the Proposed Directive are required to identify, prevent, cease, mitigate, and account for adverse human rights and environmental impacts. An 'adverse human rights impact' is defined in the Proposed Directive as an adverse impact on protected persons resulting from the violation of one of the rights or prohibitions listed in the annex to the instrument.[101] While the annex covers a range of workers' human rights, the UN Office of the High Commissioner for Human Rights (OHCHR) has expressed concerns that the use of the terms 'violation' and 'protected persons', as well as the enumeration of specific rights in the instrument, departs from the approach taken by the UNGPs and risks excluding numerous business-related human rights harms.[102]

Under the proposed EU Directive, companies are expected to undertake the six stages of due diligence elaborated upon in the OECD Guidelines for MNEs: integrate due diligence into company policies; identify actual or potential adverse impacts; cease, prevent, and mitigate adverse impacts; establish a complaints procedure; monitor the effectiveness of their due diligence actions; and publicly communicate.[103] The Proposed Directive enumerates specific actions that companies should take, 'where relevant'. These include implementing preventative/correction action plans, contractually assured codes of conduct with business partners that are third-party verified (by way of audits or industry schemes), other necessary investments to prevent or end adverse impacts, collaboration with other entities in order to prevent or bring adverse impacts to an end, and the payment of damages where harm occurs.

The proposed EU Directive imposes a narrower scope to a company's due diligence obligations than found in the UNGPs. A company is only required to undertake due diligence with respect to its own operations, the operations of its subsidiaries, and the value chain operations carried out by entities with whom the company has an 'established business relationship'. An 'established business relationship' is a direct or indirect business relationship which is, or is expected to be, lasting, in view of its intensity or duration, and which does not represent a negligible or merely ancillary part of the value chain.[104]

100 ibid art 2(1)(b), Recitals [22]

101 ibid art 3(c).

102 UN OHCHR, 'OHCHR Feedback on the Proposal for a Directive of the European Parliament and of the Council on Corporate Sustainability Due Diligence' (2022) <www.ohchr.org/sites/default/files/2022-05/eu-csddd-feedback-ohchr.pdf> accessed 20 October 2022.

103 EU Proposed Directive (n 6) art 4. These six steps are elaborated upon in arts 5–10.

104 ibid art 3(f).

With respect to the standard of due diligence required, the Proposed Directive specifies that companies must take 'appropriate measures'. An 'appropriate measure' is defined as

> a measure that is capable of achieving the objectives of due diligence, commensurate with the degree of severity and the likelihood of the adverse impact, and reasonably available to the company, taking into account the circumstances of the specific case, including characteristics of the economic sector and of the specific business relationship and the company's influence thereof, and the need to ensure prioritisation of action.[105]

There are some proposed differences in the standards of due diligence required for different categories of companies.

The Proposed Directive goes into considerable detail concerning the actions companies are required to take, 'where relevant', to address potential impacts and actual impacts.[106] While there is not the scope to examine these articles in depth here, it is important to note that these obligations—and the Proposed Directive more broadly—accords significant importance to the use of contractual clauses and third-party assurances as means through which companies may address actual and potential risks and potentially limit their exposure to civil liability. This feature of the Proposed Directive has been met with concern by the OHCHR, civil society organisations, and trade unions on the basis that it is overly legalistic and risks endorsing prevailing private labour governance practices, which are widely seen as inadequate.[107]

The proposed EU Directive refers to stakeholder consultation at various stages in the due diligence process. When identifying risks and adverse impacts, companies are to consult with 'potentially affected stakeholders' when identifying risks and adverse impacts, where this is deemed relevant.[108] When a company decides to develop a preventative action plan to respond to identified risks, it is obliged to consult with 'affected stakeholders'.[109] When a company develops a corrective action plan to respond to adverse impacts, it is to consult 'stakeholders'.[110] Companies are required to establish complaints procedures, through which affected stakeholders, trade unions, and civil society organisations can raise 'legitimate concerns

[105] ibid art 3(q).
[106] ibid arts 5 and 7.
[107] See eg UN OHCHR (n 102); Gabrielle Holly and Signe Andreasen Lysgaard, 'Legislating for Impact: Analysis of the Proposed EU Corporate Sustainability Due Diligence Directive (2022) Danish Institute for Human Rights 18–19 <www.humanrights.dk/publications/legislating-impact-analysis-proposed-eu-corporate-sustainability-due-diligence> accessed 20 October 2022; Civil Society Statement, 'Civil Society Statement on the Proposed EU Corporate Sustainability Due Diligence Directive' (2022) <https://media.business-humanrights.org/media/documents/CSO_statement_CSDDD_EN_bpByp6L.pdf> accessed 20 October 2022.
[108] EU Proposed Directive (n 6) art 6(4).
[109] ibid art 7(2)(a).
[110] ibid art 8(3)(b).

regarding actual or potential human rights impacts'.[111] The Proposed Directive makes clear that where a company receives a 'well-founded' complaint, it is obliged to address any adverse risk or impact.[112]

With respect to monitoring and enforcement, the Proposed Directive requires member states to designate one or more supervisory authorities to oversee compliance with due diligence obligations.[113] Such authorities should be independent and have appropriate powers to request information and investigate, order the cessation of infringements and remedial action, and sanction companies for non-compliance with their due diligence obligations.[114] Member states should also ensure the availability of judicial review of decisions taken by the relevant authority.[115] The Directive does not specify specific penalties for non-compliance but calls on member states to establish sanctions that are 'effective, proportionate and dissuasive'.[116] The Proposed Directive also provides for member states to ensure that persons may refer 'substantiated concerns' to the relevant supervisory body.[117]

The Proposed Directive establishes a pathway to civil liability in the event of violations of the due diligence obligations. Member states are required to ensure that a company will be liable if it fails to comply with the due diligence obligations in Articles 7 and 8, and as a result, an adverse impact that should have been addressed occurs and leads to damage.[118] The actions elaborated upon in these articles (see above) and the concept of 'appropriate measures' will be pertinent in determining whether a company has acted with due diligence for the purposes of attributing civil liability. The Proposed Directive provides a form of 'quasi-defence' by making it clear that, with respect to indirect partners with whom a company has an 'established business relationship', the company should not be held liable where it has put in place contractual obligations requiring compliance with a code of conduct and procedures in place to monitor compliance with that obligation, and it was reasonable to expect that the actions taken would be adequate.[119] The proposal is silent as to where the burden of proof should lie for the purposes of establishing corporate liability for harm caused.

III. Statutory Deference vs Statutory Elaboration

Section II above has demonstrated the growing diffusion of HRDD at the national and regional level and provided an overview of laws adopted to date, as well as

[111] ibid art 9.
[112] ibid art 9(3).
[113] ibid art 17.
[114] ibid arts 17–18.
[115] ibid arts 17–18.
[116] ibid art 20.
[117] ibid 19.
[118] ibid 22(1).
[119] ibid 22(2).

the proposed EU Directive. In this section, I argue that variation in local conditions and political dynamics has led to the emergence of two distinct approaches to HRDD. The first approach—which I term the statutory deference approach–is found in the laws adopted in countries such as the United States, the United Kingdom, and Australia. As the term suggests, this approach largely defers to—rather than challenges—a business-orientated logic when it comes to HRDD. Recall from Chapter 4, that when filtered through a managerial lens, HRDD privileges managerial prerogative, discretion, and flexibility. It privileges process over outcomes and resists the notion of external accountability for the adequacy of due diligence processes. A contrasting approach, which I term the statutory elaboration approach, is found in France and Germany and is proposed in the EU. This approach imposes some constraints on managerial discretion, although ultimately it remains too early to tell whether these will be sufficient to improve corporate performance in respecting internationally recognised workers' rights. I briefly elaborate on these two approaches below.

A. The Statutory Deference Approach: Endorsing Managerial Prerogative

In most countries adopting a statutory deference approach, the reception of HRDD has intersected with the rise of modern slavery abolitionism. This latter phenomenon, as a number of scholars have argued, has been driven by an expansion of the human trafficking concept to encompass various forms of egregious labour exploitation and the influence of powerful individuals who have zealously advocated for greater attention to be paid to recognition and eradication of the practice.[120] This modern slavery framework has generated an unprecedented breadth of support for regulatory action in the United Kingdom, Australia, and the United States, including from business. In this context, rather than being seized upon in its entirety, the HRDD framework has been drawn on by a range of actors for the overriding purpose of providing guidance on best practice on identifying and addressing modern slavery risks. While business has been a key supporter—indeed, driver—of the laws discussed above, this support has been overwhelmingly for a legislative approach that focuses solely on modern slavery and entails a 'light-touch', disclosure-based model of regulation.

[120] See Judy Fudge and Kendra Strauss (eds), *Temporary Work, Agencies and Unfree Labour: Insecurity in the New World of Work* (Routledge 2014); Judy Fudge, 'Modern Slavery, Unfree Labour and the Labour Market: The Social Dynamics of Legal Characterization' (2017) Social & Legal Studies 1; Janie A Chuang, 'Exploitation Creep and the Unmaking of Human Trafficking Law' (2014) 108 American Journal of International Law 609. For a discussion of the rise of the modern slavery frame in Australia, see Ingrid Landau and Shelley Marshall 'Should Australia be Embracing the Modern Slavery Model of Regulation? (2018) 46 Federal Law Review 313.

Further evidence of the extent and nature of corporate influence over HRDD-related laws in the United States, the United Kingdom, and Australia is found in the absence of genuine examination by policymakers of alternative models. For many of these laws, which I characterise as adopting a statutory deference approach, alternative approaches were available to, and indeed advocated for, by civil society groups and scholars. In the United States, for example, section 1502 of the Dodd–Frank Act did not begin with securities laws: rather, the law's promoters originally sought an outright ban on the import of conflict minerals.[121] In Australia, many submissions on the Modern Slavery Bill 2015 called for any reporting requirement to be broadened to encompass all human rights.[122] Scholars have also pointed to approaches in other areas of transnational activity (such as anti-bribery) which are seen as offering much more robust due diligence regulation.[123] As has been argued persuasively by Genevieve LeBaron and Andreas Rühmkorf, it is possible to explain business support for the specific type of transparency-based regulation embodied in the MSA UK model as an effective strategy through which to stave off these more robust interpretations of due diligence.[124]

As a consequence of the level of corporate influence, these legislative initiatives largely defer to, rather than challenge, managerial interpretations of due diligence. This occurs in three ways. They narrow the scope and application of HRDD as compared to the UNGPs; they distance due diligence from any overarching responsibility on businesses to take meaningful steps to address their adverse rights impacts; and they endorse unfettered managerial prerogative to determine the nature of due diligence efforts undertaken (including the extent to which, and how, stakeholders are involved in these processes). Each of these is elaborated upon briefly below.

These laws also significantly narrow HRDD when it comes to the types of businesses and rights covered and the extent to which businesses are required (or, indeed, encouraged) to consider their impacts throughout their supply chains. They only apply to large businesses. The types of rights covered are limited to the most egregious forms of labour exploitation such as forced labour, trafficking in persons, and the worst forms of child labour. Even if we presume effectiveness, a company may comply with reporting requirements and, indeed, take meaningful action to identify, prevent, and address risks of modern slavery in their supply chains without taking action to ensure that it is respecting other labour rights that constitute internationally recognised human rights, such as freedom of association, non-discrimination, health and safety, and so on. It is possible that companies may

[121] Drimmer and Phillips (n 45) 142.
[122] Landau and Marshall (n 120).
[123] LeBaron and Rühmkorf, 'Steering CSR' (n 3).
[124] LeBaron and Rühmkorf, 'The Domestic Politics of Corporate Accountability Legislation' (n 11) 709.

put in place due diligence processes to identify risks of modern slavery that are cast broadly enough to detect the existence of other (non-modern-slavery) forms of labour abuse. These companies might be compelled to address them. However, such positive outcomes for broader labour abuses would be accidental and far from guaranteed. The statutory deference approach is also significantly circumscribed in scope with respect to the extent to which due diligence efforts extend to entities in a company's supply chain. For example, neither the MSA UK nor MSA AUS provides a statutory definition of a supply chain,[125] effectively leaving it to the company to determine, to a large extent, which portions of their global operations to report on.[126]

The statutory deference approach implicitly endorses a business interpretation of HRDD in which it is the act of undertaking due diligence per se that is the ultimate measure of responsible business conduct rather than the impact or effectiveness of the company's activities. As explained in Chapter 4, when filtered through a business lens, HRDD is separated or distanced from the fundamental responsibility of a company to respect human rights. An important feature of these laws is that, to the extent that compliance is provided for and monitored, it is compliance with the act of reporting rather than with meaningful steps to address labour rights risks. There is no attempt to connect the obligation to report on due diligence measures to any overriding (or even articulated) responsibility on business to identify and address adverse human rights impacts in their own operations and supply chains.

The statutory deference approach fails to challenge managerial prerogative to determine the extent and nature of due diligence undertaken. This is manifest in several features of these laws. First, they fail to establish any public or commonly accepted baseline standard for due diligence and are not specific as to the standards to which companies should adhere. At best, they refer to, or encourage, the use of global standards (such as in the Dodd–Frank Act's section 1502 reference to the OECD Due Diligence Guidance for Responsible Supply Chains of Minerals from Conflict-Affected and High-Risk Areas or the Dutch Child Labour Due Diligence Law's reference to ILO guidance) but lack specificity as to how compliance with these standards is to be established.[127] Second, they do not provide any substantive rights to consultation and participation by affected stakeholders (including

[125] These terms are defined in non-binding guidance documents. The UK Government's statutory guidance observes that the term 'supply chain' should be interpreted in its 'everyday meaning': UK Home Office Statutory Guidance (n 21) [2.2]. The Australian guidance is more helpful, defining the term as 'the products and services (including labour) that contribute to the entity's own products and services. This includes products and services sourced in Australia or overseas and extends beyond direct suppliers': Australian Government, 'Commonwealth Modern Slavery Act 2018: Guidance for Reporting Entities' (Statutory Guidance September 2019) 34.

[126] Phillips, LeBaron, and Wallin (n 4) 16.

[127] ibid.

workers and their representatives). Rather, these initiatives leave the nature and scope of any such engagement to the company to determine. Third, they do not establish any new forms of legal or regulatory accountability for the quality of due diligence undertaken. These laws position consumers, civil society, and investors as the arbiters of company performance. The ultimate outcome of this approach, as LeBaron and Rühmkorf have observed, is that these laws have done little more than reinforce the status quo by providing statutory endorsement of existing private labour governance approaches that have long been the subject of concern, including social auditing.[128]

B. The Statutory Elaboration Approach: Challenging Managerial Prerogative?

In contrast to the first approach, the statutory elaboration model found in continental Europe did not originate with modern slavery abolitionism. The origins of the French law, for example, lie in campaigning efforts by NGO activists and jurists and an initial legislative proposal put forward in the wake of the Rana Plaza building collapse in Bangladesh in 2013. Campaigning for the bill seized upon HRDD as a means of overcoming longstanding frustrations with voluntary initiatives, and framing for the bill directly connected the initiative to global endorsement of the UNGPs, as well as to the trend towards due diligence initiatives in other countries.[129] In contrast to the high level of business support for modern slavery laws in Anglo-American jurisdictions, business opposed the French bill 'vociferously'.[130] According to Alice Evans, the societal coalition of NGOs and politicians advocating for mandatory HRDD succeeded due to a combination of 'an enabling environment, activism, and luck'.[131] Growing international support, public outcry over Rana Plaza, a political culture characterised by widespread scepticism of multinationals and acceptance of state intervention, and a centre-left government all increased the possibility for significant reform. While the French initiative was watered down after intensive lobbying by business,[132] it survived the legislative process in a much more robust form. Although important questions remain around how this law will be interpreted, it challenges business interpretations

[128] LeBaron and Rühmkorf, 'The Domestic Politics of Corporate Accountability Legislation' (n 11) 738.

[129] Alice Evans, 'Overcoming the Global Despondency Trap: Strengthening Corporate Accountability in Supply Chains' (2020) 27 Review of International Political Economy 658, 674.

[130] ibid 672.

[131] ibid 659.

[132] Sandra Cossart, Jérôme Chaplier, and Tiphaine Beau de Lomenie, 'The French Law on Duty of Care: A Historic Step towards Making Globalization Work for All' (2017) 2 Business and Human Rights Journal 317, 347. Original civil society proposals for the French law introduce a new liability regime and provide for a reversal of the burden of proof from victims to companies.

of HRDD to a greater degree than the statutory deference model. These challenges are evident in the breadth of the legislation, the extent to which stakeholders are recognised as having a legitimate role in the design and evaluation of due diligence processes, and the imposition on companies of some accountability for the quality of due diligence undertaken.

Subsequent HRDD laws in Germany and Norway, and proposed in the EU Directive, also elaborate upon HRDD in a way that has the potential to circumscribe managerial discretion with respect to the extent to which, and how, they engage in HRDD. These initiatives have also met with fierce contest over the nature of obligations they place on companies and enforcement measures.[133]

While the HRDD laws adopted in France, Germany and Norway and proposed in the EU are all significantly more limited in their scope of application (the types of companies they cover) than the UNGPs, their material scope in terms of the rights they cover is significantly broader than the statutory deference approach. The laws diverge significantly when it comes to the question of the extent to which companies are required to conduct HRDD throughout their supply chains. As explained above, the French and German laws and proposed EU Directive all significantly limit this obligation by reference to established business relationships in a manner inconsistent with the UNGPs. While the formulations adopted in these laws may provide a degree of specificity that appeals to companies, the effect is to exclude many business-related adverse human rights impacts from the scope of corporate HRDD altogether.

In contrast to the statutory deference approach, the European laws and proposed laws appear to institutionalise channels for stakeholder participation in corporate HRDD. The French law, for example, does this in several ways. First, a broad range of persons is given standing to seek an order from the competent court that a company comply with its obligation to establish, publish, and effectively implement its vigilance plan. Second, the law requires companies to consult with representative trade unions when they are developing an 'alert mechanism' through which to obtain information on the existence or the realisation of risks.[134] Third, the law appears to oblige companies to consult with stakeholders when drafting and implementing their vigilance plans.[135] The Norwegian law provides

[133] Almut Schilling-Vacaflor and Andrea Lenschow, 'Hardening Foreign Corporate Accountability through Mandatory Due Diligence in the European Union? New Trends and Persisting Challenges' (2021) 17 Regulation & Governance 677, 687; Francisca Torres-Cortés and others, 'Study on Due Diligence Requirements through the Supply Chain. Final Report' (*European Commission, Directorate-General for Justice and Consumers* 2020) <http://data.europea.eu/doi/10.2838/39830> accessed 22 October 2022.

[134] Tiphaine Beau de Lomenie and Sandra Cossart, 'Stakeholders and the Duty of Vigilance' (2017) 50 Revue Internationale de la Compliance et de l'Éthique des Affaires 1, 2.

[135] ibid 1. While the law itself does not define 'stakeholders', the explanatory memorandum (exposé des motifs) of the draft law of February 2015 referred to a definition used in a pre-existing law, in which the term 'stakeholders' was defined 'as all individuals who participate in [the enterprise's] economic life and actors of the civil society influenced, directly or indirectly, by its activities': ibid 2.

an innovative right for third parties to request information from companies. The proposed EU Directive calls for companies to consult with stakeholders at various stages of the HRDD process.

On closer analysis, however, it remains unclear how meaningful these rights will prove in practice. In the case of the French law, for example, it appears that only the first two of the three rights identified above are enforceable. Moreover, the first right pertains only to challenging a failure to adopt a plan and/or the failure of a company to implement its plan. It does not appear to enable any challenge to the *adequacy* of a plan adopted. In relation to the third potential avenue for stakeholder participation (perhaps the most potentially meaningful for workers not directly engaged by the company, their representatives and other labour rights activists), the French Constitutional Court has made clear that this provision of the law is merely hortatory.[136] The German and proposed EU laws have also come under criticism for being vague with respect to stakeholder consultation and leaving significant scope for companies to determine when consultation is considered relevant and appropriate.[137]

In contrast to the statutory deference approach, the laws adopted in continental Europe, and proposed at the EU level, impose some degree of external accountability on companies for the quality of HRDD undertaken. These measures would appear to help to ensure that HRDD plans are implemented appropriately and avoid a situation where plans are established merely for declarative purposes. However, in all cases, it appears that the responsible supervising authorities enjoy significant discretion to determine on what basis a company's HRDD plan and implementation is considered adequate. The extent to which these authorities will defer to managerial prerogative when it comes to determining precisely what compliance with the relevant HRDD obligations entails remains unclear.

The French law and proposed EU Directive appear to impose a further level of accountability on companies by way of recognising the ability of victims who have suffered harm as a result of a company's failure to comply with its HRDD obligations to sue for damages in the form of civil liability for harms caused. Again, however, the effectiveness of these provisions remains uncertain. In the case of the French law, for example, the French Constitutional Court has emphasised that the civil liability regime for harms established under the *Devoir de Vigilance Law* is based on the general French law of tort.[138] As such, the law does not overcome any of the well-recognised legal and practical obstacles encountered by victims of human rights abuses committed by French companies

[136] ibid.

[137] Christopher Patz, 'The EU's Draft Corporate Sustainability Due Diligence Directive: A First Assessment' (2022) 7 Business and Human Rights Journal 291.

[138] Stéphane Brabant and Elsa Savourey, 'France's Corporate Duty of Vigilance Law: A Closer Look at the Penalties Faced by Companies' (2017) 50 Revue Internationale de la Compliance et de l'Éthique des Affaires—Supplément à la Semaine Juridique Enterprise et Affaires 1, 2.

seeking remedy in French courts.[139] Furthermore, as Olivier De Schutter points out, it is not yet clear how this civil remedy relates to the execution of a due diligence plan, with a plausible reading of the law being that where a vigilance plan has been adopted in accordance with requirements set out in the law and a violation of human rights or an environmental harm nevertheless occurs in the group of companies or in the supply chain, the parent or lead company will not be liable.[140] It also remains unclear how the French courts will interpret key but ambiguous terms within the law, such as what constitutes a '*severe* risk', '*suitable* actions to mitigate risks or prevent serious abuses', or '*reasonable* vigilance measures' to identify risks and foresee serious violations of human rights and fundamental liberties, safety and health, and the environment. Similar types of concerns with respect to the interpretation of key terms and the potential for corporate liability to be significantly circumscribed by certain judicial interpretations of the statutorily imposed HRDD obligations have been voiced with respect to the proposed EU Directive.

IV. Conclusion

To date, state efforts to promote and mandate corporate uptake of HRDD have been limited, piecemeal, and tentative. However, in a growing number of jurisdictions, societal coalitions are securing legislative initiatives that incorporate the concept of rights-based due diligence.

Analysis of national and EU developments reveals the emergence of two distinct trajectories in HRDD-related laws. The statutory deference approach encompasses laws that focus on a narrow subset of extreme labour exploitation and impose reporting obligations on companies. By restricting the corporate focus, these laws may unintentionally incentivise businesses to prioritise efforts to address specific rights even where, objectively, these rights do not constitute salient human rights risks facing the company. These laws do not set any minimum standard on the extent or nature of due diligence undertaken. In deferring to management prerogative and failing to provide meaningful rights for stakeholders, these laws have been criticised as 'little more than an endorsement of existing voluntary CSR [corporate social responsibility] reporting'.[141] It may be argued that by mandating a certain level of transparency of due diligence efforts, these laws create 'new opportunities for public control of companies' which will be exerted by way of pressure from civil

[139] ibid 3–4.

[140] Olivier De Schutter, 'Towards Mandatory Due Diligence in Global Supply Chains' (*International Trade Union Confederation* 2020) 28 <www.ituc-csi.org/IMG/pdf/de_schutte_mandatory_due_diligence.pdf> accessed 10 September 2021.

[141] LeBaron and Rühmkorf, 'The Domestic Politics of Corporate Accountability Legislation' (n 11) 20.

society, consumers, and investors.[142] However, as Amy Sinclair and Justine Nolan emphasise, 'the assumption that greater transparency and availability of information about companies' activities will translate into both improvements in practice and increased corporate accountability remains largely untested'.[143] Many scholars are sceptical about the capacity of such reporting laws to generate 'fulsome, systematic, scaled and collaborative contributions on the part of business to ensure human rights'[144] or, indeed, to prompt companies to go beyond superficial or cosmetic forms of reporting.[145]

The statutory elaboration approach, embodied in the French *Devoir de Vigilance Law*, the German Supply Chain Due Diligence Act, and the Norwegian Transparency Act and proposed by the EU Commission is more robust. While still significantly narrowing and curtailing the concept of HRDD as articulated in the UNGPs, these instruments cover a broader range of workers' rights and impose more substantive obligations on business. These laws also provide some capacity for actors external to the company to challenge a company's failure to adopt or implement a plan. However, these laws and proposed laws also do not legalise HRDD in a manner consistent with initial expectations of the international trade union movement and other labour activists. There is no guarantee, for example, that companies that fall within the scope of these laws will consult in a meaningful fashion with workers or their representatives when drafting, implementing, or evaluating the effectiveness of their vigilance plans. Significant ambiguity remains concerning standards of compliance, and the adequacy of enforcement mechanisms has the potential to further limit the potential effectiveness of these laws as a means of strengthening corporate accountability for workers' rights.

The process of rendering soft HRDD norms into hard law at the national and regional level has, to date, led to significant narrowing and watering down of the concept. Moreover, it has advanced arguments in this book by demonstrating that there is little evidence, to date, that HRDD is being institutionalised at the national or regional level in ways that create novel and meaningful channels through which workers and their representatives can challenge extant corporate approaches with respect to working conditions in their supply chains. In many cases, features of the concept which proved so initially compelling to labour rights activists—such as the requirement for companies to respect *all* internationally recognised human rights and to consider their impacts well beyond their own operations and direct business relationships—have gone by the wayside. It is important to recognise that

142 Sabrina Zajak and Christian Scheper, 'The Dual Nature of Transparency: Corporatization and Democratization of Global Production Networks' in Stefan Berger and Dimitrij Owetschkin (eds), *Contested Transparencies, Social Movements and the Public Sphere* (Palgrave Macmillan 2019) 214.

143 Amy Sinclair and Justine Nolan, 'Modern Slavery Laws in Australia: Steps in the Right Direction?' (2020) 5 Business and Human Rights Journal 164, 169.

144 Ford and Nolan (n 10) 28–29.

145 Landau and Marshall (n 119) 326–30.

the statutory elaboration approach to HRDD adopted and proposed in continental Europe remains largely untested, and there is the potential for this approach to deliver positive outcomes for workers and trade unions. However, such outcomes are by no means assured. Furthermore, while there is little evidence, to date, to suggest that the concept is being legalised in a manner that renders it a particularly potent mechanism of transnational labour governance, these processes of HRDD legalisation are nonetheless influencing transnational labour governance in significant ways. These important but largely overlooked implications are considered in Chapter 7.

7

What Does HRDD Mean for Transnational Labour Governance?

I. Introduction

The preceding chapters of this book have examined how the concept of human rights due diligence (HRDD) has been received, contested, and institutionalised. This chapter explores what these developments mean for transnational labour governance. Drawing on the analysis in preceding chapters, the chapter presents four main findings in response to this question. First, despite the aspirations of the international union movement and others, there is little to suggest that HRDD is being legalised in a way that significantly challenges extant corporate practices with respect to the governance of labour standards in global supply chains. This is largely because, as I have demonstrated, policymakers at the international and national levels are adopting HRDD standards and laws that preserve—indeed, endorse—broad managerial discretion with respect to the extent to which, and how, labour rights issues within supply chains are addressed. The second, third, and fourth findings presented in this chapter arise from HRDD's reframing of questions around corporate accountability and labour rights in terms of risk management. It is recognised in socio-legal literature that different frames may give rise to different forms of authority and empower different actors.[1] The ascendance of the HRDD frame is facilitating a more prominent role for national courts in transnational labour governance. This development has both potential advantages and hazards. By privileging technical and professional expertise, HRDD is driving the increased presence within the field of for-profit actors. Professional management consultancies, risk advisory services, and law firms are using the legalisation of HRDD as a platform to expand and diversify their services. Again, this expansion of the for-profit intermediary in the space brings both potential benefits and risks. Finally, HRDD has enabled the Organisation for Economic Co-operation and Development (OECD) to consolidate its role as a transnational labour

[1] See eg Tim Bartley, 'How Foundations Shape Social Movements: The Construction of an Organizational Field and the Rise of Forest Certification' (2007) 54(3) Social Problems 229, 233; Sally Engle Merry, *Human Rights and Gender Violence: Translating International Law into Local Justice* (Chicago UP 2005).

Human Rights Due Diligence and Labour Governance. Ingrid Landau, Oxford University Press. © Ingrid Landau 2023.
DOI: 10.1093/oso/9780198876069.003.0007

regulator, at the expense of other intergovernmental organisations, particularly the International Labour Organization (ILO).

In this chapter, I discuss each of these four findings in turn and elaborate on why each development warrants greater reflection, dissection, and discussion among labour activists who prioritise HRDD as a strategic objective and among international labour scholars.

II. A Blunt Instrument of Transnational Labour Law

To what extent has the rise of HRDD transformed transnational labour governance through the introduction of a new and meaningful channel to promote and secure workers' rights in global supply chains? As discussed in Chapters 2 and 4, HRDD has been embraced by the international trade union movement on the presumption that legalisation of HRDD will lead to this outcome. These actors believed that the adoption of HRDD would compel businesses to both deepen and broaden their respect for workers' human rights. More specifically, HRDD held out the promise of addressing perceived shortcomings of private labour governance approaches. These included the selectivity exhibited in many private governance initiatives when it comes to which labour standards are promoted and enforced; the absence of meaningful channels for workers, their representatives, and other stakeholders to voice concerns and challenge private labour governance approaches perceived as inadequate (such as social auditing); and the absence of sufficient public accountability for the impact of corporate practices on workers' rights.

The analysis in preceding chapters suggests that these ambitions for the concept have, to date, gone largely unfulfilled. This is principally because, as I have shown, HRDD as articulated in the UNGPs is ambiguous and leaves broad scope for actors to shape the meaning of the concept during subsequent processes of legalisation. Analysis of these processes—at the international level (Chapter 5) and national level (Chapter 6)—has shown that business actors have successfully influenced public norm-making processes. At the international level, efforts to secure substantive HRDD standards through the ILO have proven unsuccessful. While there has been much activity at the OECD in relation to HRDD, these activities have been overwhelmingly limited to discussions and to the publication of non-binding technical guidance. At the national level, many HRDD-related initiatives have focused on a narrow subset of labour rights and have only required public disclosure of due diligence efforts undertaken. Mandatory HRDD laws in Europe show more promise; however, these initiatives have also not legalised HRDD in a manner consistent with the initial expectations accorded to the concept by labour activists. Moreover, such laws have yet to be used effectively by civil society to hold companies to account for the extent or nature of their due diligence efforts. Overall, the analysis in this book suggests not only that the legalisation of HRDD is not substantially challenging corporate processes with respect to working conditions in global supply chains but also that it carries the potential to *reinforce* prevailing private labour governance approaches.

This finding—that HRDD is proving a blunt instrument of transnational labour law—has important implications for those who advocate for the increased legalisation of the concept. It questions the presumption that incorporation of HRDD requirements in national and international law per se will lead to improved corporate performance with respect to workers' rights in supply chains. There is a significant risk that regulatory interventions may be crafted in such a way as to preserve and legitimise, rather than challenge, corporate discretion when it comes to the extent to which, and how, a company considers and addresses labour rights issues in its own operations and supply chains. In doing so, regulatory interventions may ultimately fail to achieve the public goal they are designed to achieve, that is, the reduction or elimination of adverse human rights impacts. There is also a risk that these interventions foreclose other possibilities. These findings underscore the need for labour rights advocates and others who support and advocate for the further legalisation of HRDD to engage in more reflection and debate over the question of how HRDD-related regulatory interventions should be designed so as to ensure that they open up possibilities and empower, rather than disempower, workers and their organisations. The question as to how this could be done is taken up in Chapter 8.

III. A More Prominent Role for the Courts

A second important implication arising from HRDD's ascendance concerns the position and authority of national courts within transnational labour governance. As discussed in Chapter 6, some national HRDD-related laws enacted to date merely impose reporting requirements. However, an increasing number of laws at the national and regional level are recognising a role for judicial scrutiny of corporate HRDD practices. To date, such laws include the French Duty of Vigilance Law[2] and the proposed EU Directive.[3] This trend towards the adoption of HRDD laws that provide a role for the courts in scrutinising corporate compliance with HRDD obligations is only likely to continue, given ongoing domestic and transnational activist campaigns to secure mandatory HRDD laws in other jurisdictions. Other international developments beyond the scope of this book—including negotiations towards a draft Business and Human Rights Treaty—also suggest that,

[2] *Loi 2017-399 du 27 Mars 2017 Relative au Devoir de Vigilance des Sociétés Mères et des Enterprises Donneuses D'ordre.*

[3] European Commission, 'Proposal for a Directive on Corporate Sustainability Due Diligence and Annex 2022' (2022) <https://ec.europa.eu/info/publications/proposal-directive-corporate-sustainable-due-diligence-and-annex_en> accessed 5 October 2022.

in the future, national courts may play a greater role in scrutinising corporate compliance with HRDD laws.[4]

An enhanced role for domestic courts in overseeing and enforcing HRDD is likely to have significant consequences for transnational labour governance. Some of these are self-evident. Assuming victims can surmount the many practical barriers to bringing a legal claim transnationally (which is by no means assured), they may have greater access to remedy for corporate labour-rights related harms. Presumably too, such developments may increase the volume of litigation in domestic courts concerning corporate responsibilities with respect to labour rights in global supply chains.[5] Other consequences, however, may be less considered and intended. Below, and drawing on the analysis in preceding chapters, I identify two potential implications to arise from judicial control of interpretation of HRDD norms that, I suggest, warrant greater consideration by labour rights advocates and others who seek further legalisation of HRDD. The first is the high probability that courts will defer to business practice, and the second is that courts will curtail HRDD to 'fit' within existing legal doctrines.

A. Judicial Deference to Business Practice

HRDD legislation may result in the judicial endorsement of existing corporate responsibility practices that have long been regarded by labour and human rights activists as inadequate, and indeed, somewhat paradoxically, a motivating force for labour support for HRDD in the first place. Through lawsuits (whether by victims or activists), national courts will be asked to determine what constitutes compliance with the law. This will require judicial interpretation of questions such as what constitutes 'reasonable' due diligence and 'adequate' mitigation measures. This study has shown that understandings of these terms vary significantly between actors. Chapter 3 of this book introduced legal endogeneity theory. This theory suggests that courts may interpret concepts, and legislative requirements,

[4] See UNHRC (United Nations Human Rights Commission) Open-Ended Intergovernmental Working Group on Transnational Corporations and Other Business Enterprises with Respect to Human Rights, 'Legally Binding Instrument to Regulate, in International Human Rights Law, the Activities of Transnational Corporations and Other Business Enterprises: Third Revised Draft' (*Office of the High Commissioner of Human Rights* 17 August 2021) <www.ohchr.org/en/hr-bodies/hrc/wg-trans-corp/igwg-on-tnc> accessed 23 October 2022.

[5] Of course, efforts by labour and human rights activists to use national courts to hold companies accountable for labour rights violations in global supply chains are not new. For years now, these actors have creatively (but rather unsuccessfully) used a range of statutes and common law doctrines to pursue corporate accountability for labour rights violations abroad. See eg Martin Spitzer, 'Human Rights, Global Supply Chains and the Role of Tort' (2019) 10 Journal of European Tort Law 95; David Cabrelli, 'Liability for the Violations of Human Rights and Labour Standards in Global Supply Chains: A Common Law Perspective' (2019) 10 Journal of European Tort Law 108; André Sobczak, 'Are Codes of Conduct in Global Supply Chains Really Voluntary? From Soft Law Regulation of Labour Relations to Consumer Law' (2015) 16 Business Ethics Quarterly 167.

in ways that defer to, rather than challenge, managerial interpretations of HRDD. According to legal endogeneity theorists, when faced with legislation that mandates broad standards without specifying precisely what is necessary for compliance, companies will respond by creating 'symbolic structures' to show that they are complying with the law. When asked to rule on what constitutes compliance, judges tend to be impressed by these formal policies and strategies that symbolise legality and rationality and endorse them as constituting compliance.[6]

A recent case in Canada demonstrates this potential for judicial deference to corporate practice. The case involved a class action negligence lawsuit brought against Canadian grocery store chain Loblaws on behalf of victims of the Rana Plaza building collapse in April 2013. Loblaws had an 'impressive sounding' corporate social responsibility (CSR) programme, which included a Supplier Code of Conduct that clearly stated the company's desire to do business only with suppliers whose practices were consistent with its ethics, principles, and enumerated standards. It had engaged an auditing company to monitor compliance with its Supplier Code in Bangladesh. However, this audit company had been engaged only to undertake a 'basic audit', which did not cover inspection of the structural integrity of the buildings that housed its supplier factories.[7] David Doorey has shown how the court in this case, while it engaged with notions of control and responsibility in CSR, did not do so in a way that corresponded to how these concepts are understood and used in private labour governance. Not only did the court reject the claims, but it also praised Loblaws for its CSR efforts.[8] In explaining the decision, Doorey has argued that the judge failed to appreciate the important difference 'between genuine and window-dressing CSR and between code monitoring on the one hand, and enforcement and remediation on the other'.[9] While this action was taken under tort law rather than any HRDD legislation, it hints at the significant potential for judicial deference to symbolic structures adopted by companies when it comes to considering what constitutes adequate due diligence on workers' human rights in supply chains.

This risk of judicial deference to prevailing managerial practices would appear particularly acute in the case of HRDD laws that explicitly identify mechanisms such as codes of conduct and social audits as indicators of due diligence. This is the approach taken, for example, by the proposed EU Directive, discussed briefly in Chapter 6. As Patz points out, the proposed Directive effectively privileges and promotes the use of codes of conduct, contractual clauses, and third-party

[6] Lauren B Edelman, *Working Law: Courts, Corporations and Symbolic Civil Rights* (Chicago University Press 2016).

[7] David J Doorey, 'Lost in Translation: Rana Plaza, Loblaw, and the Disconnect between Legal Formality and Corporate Social Responsibility' (2018) 2–3 <http://ssrn.com/abstract=3265826> accessed 20 September 2021.

[8] ibid.

[9] ibid.

verification by audit companies or industry initiatives.[10] At the same time, it fails to articulate any expectation on companies to consider the impact of their purchasing practices on working conditions in their supply chains. In this context, it appears highly likely that courts asked to consider the reasonableness of company actions (including of reliance on contractual clauses and audits) will defer to longstanding CSR practices, despite the abundance of evidence to indicate that these have proven incapable of adequately protecting workers' human rights.

B. The Disciplining Power of Legal Doctrine

Placing HRDD in the courts is also likely to be subject to the concept of 'the disciplining power of legal doctrine'.[11] This term is used by Jan Smits to describe the common process by which a new solution is 'fitted' within the system that is accepted and used by the legal community. HRDD legislation will inevitably provide broad scope for judicial interpretation. This includes, for example, interpretation as to what extent a company should be expected to exercise due diligence, as well as at what point it may be unreasonable to impose liability on a company for labour rights violations within its supply chain. Faced with these ambiguities, legislatures and courts are likely to interpret HRDD in the light of existing legal doctrines and concepts. The French Duty of Vigilance Law exemplifies this dynamic with respect to the legislative process. Under this law, the scope of a company's due diligence is limited by principles drawn from French commercial law, and the nature of liability is based on French tort law.

While the extent to which HRDD will be diluted to align with existing legal doctrines or concepts will depend, to a large extent, on how the legislative provisions are drafted, legislatures and courts are likely to be influenced in their interpretation of the legislation by established private law doctrines and concepts. This may have the paradoxical outcome of further legitimising the application of concepts drawn from tort law and contract to the question of corporate responsibility for labour rights violations in global supply chains, despite HRDD being embraced precisely for its capacity to respond to the limitations of these legal doctrines as mechanisms to promote and secure labour and human rights.

The potential for the imposition of civil liability for failure to engage in HRDD to blunt much of the transformative potential of the concept for workers and their organisations has been recognised by longstanding calls by scholars, trade unions, and non-governmental organisations (NGOs) to ensure that the obligation to

[10] Christopher Patz, 'The EU's Draft Corporate Sustainability Due Diligence Directive: A First Assessment' (2022) 7 Business and Human Rights Journal 291, 298.

[11] Jan M Smits, 'Enforcing Corporate Social Responsibility Codes Under Private Law: On the Disciplining Power of Legal Doctrine' (2017) 24 Indiana Journal of Global Legal Studies 99, 108.

practice HRDD and the requirement to remedy any harm resulting from human rights violations are treated as two separate and complementary obligations.[12] This dual approach, which has been adopted in the French Duty of Vigilance Law and the proposed EU Directive, may limit the influence of the courts on the trajectory of HRDD to a significant degree and enable more open contest over the adequacy of HRDD measures taken by companies. However, it rests on the presumption that there is a public authority willing to take a robust and active approach to enforcing the initial obligation to undertake HRDD. I return to this question in Chapter 8.

C. Alternative Approaches

To further elicit implications arising from an increasingly prominent role for national courts in enforcing a legally binding duty on businesses to conduct HRDD, it is useful to contrast this with an alternative approach to addressing working conditions in corporate supply chains that, I suggest, is more consistent with a transnational labour law orientation.[13] This is the 'transnational industrial relations agreement' (TIRA) or 'enforceable brand agreement'. While the origins of this approach lie in international framework agreements (IFAs),[14] it is a labour governance approach identified as new and distinct.[15] One example of this approach is the Accord on Fire and Building Safety in Bangladesh, an agreement reached in the wake of the Rana Plaza factory building collapse in 2013 involving more than 200 garment brands and retailers and two global unions. Another example is the Action, Collaboration, Transformation (ACT) initiative. Founded in 2015, also in the global garment industry, ACT is an agreement reached between the global union IndustriALL and fifteen global garment brands that is designed to secure living wages for workers in garment supply chains through industry-wide collective bargaining agreements in selected garment-exporting countries and improved purchasing practices of buyers. A further example is found in the 2019 agreements reached between leading apparel brands, trade unions, and womens' rights organisations to address gender-based violence and harassment in Lesotho's garment sector.[16] While a legally enforceable duty of HRDD, and TIRAs are not

[12] See eg Olivier De Schutter, 'Towards Mandatory Due Diligence in Global Supply Chains' (*International Trade Union Confederation* 2020) 50 <www.ituc-csi.org/IMG/pdf/de_schutte_mandatory_due_diligence.pdf> accessed 10 September 2021.

[13] See Chapter 1.

[14] See Chapter 2.

[15] See eg Sarah Ashwin and others, 'Spillover Effects across Transnational Industrial Relations Agreements: The Potential and Limits of Collective Action in Global Supply Chains' (2020) 73 Industrial and Labour Relations Review 995; Mark Anner, Jennifer Bair, and Jeremy Blasi, 'Toward Joint Liability in Global Supply Chains: Addressing the Root Causes of Labor Violations in International Subcontracting Networks' (2013) 35 Comparative Labor Law & Policy Journal 1.

[16] See Worker Rights, 'Combating Gender-Based Violence in Lesotho' (*Worker Rights Consortium* 2022) <www.workersrights.org/issues/gender-based-violence-and-discrimination/gender-based-violence-in-lesotho> accessed 25 October 2022.

mutually exclusive approaches, a number of features of the latter can usefully be contrasted with the former: these include TIRAs' recognition of the need for collective action, the nature of the parties involved, the centrality of freedom of association and collective representation, and how commitments are monitored and enforced.[17]

In contrast to a judicially enforceable HRDD standard, TIRAs do not necessarily focus solely on the responsibilities and actions of an individual business enterprise. Rather, these initiatives recognise that poor working conditions and unjust outcomes in global supply chains are often created and sustained by the actions of multiple parties and require some acknowledgement of collective responsibility and multi-firm coordination in response.[18] In the case of the Bangladesh Accord, for example, apparel brands and retailers at the top of the supply chain are jointly responsible, along with contractors, for working conditions in the supply chain. In the case of ACT, it is envisaged that brands and IndustriALL will work with their supplier factories and affiliated unions, respectively, 'to bring them together to negotiate towards a living wage'[19] and will make 'joint approaches to governments in support of higher minimum wage outcomes, including brand commitments to continued sourcing'.[20] Brands also commit to ensuring that their purchasing practices facilitate the payment of a living wage.[21]

TIRAs affirm the 'crucial role' of collective representation and collective bargaining.[22] Organised labour (local and/or global) is a key actor in devising and implementing the agreement. The agreement itself is 'the negotiated result of interest representation ... for the pursuit of global labor relations'[23] in which the parties jointly agree on the content, the actors, the processes, and the accountability mechanisms. The Accord and ACT both assign workers' organisations key roles in their governance structures. Furthermore, they are (at least as envisaged by global union federations (GUFs)) frameworks through which to organise workers and build industrial relations at the transnational level.[24] They provide implementation mechanisms in which worker representatives can play a role. ACT

[17] Ashwin and others (n 15) 997.

[18] On the need for collective responsibilities to address labour rights issues in global supply chains, see eg Anner, Bair, and Blasi (n 15).

[19] Act on Living Wages, 'Memorandum of Understanding between ACT Corporate Signatories and IndustriALL Global Union on Establishing within Global Supply Chains Freedom of Association, Collective Bargaining, and Living Wages' (2017) art 8 <https://actonlivingwages.com/memorandum-of-understanding> accessed 10 February 2022.

[20] ibid art 14.

[21] ibid art 5.

[22] Adelle Blackett and Anne Trebilcock, 'Conceptualizing Transnational Labour Law' in Adelle Blackett and Anne Trebilcock (eds), *Research Handbook on Transnational Labour Law* (Edward Elgar 2015) 8.

[23] Ashwin and others, '(n 15) 1000.

[24] Renée-Claude Drouin, 'Freedom of Association in International Framework Agreements' in Blackett and Trebilcock, *Research Handbook on Transnational Labour Law* (n 22) 219.

> thus envisages multilevel industrial relations mechanisms, with IndustriALL negotiating with signatory brands regarding purchasing practices, IndustriALL and signatory brands encouraging industrial relations actors in garment-producing countries to the bargaining table, and local industrial relations actors negotiating industry-wide collective agreements.[25]

Unlike a statutorily imposed broad obligation upon a business to engage in HRDD, TIRAs impose specific, substantive, and legally enforceable obligations on business enterprises. The Bangladesh Accord imposes legally binding commitments on brands to financially support remediation efforts needed by unsafe factories, as well as commitments to continue sourcing from them during the agreement. Disputes arising between the parties may be subject to a final and binding arbitration process and the award enforceable in a court of law of the domicile of the signatory against whom enforcement is sought. While ACT is not legally binding, it has an (internal and external) grievance mechanism and envisages third-party monitoring of brands' sourcing practices.

TIRAs have their limitations in scope and effectiveness,[26] and unlike HRDD, there is no momentum to establish national or international institutional frameworks through which to support or foster such agreements.[27] It is also, of course, the case that the two approaches are not mutually exclusive. Nonetheless, as an approach, TIRAs usefully highlight some of the significant limitations from a transnational labour law perspective of a duty to conduct HRDD enforceable in a court of law. In the case of mandatory HRDD, corporate management maintains the prerogative to determine which rights to prioritise and resource, as well as how to go about monitoring and implementation, largely on a unilateral basis. These decisions may—where harm is caused—be subject to some level of scrutiny by a court, whose willingness to closely examine these decisions remains unknown. TIRAs would appear to offer a markedly more collaborative and inclusive approach to the promotion of greater corporate respect for workers' rights and interests across national borders.

IV. Expansion of the HRDD Intermediary

The third development in transnational labour governance precipitated by the rise of HRDD is the expansion of for-profit intermediaries in the field. The term 'intermediaries' in this context refers to actors that are situated between regulators and regulatory targets and that perform roles in interpreting or translating regulatory

[25] Ashwin and others (n 15) 998.
[26] ibid.
[27] Drouin (n 23) 228–29.

standards.[28] New transnational norms often give rise to new markets for professional expertise. They may require new professional specialisations and shifts in professional authority.[29] In this section, I elaborate on how legalisation of HRDD is driving the expansion of a specific group of actors—large professional services firms (PSFs) that provide consultancy and assurance services and legal services—in transnational labour governance.[30] These include, for example, the 'Big Four' audit firms (Deloitte, Ernst & Young (EY), KPMG, and PricewaterhouseCoopers (PwC) and global law firms.[31] The role of other for-profit intermediaries already established in the field of transnational labour governance, such as auditors, is also being consolidated.

A. Professional Services Firms and the Emerging HRDD Market

The presence of PSFs in transnational labour governance is far from a new phenomenon. A range of for-profit service markets have evolved over the past three decades alongside private transnational governance to assist firms in developing and monitoring private regulatory commitments.[32] However, features of HRDD identified and elaborated upon in preceding chapters of this book are facilitating the entry and further expansion of these firms in the field. Reframing labour and human rights issues in global supply chains as 'risk management' requiring 'due diligence' is leading to increased demand for HRDD-related advisory services and products. As discussed in Chapter 3, HRDD demands a specific and extensive assemblage of knowledge and expertise. It requires knowledge of enterprise, sector, and geographic-specific risks and of human rights and of relevant international and national laws. It also demands expertise in business operational systems and practices, and in processes of risk assessment, and the implementation and evaluation of prevention and mitigation strategies. With their range of expertise and

[28] See Kenneth W Abbott, David Levi-Faur, and Duncan Snidal, 'Theorizing Regulatory Intermediaries: The RIT Model' (2017) 670 Annals of the American Academy of Political and Social Science 14, 18.

[29] Gregory Shaffer, 'Transnational Legal Process and State Change' (2021) 37 Law & Social Inquiry 229, 246.

[30] While the abbreviation PSF is used here to refer only to these three types of actors, it is recognised that common definitions of professional services firms capture a broader range of firms. See Laura Empson and others, 'Researching Professional Services Firms: An Introduction and Overview' in Laura Empson and others (eds), *The Oxford Handbook of Professional Services Firms* (OUP 2015).

[31] The term 'global law firm' is used to describe law firms which attain an international reach by having their own offices in different jurisdictions and which have a presence in key global cities: Glenn Morgan and Sigrid Quack, 'Global Networks or Global Firms? The Organizational Implications of the Internationalization of Law Firms' in Anthony Ferner, Javier Quintanilla, and Carlos Sánchez-Runde (eds), *Multinationals, Institutions and the Construction of Transnational Practice* (Palgrave Macmillan 2006) 225.

[32] See eg David Vogel, *The Market for Virtue: The Potential and Limits of Corporate Social Responsibility* (Brookings Institute Press 2005).

capacity to commodify managerial knowledge into useable, portable, and saleable forms,[33] PSFs are well positioned to market themselves as actors with this unique skill set. Processes of HRDD legalisation (discussed in Chapter 6) are further fuelling demand for specific types of expertise. As Stéphane Brabant and Elsa Savourey explain, for example, lawyers advising business enterprises are 'in a privileged position' to advise on human rights in the evolving legal context because

> they already have a deep understanding of how businesses operate, the legal frameworks applicable to businesses' activities and the means to ensure compliance with such frameworks. They also have expertise in structuring deals, contractual drafting, transactional work, due diligence, crisis management, [and] judicial and non-judicial proceedings.[34]

According to the International Bar Association (IBA), lawyers can become 'wise professional counselor[s] or trusted advisor[s]' as well as 'go-to counselors' to advise businesses on soft and hard law requiring businesses to respect human rights.[35]

Professional services firms are responding to the rise of HRDD transnationally, effectively using the expansion of risk management and legal concepts into human rights as a platform from which to extend the scale and scope of their services into new territory. Major risk advisory firms, management consultancies, and global law firms now market HRDD-related products and services. In doing so, they draw on their significant knowledge, expertise, and legitimacy in the risk management market.[36] Alongside their skills, PSFs market their transnational capabilities, which enable them to keep abreast of regulatory developments and offer consultancy on 'best practices' and emerging trends. As they consolidate their position in the market, PSFs are also able to promote their active participation in business and human rights epistemic communities.[37] Strong networks, both within local business communities and internationally, provide PSFs with a comparative advantage in the emerging HRDD market, and many can capitalise on established client relationships. The IBA, for example, notes that 'businesses are increasingly expecting

[33] Roy Suddaby and Royston Greenwood, 'Colonizing Knowledge: Commodification as a Dynamic of Jurisdictional Expansion in Professional Services Firms' (2001) 54 Human Relations 933, 938.

[34] Stéphane Brabant and Elsa Savourey, 'From Global Toolbox to Local Implementation: The IBA Practical Guide on Business and Human Rights for Business Lawyers' (2017) 2 Business and Human Rights Journal 343, 345–46.

[35] IBA (International Bar Association), 'Practical Guide on Business and Human Rights for Business Lawyers' (2016) 36 <www.ibanet.org/MediaHandler?id=D6306C84-E2F8-4C82-A86F-93940D6736C4>> accessed 10 June 2021.

[36] Luc Brès and Jean-Pascal Gond, 'The Visible Hand of Consultants in the Markets for Virtue: Translating Issues, Negotiating Boundaries and Enacting Responsive Regulations' (2014) 67 Human Relations 1347, 1351.

[37] An epistemic community is a loose collection of knowledge-based experts who share certain attitudes and values and substantive knowledge, as well as ways of thinking about how to use that knowledge: Peter M Haas, 'Epistemic Communities' in Daniel Bodansky, Jutta Brunnée, and Ellen Hey (eds), *The Oxford Handbook of International Environmental Law* (OUP 2008) 792.

their preferred external counsel to act as partners in the identification or management of human rights risks'.[38]

B. The Brighter and Darker Sides of PSF Intermediation

As PSFs continue to expand their HRDD-related services and acquire knowledge as they translate due diligence rules and guidance into practical forms applicable to specific businesses, they are likely to gain greater legitimacy as actors in the field. Yet, the role of these actors in transnational labour governance remains under-examined.[39] There are both 'brighter' and 'darker' sides to their intermediation.[40]

With a professional stake in HRDD, these actors may facilitate its diffusion as a transnational norm.[41] At the national level, they may become important allies for civil society efforts to further embed HRDD in regulatory frameworks.[42] They may help to raise the business community's awareness of binding and non-binding due diligence regulatory initiatives.[43] Already, the potential to secure more business opportunities is prompting PSFs to emphasise the importance of HRDD as an emerging norm: the 'heightened global expectation' that companies perform HRDD and the rapid and ongoing evolution of these norms into 'hard law'.[44] Law firms point to the reputational, financial, and litigation risks for businesses that fail to take action.

The ever-increasing presence of PSFs in transnational labour governance is likely to enhance their capacity to exert influence on public regulatory processes.[45] To date, relatively little is known about the extent to which, and how, this important subset of actors influences national and international lawmaking efforts in transnational labour governance. However, a recent study by LeBaron and Rühmkorf suggests that these influences may be significant and complex. Examining the role of the Big Four during the drafting of the Modern Slavery Act 2015 (UK) (MSA UK), these scholars found that, having entered into regulatory support roles on the basis of their operational capacity, perceived expertise, and independence,

[38] IBA (n 35) 31.

[39] Cf Genevieve LeBaron and Andreas Rühmkorf, 'The Domestic Politics of Corporate Accountability Legislation: Struggles over the 2015 UK Modern Slavery Act' (2019) 17 Socio-Economic Review 709; Luc Fransen and Genevieve LeBaron, 'Big Audit Firms as Regulatory Intermediaries in Transnational Labour Governance' (2019) 13 Regulation & Governance 260; Phillip Paiement, 'Jurisgenerative Role of Auditors in Transnational Labor Governance' (2018) 13 Regulation & Governance 280.

[40] Jeroen van der Heijden, 'Brighter and Darker Sides of Intermediation: Target-Oriented and Self-Interested Intermediaries in the Regulatory Governance of Buildings' (2017) 670 Annals of the American Academy of Political and Social Science 207.

[41] Shaffer (n 29) 254.

[42] ibid.

[43] Brès and Gond (n 36) 1371–73.

[44] ibid.

[45] ibid.

PSFs were invited by the UK Government to offer insights on subsequently regulatory reforms. The Big Four perceived that neutrality, and their proximity to large consumer-facing companies, make them an attractive industry ally for government.[46] LeBaron and Rühmkorf also found that the firms promoted a political agenda in the modern slavery arena of incrementalism, soft-law governance, business roles in regulation, and partnership between civil society parties and businesses. Conversely, they opposed features proposed for inclusion by labour and human rights activists, such as the imposition of concrete performance targets, more binding public regulation, and an independent watchdog role for civil society.[47]

Professional services firms are likely to play increasingly important roles as interpreters and implementers of HRDD-related regulatory initiatives. In their service roles, these actors are taking international or national standards and 'translating' these for businesses: repackaging them into practical and/or simpler forms, providing assistance, and evaluating alternative modes of implementation in the process.[48] In bridging the gap between regulatory standards and their application, these actors will enjoy considerable influence over how standards are understood and implemented by business.

V. The OECD Takes Centre Stage

As the UN agency responsible for the world of work and with its global membership, the ILO would initially have appeared to be the intergovernmental organisation (IGO) best equipped to elaborate on HRDD as it pertains to workers' rights. However, as shown in Chapter 5, the ILO has struggled to establish itself as an authority on the subject. In contrast, the OECD has benefited from perceived technical competence, smaller constituency, and more flexible committee-based structures and pursued an active and broad-ranging work programme on labour rights due diligence. This work programme is both normative (by way of the revision of the OECD Guidelines for Multinational Enterprises (OECD Guidelines for MNEs) and production of accompanying guidance) and operational (by reinvigorating the OECD National Contact Points (NCPs)). Below, I briefly identify and discuss two sets of questions that arise as a consequence of the Organisation's increasingly influential role in transnational labour governance. These involve transparency and representativity at the OECD and the nature and effectiveness of its regulatory methods.

[46] LeBaron and Rühmkorf (n 39) 263.
[47] ibid.
[48] Kenneth W Abbott, David Levi-Faur, and Duncan Snidal, 'Introducing Regulatory Intermediaries' (2017) 670 Annals of the American Academy of Political and Social Science 6, 7.

A. Transparency and Representativity

The increasing prominence of the OECD as the pre-eminent global standard-setter in the area of responsible business governance (and HRDD specifically) prompts important normative and empirical questions concerning the legitimacy of its rule-making activities, including with respect to transparency and representativity. These questions are no less salient simply because the labour governance activities undertaken by the organisation largely involve the use of soft law or other instruments.[49]

Transparency is widely viewed as a key precept for the accountability of international organisations (IOs) and other transnational regulators,[50] requiring those who are affected by an actor's decision to be able to see what the affecting actor is doing and how.[51] Yet, the OECD is a notoriously opaque organisation. As explained in Chapter 5, the OECD adopts a closed working style and makes decisions at committee level by consensus. No OECD document may be released publicly without approval by all member countries, and internal documents are not publicly available. Membership of ad hoc committees is also not disclosed. These decision-making processes, as Rianne Mahon and Stephen McBride observe, work 'to obscure OECD decision making and insulate it against participation from member nations' democratic publics'.[52] These practices render it very difficult, if not impossible, for outsiders to gain insight into precisely which actors are shaping policy or guidance documents, issues of contention, or views not adopted. Indeed, at the time of the 2011 revisions to the OECD Guidelines for MNEs,[53] a number of NGOs voiced concern over the lack of transparency in the revision process. The International Federation for Human Rights (IFHR), for example, observed that 'at no stage have the negotiated drafts been made available online nor made accessible otherwise in the public domain for stakeholders within and outside adhering countries'.[54] The OECD appears to have taken significant steps to address these concerns: for example, it now releases submissions to various consultation processes on the OECD Guidelines for MNEs and proposed instruments online. However, there remains little information available on the process through which influential

[49] Franz Christian Ebert and Tonia Novitz, 'Introduction: International Institutions, Public Governance and Future Regulation of Work: Taking Stock at the International Labour Organization's Centenary' (2020) 17 International Organizations Law Review 1, 2.

[50] Franz Christian Ebert, 'A Public Law Perspective on Labour Governance by International Financial Institutions' (2020) 17 International Organizations Law Review 105.

[51] Jan Aart Scholte, 'Global Governance, Accountability and Civil Society' in Jan Aart Scholte (ed), *Building Global Democracy? Civil Society and Accountable Global Governance* (CUP 2011) 16.

[52] Rianne Mahon and Stephen McBride, 'Introduction' in Rianne Mahon and Stephen McBride (eds), *The OECD and Transnational Governance* (University of British Columbia Press 2008) 15.

[53] See Chapter 6.

[54] FIDH (International Federation for Human Rights), 'Open Letter to OECD Investment Committee on the Review Process of the OECD Guidelines for Multinational Enterprises' (*Press Release* 28 April 2011) <www.fidh.org/en/issues/globalisation-human-rights/Open-Letter-to-OECD-Investment> accessed 22 September 2021.

quasi-standards, such as the general and sector-specific due diligence guidance, have been produced, and membership of the ad hoc committees responsible for drafting these standards (which include states, MNEs, and others) is not disclosed.

Questions of representativity arise with respect to both the OECD's restricted membership and the extent to which the organisation includes civil society groups in its internal decision-making processes. State membership of the OECD has expanded in recent years. It stands today at thirty-eight, rendering it much less globally representative than other organisations, such as the ILO. The OECD has sought to enhance its normative legitimacy through intensified outreach activities to non-member states.[55] Its relatively homogeneous membership has enabled it to maintain a 'collegial, club-like culture'[56] and to reach consensus that would be elusive at more inclusive fora.[57] Indeed, as Salzman observes, while it is not voiced openly, 'many OECD country delegates think of the closed-door meetings of the OECD as a welcome alternative forum to what is often viewed as the developing country dominated and politicized United Nations system'.[58] Many states, including some of the world's largest economies, such as China and India, remain outside the OECD's formal decision-making structures.

While the OECD has formal channels for civil society input, there are notable limits to this participation. As explained in Chapter 5, since its creation, the organisation has institutionalised worker and employer representation through the Business and Industry Advisory Council (BIAC) and the Trade Union Advisory Committee to the OECD (TUAC). In response to pressure from civil society groups and some nation-states, the organisation has significantly expanded civil society involvement in its work since the early 2000s by way of the formal participation of OECD Watch.[59] TUAC and OECD Watch's participation in the OECD is no doubt immensely valuable in inserting worker and civil society voices and interests into the organisation's deliberations.[60] The OECD frequently cites the involvement of these actors and other civil society organisations in the revision of the OECD Guidelines for MNEs and the OECD's proactive agenda to promote the legitimacy of its normative instruments.[61] Civil society observers have also noted that 'because of their multistakeholder development and buy-in, [the due

[55] See Chapter 6.

[56] Richard Eccleston, 'The OECD and Global Economic Governance' (2011) 65 Australian Journal of International Affairs 243, 245..

[57] ibid.

[58] James Salzman, 'Labor Rights, Globalization and Institutions: The Role and Influence of the Organization for Economic Cooperation and Development' (2000) 21 Michigan Journal of International Law 769, 776–77.

[59] Morten Ougaard, 'Civil Society and Patterns of Accountability in the OECD' in Scholte, *Building Global Democracy?* (n 51) 163.

[60] See further Jean-Marc Thouvenin, 'Diffusion and Leveraging of Transnational Labour Norms by the OECD' in Blackett and Trebilcock, *Research Handbook on Transnational Labour Law* (n 22) 387–89.

[61] See eg Roel Nieuwenkamp, 'The OECD Guidelines for Multinational Enterprises on Responsible Business Conduct: Soft Law with Hard Consequences' (2013) 4 Dovenschmidt Quarterly 171, 172.

diligence standards] offer regulators significant comfort'.[62] However, other civil society organisations have expressed serious concerns over the inclusiveness of these processes.[63]

TUAC's affiliated trade union centres are limited to OECD countries, and OECD Watch's network is also limited. TUAC and BIAC enjoy only consultative status in the organisation and are staffed by small secretariats. The two groups do not, for example, have voting rights in the organisation, as the workers and employer groups do within the ILO's legislative and executive organs. Even where NGOs are admitted, in practice, participation in OECD committees, working parties, and expert groups requires considerable resources that may be beyond the capacity of many organisations.[64] Scholars writing on the OECD have emphasised the uneven and limited nature of civil society participation and characterised the organisation's approach to civil society as narrow and instrumental. According to Richard Woodward, the organisation uses civil society as a means of fortifying, rather than challenging, its prevailing philosophy and approaches.[65] He observes that the OECD has

> judiciously selected its civil society acquaintances and the domains to which they are admitted. The suspicion persists that this is a deliberate manoeuvre by elites to ensure that civil society acquiesces to their neoliberal agenda.[66]

Overall, it is difficult to discern how, if at all, the voices of non-members, and workers and civil society within those states, are heard, despite the centrality of these states in the context of global supply chains to which the OECD's regulatory efforts and influence are increasingly directed.

B. The OECD as a Transnational Labour Regulator

Extant literature tends to view the OECD overwhelmingly as an 'intermediary' in transnational labour governance.[67] The OECD's regulatory contribution is seen

[62] Amol Mehra, 'Always in All Ways: Ensuring Business Respect for Human Rights' in César Rodriquez-Garavito (ed), *Business and Human Rights: Beyond the End of the Beginning* (CUP 2017) 138, 144.

[63] See eg OECD Watch, 'OECD Watch Comments on the OECD Due Diligence Guidance for Responsible Business Conduct and the Due Diligence Companion' (2017) <www.oecdwatch.org/wp-content/uploads/sites/8/2017/02/OECD-Watch-comments-on-the-OECD-Due-Diligence-Guidance-for-Responsible-Business-Conduct-and-Due-Dilligence-Companion.pdf> accessed 20 October 2022.

[64] Peter Carroll and Aynsley Kellow, *The OECD: A Study of Organisational Adaptation* (Edward Elgar 2011) 175–76.

[65] Richard Woodward, 'Towards Complex Multilateralism? Civil Society and the OECD' in Mahon and McBride, *The OECD and Transnational Governance* (n 52).

[66] ibid 77–78.

[67] Axel Marx and Jan Wouters, 'Rule Intermediaries in Global Labor Governance' (2007) 670 Annals of the American Academy of Political and Social Science 14, 189.

as 'translating' international labour rights norms, established by other organisations (such as the ILO) and applicable to states, into guidelines that are capable of being implemented by multinational enterprises. However, close analysis of the organisation's HRDD-related activities, as undertaken in this book, reveals that the OECD is a much more dynamic and sophisticated transnational labour regulator than this characterisation suggests. As Table 3 below indicates, the organisation engages in all five commonly recognised stages of the regulatory process: agenda-setting, rulemaking, implementation, monitoring, and enforcement.[68] The

Table 3 Indicative List of OECD Regulatory Activities with respect to HRDD

Agenda setting	Strategic support to G7 and G20 Annual Forum on Responsible Business Conduct Sector-specific forums Annual Government Policy Roundtable on RBC
Negotiation (rule making)	Revisions to OECD Guidelines for Multinational Enterprises Sector-specific due diligence guidance (minerals, agriculture, and garment and footwear supply chains); general due diligence guidance; good practice papers for the extractives and financial sectors Draft Recommendation on the Role of Government in Promoting Responsible Business Conduct
Implementation	Strengthening of National Contact Points WPRBC activities Sector-specific implementation programmes (minerals, garment and footwear, agriculture) Direct engagement with business through annual and sector-specific forums, ad-hoc working groups, and sector-specific implementation programmes Alignment Assessment of Industry Initiatives and MSI Methodology (and undertaking of voluntary assessments in garment and footwear sector) Recommendations on due diligence guidance (implementation via states) Launch of Due Diligence Policy Hub
Monitoring	Strengthening of NCPs (limited)
Enforcement	State withdrawal of various forms of public support in response to failure to participate in or adverse decision of NCP (indirect enforcement and very limited)

Source: author.

[68] Kenneth W Abbott and others, 'Orchestration: Global Governance through Intermediaries' in Kenneth W Abbott and others (eds), *International Organizations as Orchestrators* (CUP 2015).

organisation is an increasingly influential agenda-setter and rule-maker in transnational labour governance. It also implements and monitors the standards it sets for business in a range of direct and indirect ways. Significantly, it has also expanded its regulatory activities with respect to *state* regulation of MNE conduct, including through seeking to influence national policymaking on HRDD legislation.

Through its proactive agenda, the OECD has shifted its focus from the specific instance procedure as the key, if not exclusive, means through which to promote and implement the OECD Guidelines for MNEs to embracing a broader and more multifaceted approach to promoting OECD standards in the global economy. It is increasingly bringing to bear its longstanding methods including research, production of best practice guidance, and benchmarking to bear on its HRDD-related activities. It is increasingly active in promoting and supporting the integration of its instruments into national and regional due diligence laws. Yet, little is known about the nature or effectiveness of these methods.

VI. Conclusion

This chapter has sought to draw together the findings in earlier chapters to consider what the rise of HRDD means for transnational labour governance as a field of scholarship and activism. It has offered four main findings in response to this question. First, the chapter has suggested that HRDD is proving to be a blunt instrument of transnational labour law. I argue that this is because international and national policymakers are deferring to managerial interpretations of the concept. Consequently, due diligence-related laws are preserving—if not endorsing—broad managerial discretion to determine the nature and extent of HRDD undertaken. Considering this trajectory, I have cautioned against the presumption that further legalisation of HRDD per se would be a positive development for transnational labour law.

The remaining three findings concern how the rise of the HRDD frame has empowered certain actors, potentially at the expense of others. The rise of HRDD—and accompanying movements towards mandatory HRDD at the national level—foreshadow that national courts will adopt a more prominent role in applying and interpreting HRDD. The due diligence and risk management framework has also enabled for-profit intermediaries to consolidate their position in the field. This chapter has questioned whether this development is desirable from a transnational labour law perspective.

Finally, the chapter has drawn attention to the OECD's increasing prominence in transnational labour governance. This development has been facilitated by the organisation's embrace of HRDD and its extensive work programme on labour rights due diligence in particular. In short, the OECD has emerged as the frontrunner in setting, defining, and promoting due diligence as a global standard of business conduct. Yet, relatively little is known about this low-profile institution and the extent to which, and how, it exerts influence in transnational labour governance. This chapter has identified aspects of the OECD's work that demand greater attention from international labour law scholars. These include questions around the organisation's representativity, transparency, and accountability and the nature and impact of its working methods and approaches.

8
Towards a More Promising Trajectory for Human Rights Due Diligence as Transnational Labour Law

I. Introduction

This book has traced the ascension of human rights due diligence (HRDD) as a common frame through which public and private actors in transnational labour governance are engaging with, and contesting, issues around corporate responsibility for working conditions in supply chains. It has also examined the legalisation of the concept at multiple levels. I have shown that, contrary to initial expectations of the international labour movement and others, HRDD is not proving to be a robust mechanism to protect and promote workers' human rights in the global economy. I have argued that a key reason for this is because ambiguities in the concept are being resolved at multiple levels and in multiple forums in ways that enshrine managerial prerogative and cast workers as passive beneficiaries of corporate human rights initiatives. Legalisation of the concept thus risks further legitimising corporate social responsibility (CSR) practices that have long been criticised as inadequate by labour activists and scholars and ultimately reproducing, rather than overcoming, the 'accountability traps'[1] that inspired trade union and civil society support for the concept in the first place.

These dynamics present a dilemma for those concerned with improving protections for workers' rights in the global economy. On the one hand, as Surya Deva has recently observed, 'mandatory HRDD legislation as a new avatar of domestic regulation is here to stay'.[2] There is broad civil society support for ongoing legalisation of the concept and what appears to be unprecedented (albeit still limited) appetite among states for law reform in this area. Thus, there are strategic reasons for supporting legalisation of the concept. On the other hand, the trajectory of HRDD regulation to date provides reason to be wary of the concept's

[1] Almut Schilling-Vacaflor and Andrea Lenschow, 'Hardening Foreign Corporate Accountability through Mandatory Due Diligence in the European Union? New Trends and Persisting Challenges' (2023) 17 Regulation & Governance 677, 678.

[2] Surya Deva, 'Business and Human Rights: Alternative Approaches to Transnational Regulation' (2021) 17 Annual Review of Law and Social Science 139, 146.

Human Rights Due Diligence and Labour Governance. Ingrid Landau, Oxford University Press.
DOI: 10.1093/oso/9780198876069.003.0008

capacity to strengthen corporate accountability for labour rights violations in supply chains.

Recognising the significant momentum around HRDD in transnational governance and drawing on the preceding analysis, this chapter begins the task of considering what measures could potentially help to steer HRDD towards a regulatory form that opens up, rather than forecloses, spaces for workers and trade unions to challenge extant corporate practices where these cause, or contribute to, labour rights violations in transnational supply chains. Consistent with the scope of this study and anticipating that binding instruments on HRDD at the international level will remain elusive for some time to come, it focuses on potential measures that could be implemented at the national level and within the confines of the Organisation for Economic Cooperation and Development (OECD) system.

In gesturing at a vision of a more transnationally labour law orientated HRDD, this chapter draws on three strands of literature that have been introduced earlier in this book. Adopting a transnational labour law perspective,[3] this chapter seeks to identify measures that would promote not only worker protection but also worker agency and that would help to counteract the asymmetries of power that exist between workers and those who benefit from their labour. Recognising the role of HRDD as business regulation,[4] the proposals advanced in this chapter are informed by insights from regulatory studies and, more specifically, by scholarship that has theorised and empirically explored the various ways in which the regulatory capacities of the state and other actors (such as workers, trade unions, and non-governmental organisations (NGOs)) can be harnessed to steer and oversee corporate self-regulatory processes to achieve public policy objectives.[5] Finally, consistent with legal endogeneity theory,[6] this chapter recognises that law may create normative environments that prompt business to respond by creating the appearance of compliance (by way of adopting policies and processes) without necessarily complying substantively with the objectives of the regulation. It also draws on contributions to legal endogeneity theory that recognise the importance of considering how interpretive authority over ambiguous norms is exercised and by whom.

This chapter has eight sections. Following this introductory section, section II briefly addresses questions around HRDD's purpose and scope. Section III identifies the embedding of enforceable rights for workers and their representatives as a

[3] See Chapter 1.

[4] See Chapter 3.

[5] These include theories such as 'enforced self-regulation', 'co-regulation', and 'meta-regulation': see further John Braithwaite and Christine Parker, 'Regulation' in Mark Tushnet and Peter Cane (eds), *The Oxford Handbook of Legal Studies* (OUP 2003) 141–42. For an application of meta-regulatory theory to HRDD, see Ingrid Landau, 'Human Rights Due Diligence and the Risk of Cosmetic Compliance' (2019) 20 Melbourne Journal of International Law 221.

[6] See Chapter 3.

key measure that would help to alter the trajectory of HRDD regulation. These enforceable rights include rights to information, to consultation, and to enforcement. Sections IV to VII discuss state supervisory authorities, national-level commissions or tribunals, liability regimes and the role of the courts, and the strengthening of OECD National Contact Points respectively. Concluding observations are offered in section VIII.

Before proceeding, it is important to emphasise that this discussion on measures that could help to ensure HRDD initiatives are not simply more 'grist for the CSR mill'[7] is not intended to detract from the critical importance of pursuing other public and private regulatory responses to tackling worker exploitation in transnational supply chains. While, as this study attests, HRDD has enjoyed a rapid ascension in transnational labour governance, it remains but one among multiple mechanisms by which greater corporate accountability for working conditions may be achieved. Other mechanisms include, critically and centrally, the enforcement by states of domestic and international labour law.[8] Alternative approaches to the setting, monitoring, and enforcement of minimum standards in supply chains, including by way of transnational industrial relations agreements and ongoing efforts to create a supportive transnational architecture for international labour arbitration, also demand attention.[9]

II. Safeguarding HRDD's Purpose and Scope

This chapter focuses largely on envisaging a more supportive institutional architecture through which HRDD could be implemented and businesses could be held to account. However, it is important as a preliminary step to emphasise that, to constitute a significant advance for workers and trade unions, it is important that HRDD laws not curtail the innovative scope of the concept or overlook the importance of anchoring due diligence obligations in a general duty on business to avoid causing, or contributing to, adverse human rights impacts.

With respect to scope, this study has revealed how legalisation of HRDD at the national level is leading to a significant narrowing of the concept. This has occurred by way of limiting the application of the duty to undertake HRDD to companies of

[7] Cynthia Estlund, 'Enforcement of Private Transnational Labor Regulation: A New Frontier in the Anti-Sweatshop Movement' in Fabrizio Cafaggi (ed), *Enforcement of Transnational Regulation: Ensuring Compliance in a Global World* (Edward Elgar 2012) 252.

[8] See eg Tim Bartley, *Rules without Rights: Land, Labor and Private Authority in the Global Economy* (OUP 2018); Genevieve LeBaron, *Combatting Modern Slavery: Why Labour Governance Is Failing and What We Can Do About It* (Wiley 2020) Ch 6.

[9] See Chapter 7; Aaron Gladstone, 'Worker Driven Social Responsibility Agreements: A New Future in Labor Rights Protections' (2020) 44 Fordham International Law Journal 549; Isabelle Glimcher, 'Arbitration of Labor and Human Rights: The Bangladesh Experience' (2019) 52 International Law and Politics 231.

certain sizes and types and limiting the extent to which companies are required to undertake HRDD throughout their supply chains and business relationships. These limitations, often justified on the basis of providing clarity for business, have removed much of the value and innovative potential of the concept for workers. Limiting the obligation to undertake HRDD to 'established business relationships', for example, removes the need for companies to consider how their acts and omissions, and their purchasing practices, may be impacting upon workers throughout their supply chains. This is the case even where these more distant tiers embody the most severe risks and impacts. It also contributes to the risk of companies deploying various forms of 'creative compliance', such as making legal or tactical decisions to ensure that certain suppliers do not fall 'within scope'.[10] HRDD legislation should be consistent with international standards; that is, it should apply to companies of all sizes and types and should require due diligence to the full scope of the supply chain. As many others have already pointed out, the concept of HRDD as articulated in the United Nations Guiding Principles on Business and Human Rights (UNGPs) takes into account factors such as size, industry sector, and the seriousness of human rights impacts to which the company's activities may give rise through the notion of 'due diligence'.[11] The formulation of binding industry codes (see below) could also help to obviate concerns of a 'one-size-fits-all' approach.

HRDD laws should impose a general duty on business to avoid causing, or contributing to, adverse human rights impacts in their operations and supply chains and to address such impacts where they occur. This study has revealed a number of ways in which business has successfully secured endorsement of an interpretation of HRDD that distances business from substantive obligations to respect human rights in their supply chains. One way this has been achieved is by privileging HRDD as the ultimate regulatory objective, despite its original formulation in the UNGPs as a subsidiary element of the fundamental responsibility to respect human rights. It has also been achieved by casting HRDD as a *process* in its own right rather than as one directed at securing a clearly established outcome. To the extent that HRDD regulation at the national level has endorsed this approach, it has met with considerably less business opposition. As noted in Chapter 6, for example, disclosure-based modern slavery legislation in the United Kingdom and Australia has largely been supported by business communities.

[10] Creative compliance entails creatively interpreting regulatory requirements to avoid substantive compliance: Doreen McBarnet, 'It's Not What You Do But The Way That You Do It: Tax Evasion, Tax Avoidance and the Boundaries of Deviance' in David Downes (ed), *Unravelling Criminal Justice* (MacMillan 1992) 253.

[11] UN OHCHR (United Nations Office of the High Commissioner for Human Rights), 'Guiding Principles on Business and Human Rights: Implementing the United Nations 'Protect, Respect, and Remedy' Framework' (2011) Guiding Principle 14 (hereafter UNGPs).

Yet, laws that simply require businesses to engage in HRDD, without stipulating outcomes against which the success of these efforts are to be evaluated (either internally or externally), render it difficult, if not impossible, for external actors to hold businesses accountable for the extent and quality of their due diligence processes. In many cases, they enable businesses to simply rebadge existing CSR approaches as due diligence. They leave broad discretion for management to interpret the requirements as they see fit and to avoid difficult issues, such as the extent to which certain business models may be causing or contributing to adverse human rights impacts.

While empirical studies of HRDD remain limited in scale and scope, there is reason to believe that these concerns are not merely academic. Superficial forms of compliance have been found to dominate business responses to Australia's and the United Kingdom's Modern Slavery Acts,[12] the California Transparency in Supply Chains Act,[13] and section 1502 of the US Dodd–Frank Act.[14] It has also been identified as a common business response to the French Duty of Vigilance Law.[15] As argued elsewhere by the author and others, for HRDD regulation to constitute a significant advance in corporate accountability, it must clearly articulate non-delegable standards or outcomes against which corporate processes are to be directed and against which they can be evaluated.[16]

III. Embedding Rights in HRDD Laws

Recognition of the instrumental and normative value of enforceable rights for workers and others to challenge the managerial formulation and implementation of HRDD would constitute an important step towards more robust HRDD laws. The inclusion of such rights should be considered as a priority in further standard-setting on HRDD at the national and international levels. These include rights to information, consultation, and enforcement.

[12] See eg Amy Sinclair and Freya Dinshaw, 'Paper Promises? Evaluating the Early Impact of Australia's Modern Slavery Act' (2022) <www.hrlc.org.au/reports/2022/2/3/paper-promises-evaluating-the-early-impact-of-australias-modern-slavery-act> accessed 10 September 2022.

[13] See eg Rachel N Birkey and others, 'Mandated Social Disclosure: An Analysis of the Response to the California Transparency in Supply Chains Act of 2010' (2018) 152 Journal of Business Ethics 827.

[14] See eg Galit A Safarty, 'Shining Light on Global Supply Chains' (2015) 56 Harvard International Law Journal 419.

[15] See eg Elsa Savourey and Stephane Brabant, 'The French Law on the Duty of Vigilance: Theoretical and Practical Challenges Since its Adoption' (2021) 6 Business and Human Rights Journal 141, 147–48.

[16] See eg Landau (n 5) 221; Joseph Wilde-Ramsing, Ben Vanpeperstraete, and David Hachfeld, 'Legislating Human Rights Due Diligence: Respecting Rights and Ticking Boxes' (*SOMO* 2022) CCC (Clean Clothes Campaign), European Center for Constitutional and Human Rights (ECCHR), Public Eye, and Centre for Research on Multinational Corporations (SOMO) Briefing Paper <www.somo.nl/respecting-rights-or-ticking-boxes> accessed 20 October 2022; Rachel Davis, 'Legislating for Human Rights Due Diligence: How Outcomes for People Connect to the Standard of Conduct' (2021) <https://shiftproject.org/hrdd-outcomes-standard> accessed 5 October 2022.

A. Rights to Information

Access to information can play a powerful role in promoting transparency and accountability. It can also help to combat information asymmetries and help to alter the power dynamics in negotiations between various actors.[17] In the context of transnational labour activism, information disclosure is a particularly useful regulatory approach, given the often prohibitive costs for non-state actors associated with collecting information about a company's supply chains where these extend offshore.[18] Extant HRDD laws recognise the value of information disclosure through requiring businesses to publish details of their HRDD policies and processes. However, these laws generally do not go far enough in recognising, or seeking to address, the significant obstacle that lack of transparency can pose to efforts to hold companies to account for working conditions in their supply chains. Extant laws tend to cast disclosure requirements so broadly and generally as to be of little use to the intended audience. They thus fail to achieve the goal of empowering private actors (including unions) to place pressure on companies to adjust their behaviour.[19]

HRDD legislation or subsidiary regulations could require detailed regular disclosure on consistent and meaningful metrics, made available on a publicly accessible and centralised platform, supervised by the competent national authorities.[20] These general information disclosure requirements could be complemented by enforceable rights for third parties to request additional information on a company's supply chains and HRDD processes where this information is not adequately provided in the general disclosure. While this right may be subject to certain enumerated grounds upon which a business may refuse to disclose information, it could conceivably extend to, for example, requests for information on supplier lists, including company names and addresses, as well as detailed information on the methodology used in a company's HRDD and the effectiveness of HRDD efforts taken. This right could also potentially extend to requesting the disclosure of social audits, which would recognise the value of making publicly available details of working conditions in supply chains and render it easier for workers and unions to seek accountability for companies and social auditing firms.[21] To date, a general right to information appears to be found only in the Norwegian Transparency Act.[22] As noted in Chapter 6, this law provides a statutory right for any person to

[17] David Doorey (2005) 'Who Made That? Influencing Foreign Labour Practices through Reflexive Domestic Disclosure Regulation' (2005) 43 Osgoode Hall Law Journal 353, 376.

[18] ibid 375–76.

[19] See eg Sinclair and Dinshaw (n 12).

[20] LeBaron (n 8) 164.

[21] On confidentiality and social audits, see Tara Van Ho and Carolijn Terwindt, 'Assessing the Duty of Care for Social Auditors' (2019) 2 European Review of Private Law 379, 384; LeBaron (n 8) Ch 5.

[22] *Lov om virksomheters åpenhet og arbeid med grunnleggende menneskerettigheter og anstendige arbeidsforhold (åpenhetsloven)* [Act relating to Enterprises' Transparency and Work on Fundamental Human Rights and Decent Working Conditions] LOV-2021-06-18-99.

request information from a company on how it addresses its actual and potential impacts on human rights and working conditions.[23] Responses to such requests must be 'adequate and comprehensible' and provided within certain time frames. The broader inclusion of such rights in HRDD laws would constitute a powerful incentive for companies to ensure that their processes of HRDD (including in relation to areas susceptible to 'slippage', such as prioritising risk) are more than cosmetic. Access to such information would also facilitate worker organising, which is recognised as having a critical role in preventing and addressing labour exploitation.[24]

B. Rights to Consultation

The UNGPs and various HRDD initiatives at the regional and national level recognise the value of 'stakeholder consultation' to ensuring effective HRDD. Yet, as the analysis in this book has revealed, the institutionalisation of HRDD to date has largely deferred to a model in which the extent and nature of this consultation is ultimately cast as a matter for the discretion and authority of corporate management. Where requirements to consult with rights-holders and others have made it into the text of HRDD laws, such as in the French Duty of Vigilance Law and proposed EU Directive, these requirements are limited both by the use of broad terms such as 'where relevant' and to certain stages in the HRDD process. Moreover, there are inadequate safeguards against *pro forma* participation; for example, there are no mandated requirements going to the quality of consultation, such as that it be carried out in good faith or be timely and informed. The findings in this book thus reinforce human rights critiques of HRDD that have voiced serious concerns over the absence of any rights to participation or institutional pathways through which rights-holders and others can play a role in identifying cause of abuse and formulating contextually appropriate mechanisms and procedures for their prevention and mitigation.[25]

The absence of any capacity for workers and trade unions to be consulted in corporate HRDD as a matter of right is problematic. From an instrumental perspective, it cannot be presumed that, without express and enforceable rights to consultation, companies will adequately identify and consult with these actors. As is recognised in other areas of labour regulation, such as workplace health and safety, workers and their representatives are often in the best position to inform understanding of

[23] ibid ss 6–7.
[24] LeBaron (n 8) 178.
[25] See eg Tara J Melish, 'Putting "Human Rights" Back into the UN Guiding Principles on Business and Human Rights: Shifting Frames and Embedding Participation Rights' in Cesar Rodriquez-Garavito (ed), *Business and Human Rights: Beyond the End of the Beginning* (CUP 2017) 76.

actual and potential risks, as well as ways to address them. Consultation also has the potential to enhance worker awareness of HRDD processes.

The importance of consultation rights is also underscored by leading theories of 'meta-regulation' or 'regulated self-regulation'. Opening up companies to external scrutiny and critique significantly decreases the potential for companies to engage in HRDD superficially or cosmetically, that is, in a way that exhibits all the formal hallmarks of HRDD but fails to lead to genuine and substantial improvements in practice.[26] Scholars have already identified this as a danger inherent in HRDD, extrapolating from other areas of corporate or regulatory life.[27] Mandating rights would help to militate against the concerning trend, as identified in this study, towards quasi-state endorsement of managerialist approaches to private labour governance that have proven, time and time again, to be inadequate.

From a normative perspective, implementing *rights* to consultation is consistent with a transnational labour law perspective which promotes worker participation. Mandating rights would help to push HRDD beyond a narrow and managerialist view of employee involvement as beneficial for its capacity to help deliver on the managerial agenda and help to create space for worker representation that is collectivist and representative in nature. It would promote a pluralistic conception of HRDD which recognises the reality of divergent interests and promotes opportunities for dialogue and negotiated approaches. In this context, workers having a voice is viewed as an outcome as well as an 'input' capable of strengthening managerial systems of labour governance.[28]

HRDD legislation could provide enforceable rights for stakeholders to be consulted in the development, implementation, and evaluation of due diligence plans at a company level. Laws could make clear that workers and trade unions are stakeholders for these purposes and that consultation be undertaken regularly, in good faith, and in a timely manner. Consultation rights for workers and trade unions should extend to the design, monitoring, and evaluation of company-level grievance mechanisms. To promote transparency, companies could be required to report on the outcomes of consultations.

To date, little consideration appears to have been paid to possible institutional structures through which worker consultation could be achieved in the context of corporate HRDD. Such mechanisms would evidently vary between national jurisdictions and be influenced by established approaches to worker consultation. In

[26] See further Landau (n 5); Cynthia Estlund, 'A Return to Governance in the Law of the Workplace' in David Levi-Faur (ed), *The Oxford Handbook of Governance* (OUP 2012) 540.

[27] See eg Landau (n 5); Christine Parker and John Howe, 'Ruggie's Diplomatic Project and Its Missing Regulatory Infrastructure' in Radu Mares (ed), *The UN Guiding Principles on Business and Human Rights: Foundations and Implementation* (Martinus Nijhoff 2012).

[28] Juliane Reinecke and Jimmy Donaghey, 'Towards Worker-Driven Supply Chain Governance: Developing Decent Work through Democratic Worker Participation' (2021) 57 Journal of Supply Chain Management 14, 19.

Europe, for example, trade unions have drawn attention to the potential to link HRDD obligations expressly with European Union (EU) regulations on workers' rights of information, consultation, and participation, as well as collective bargaining. They have also highlighted the potential roles of works councils and workers' representatives on company boards in HRDD.[29] Recommendations in the European Parliament's report on corporate due diligence and corporate accountability,[30] many of which did not find their way into the proposed EU Directive on Corporate Sustainability Due Diligence,[31] also address this question to some extent. This report proposes that member states be required to carry out 'in good faith effective, meaningful and informed discussions with relevant stakeholders' when discussing and implementing HRDD.[32] It further stipulated that 'Member-states shall guarantee, in particular, the right for trade unions at the relevant level, including sectoral, national, European and global levels, and for workers representatives to be involved in the establishment and implementation of the due diligence strategy in good faith with their undertaking.'[33] It emphasised the importance of ensuring that adequate anti-retaliation measures were in place, recommending that member states ensure that affected, or potentially affected, stakeholders were not put at risk due to participating in discussions.[34] In other jurisdictions such as Australia, consideration could be given to a requirement to establish HRDD committees in all businesses above a certain threshold size, akin to the type of committees mandated under work health and safety legislation.

Of course, embedding rights to consultation in HRDD laws would not overcome many of the conceptual and practical challenges associated with promoting and securing a worker voice in the context of transnational supply chains. Recognising that 'those affected by governance need to be part of it', if it is to be meaningful, is a principle that is easier to articulate than to implement in transnational governance.[35] The question of how to expand the concept of industrial democracy, a

[29] ETUC (European Trade Union Confederation), 'ETUC Position for a European Directive on Mandatory Human Rights Due Diligence and Responsible Business Conduct' (2019) <www.etuc.org/en/document/etuc-position-european-directive-mandatory-human-rights-due-diligence-and-responsible> accessed 28 September 2022; ETUC, 'ETUC Initial Analysis of the Commission's Proposal for a Directive on Corporate Sustainability Due Diligence and Updated Roadmap for ETUC Actions in 2022–2023' (2022) <www.etuc.org/en/document/etuc-initial-analysis-commissions-proposal-directive-corporate-sustainability-due> accessed 28 September 2022.

[30] European Parliament, 'Resolution of 10 March 2021 with recommendations to the Commission on corporate due diligence and corporate accountability' (2021) 2020/2129(INL).

[31] European Commission, 'Proposal for a Directive of the European Parliament and of the Council on Corporate Sustainability Due Diligence and Amending Directive (EU) 2019/1937', COM (2022) 71 final. For discussion see Chapter 7.

[32] European Parliament, 'Resolution of 21 March 2021' (n 30) art 5(1).

[33] ibid.

[34] ibid art 5(3).

[35] Juliane Reinecke and Jimmy Donaghey, 'When Industrial Democracy Meets Corporate Social Responsibility—A Comparison of the Bangladesh Accord and Alliance as Responses to the Rana Plaza Disaster' (2018) 56 British Journal of Industrial Relations 14, 14.

principle that developed mainly in the context of national economies, to the radically different context of transnational supply chains is a question that continues to challenge labour scholars and others. However, as Reinecke and Donaghey remind us, industrial democracy in the traditional sense (at the workplace level) did not emerge spontaneously but rather as a result of significant political struggle and in a context in which states have played key roles in 'setting the rules of the game'.[36] Through mandating participatory rights in HRDD, states have an opportunity to begin to foster more inclusive and democratic approaches to labour governance in the context of transnational supply chains.

C. Rights to Enforcement

The absence of meaningful rights to enforce HRDD obligations risks the replication of CSR approaches that marginalise, rather than empower, workers and their representatives. HRDD laws could take steps to counter this risk through recognising and safeguarding the existence of multiple channels through which workers, trade unions, and other stakeholders potentially and actually impacted by a company's decision-making could hold businesses to account for the quality of their due diligence processes. Giving workers and their advocates the ability to enforce HRDD obligations would also complement state monitoring and enforcement efforts in a manner consistent with leading regulatory theories that recognise the influential roles that non-state actors can play in implementing state regulation.[37]

HRDD laws could recognise a broad class of persons with the capacity to bring concerns relating to non-compliance with the HRDD laws to the attention of the relevant regulator, as well as to pursue disputes concerning alleged non-compliance in their own right (see below). These should include workers and worker representatives, as well as other persons with an interest in the matter. As is already required by certain HRDD laws, businesses could also be required to establish or participate in appropriate operational-level grievance mechanisms directed at identifying and remediating adverse human rights impacts. To promote effective operational-level grievance mechanisms, HRDD laws could prescribe criteria on the quality of such mechanisms, as well as reporting requirements. As is the case in the French and German due diligence laws (see Chapter 6), companies could be obliged to address any adverse risk or impact arising from a well-founded stakeholder complaint. Dispute resolution could be made accessible via a public dispute-resolution body, and judicial remedies should be available as a last resort (see below).

[36] Reinecke and Donaghey, 'Towards Worker-Driven Supply Chain Governance' (n 28) 19.

[37] See eg Ian Ayres and John Braithwaite, *Responsive Regulation: Transcending the Deregulation Debate* (1st edn, OUP 1992); Neil Gunningham and Peter Grabosky, *Smart Regulation: Designing Environmental Policy* (OUP 1998).

IV. State Supervisory Authorities

As articulated in the UNGPs, HRDD constitutes a positive *ex ante* duty on companies to assess actual and potential human rights impacts, integrate and act upon these findings, track responses, and communicate on how impacts are addressed. However, as observed in Chapter 6 and incorporating aspects of the third pillar of the UNGPs concerning remedy,[38] an increasing number of extant HRDD laws also recognise and/or provide for *ex post* remedies for victims where companies have failed to take adequate preventative measures and harm to rights-holders has eventuated. As many have argued, these two approaches to enforcement of HRDD laws are best seen as separate and complementary, with both performing important roles in securing accountability where a company has failed to meet their HRDD obligations.[39]

With respect to *ex ante* HRDD obligations, and as indicated in Chapter 6, an increasing number of HRDD laws are recognising that the state should play a role in supervising and administering HRDD laws. However, to whom this supervisory function should be entrusted, and the nature and scope of this supervision remain contested issues. While recognising that different jurisdictions will have different traditions and approaches to enforcement, I argue in this section that *administrative enforcement* should play a central role in any state-based HRDD regulatory architecture. Administrative supervision and enforcement have the potential to regulate a much broader range of situations and business relationships than courts applying conventional legal tests for civil liability[40] and to constitute a more ambitious and responsive approach to implementation of HRDD legislation.

A strong theme throughout this book has been that the exercise of interpretive authority is a critical factor in determining the ultimate usefulness of HRDD as a regulatory concept. Where the authority to clarify and determine what constitutes compliance with broadly stipulated HRDD requirements rests with business itself or with an institution or actor that is overly sympathetic to business frames and objectives, it is unlikely to result in meaningful change. Yet, the nature of HRDD makes it difficult, if not impossible, to statutorily specify prescriptive standards. In this context, the nature of the state regulator assumes particular importance in helping to ensure that businesses take their responsibilities seriously. What is needed with respect to HRDD laws are regulators that are not only independent and adequately resourced but that also have the appropriate orientation

[38] See Chapter 2.

[39] See eg Shift and UN OHCHR, 'Enforcement of Mandatory Due Diligence: Key Design Considerations for Administrative Supervision' (*Shift*, 2021) Policy Paper <https://shiftproject.org/wp-content/uploads/2021/10/Enforcement-of-Mandatory-Due-Diligence_Shift_UN-Human-Rights_Policy-Paper-2.pdf> accessed 5 October 2022..

[40] ibid 5.

or statutory mandate and expertise. These regulators should be entrusted with a broad range of functions and a suite of enforcement tools.

While it is tempting to assign regulatory oversight of HRDD laws to existing state bodies with responsibility for trade and investment or consumer protection, assigning supervision to such entities is likely to significantly curtail the effectiveness of the legislative interventions. As Marshall and others have cautioned, basing human rights mechanisms in government agencies responsible for promoting trade and investment may lead to conflicts of interest and prejudice outcomes.[41] Supervisory responsibility should be assigned to an existing or new regulator that has expertise in human rights and a clear statutory mandate to exercise its functions in a manner that promotes public objectives, such as respect for human rights, as well as transparency, participation, and accountability. This supervisory authority should have expertise in both domestic and international labour and human rights standards.

Regulators could be given a range of functions directed towards ensuring that companies meet the minimum standards set out in the relevant legislation. This includes by way of monitoring and promoting compliance with the statute and subsidiary regulations, investigating suspected contraventions, and instituting appropriate enforcement action in the case of non-compliance. They should be given broad powers to carry out these functions. These powers could include, for example, powers to investigate alleged breaches (including by way of obtaining relevant information and documentation and interviewing persons) and to impose administrative sanctions, including pecuniary penalties. Regulators should have a range of enforcement tools available to them that can be drawn upon in the case of suspected non-compliance. These could include a capacity to 'settle' potential regulatory enforcement action with businesses on the condition that they agree to implement specific changes to their HRDD policies and processes.[42] Sanctions could go beyond monetary fines to include recommendations concerning exclusion from other state benefits, such as access to public procurement opportunities.

V. Envisaging a Role for National-Level Commissions or Tribunals

An independent and well-resourced public regulator with appropriate powers and expertise would go a significant way to ensuring that HRDD laws are capable of

[41] Shelley Marshall and others 'Mandatory Human Rights Due Diligence: Risks and Opportunities for Workers and Unions' (*Royal Melbourne Institute of Technology University Business and Human Rights Centre, TraffLab European Research Council, and Labour Equality and Human Rights (LEAH) Research Group, Monash Business School*, 2023).

[42] This type of enforcement technique is used in multiple jurisdictions and referred to as an 'enforceable undertaking' in Australia.

achieving the regulatory objectives to which they are directed. However, HRDD laws could also facilitate more pluralistic and dynamic norm elaboration processes by providing a role for specialist commissions or tribunals. As part of a bold, three-pronged regulatory proposal to address informality in global supply chains, Shelley Marshall has proposed the establishment of national supply chain tribunals with wide-ranging standard-setting and dispute resolution powers.[43] I suggest that there is considerable merit in considering a similar type of tribunal model for HRDD.

As Marshall notes, there is a significant literature on the benefits of tribunals as deliberative forums.[44] These benefits include accessibility and affordability and the adoption of less technical and legalistic approaches, and enable the generation and application of subject-specific expert knowledge by tribunal members. Tribunals enable 'reasoned judgments which allow for both sides to make amendments, for appeals, and for justice to be seen to be done'.[45] Assigning certain HRDD-related functions to a commission or tribunal would recognise the political, rather than technical, nature of the regulation of working conditions in supply chains.[46] It would facilitate and enable a more pluralist perspective to HRDD and one which creates spaces in which diverse views on what constitutes adequate HRDD can be heard and interact and authoritative decisions can be made. It would recognise the dynamic and evolving nature of HRDD expectations concerning corporate accountability with respect to working conditions in global supply chains across different industries.

HRDD laws could assign a commission or tribunal with a range of standard-setting and dispute resolution functions. With respect to standard-setting, HRDD laws could establish broad HRDD obligations and a framework through which a commission or tribunal could establish, and amend, sector- or industry-specific HRDD codes through multi-stakeholder processes. Such an approach would resemble a form of 'enforced self-regulation'[47] that is commonly found in labour law and in many other policy areas, with collective bargaining being the most recognisable example. The negotiation of more detailed standards on an industry-specific basis is also, of course, a well-established approach in business and human rights, as embodied in multi-stakeholder initiatives (MSIs) and the sectoral-specific due diligence guidance developed by the OECD.[48]

Industry-level negotiated HRDD codes would help to obviate concerns over a 'one-size-fits-all' approach to HRDD that may arise from maintaining a broad

[43] Shelley Marshall, *Living Wage: Regulatory Solutions to Informal and Precarious Work in Global Supply Chains* (OUP 2019) Ch 9.
[44] ibid 174.
[45] ibid.
[46] Reinecke and Donaghey, 'Towards Worker-Driven Supply Chain Governance' (n 28) 14.
[47] Ayres and Braithwaite (n 37) 101.
[48] See Chapter 5.

scope to HRDD laws. From a regulatory perspective, such codes can also help to enhance the legitimacy of standards by enabling stakeholders to contribute to the formulation of appropriate standards of conduct and enforcement procedures.[49] The process of formulating industry-specific codes could take place by way of collaborative or adversarial-type proceedings in a manner that would enable stakeholders to present oral and written evidence and arguments. To facilitate the generation of appropriate expertise and legitimacy, the commission or tribunal could comprise panels with sector-specific expertise, potentially supported by an independent research capacity. The negotiation of industry-specific codes could potentially be encouraged by the prospect of the state developing sector-specific standards if actors fail to do so voluntarily through tribunal processes.[50] By virtue of appropriate provisions in the HRDD law, negotiated codes could be rendered mandatory; that is, failure to comply with an applicable industry code would constitute a civil penalty offence. As discussed above, the state regulator, as well as other parties, could be given rights under the legislation to enforce the codes.

A commission or tribunal could assist in the resolution of disputes arising under the relevant HRDD law. It could perform mediation and conciliation functions, potentially as a pre-condition to arbitration or litigation. It could also be assigned the task of resolving disputes arising from the exercise, or attempted exercise, of rights to information and consultation (discussed above). A commission or tribunal with appropriate expertise and legitimacy could also play an important role in facilitating the making of additional and binding agreements on a sectoral or multi-stakeholder basis. Finally, an adequately resourced and expert commission could play an important role in providing relevant information and research to support effective implementation of HRDD requirements. This could potentially include providing information and assessments of relevant MSIs.

VI. Liability Regimes and the Role of the Courts

This book has cautioned against assigning courts with the primary responsibility in interpreting what HRDD requires of business. Drawing on legal endogeneity theory, I have argued that the courts are likely to defer to extant corporate practices, to formal policies and processes, and to managerial interpretations of what constitutes reasonable due diligence measures. Ultimately, this approach leaves it to the courts to determine important political questions. Yet, as Judy Fudge and

[49] Ayres and Braithwaite (n 37).

[50] This approach was taken in the context of Australian regulation of employment practices in the textile and clothing industry. See Michael Rawling, 'A Generic Model of Regulating Supply Chain Outsourcing' in Christopher Arup and others (eds), *Labour Law and Labour Market Regulation: Essays on the Construction, Constitution and Regulation of Labour Markets and Work Relationships* (Federation Press 2006).

Guy Mundlak remind us, the courts—across multiple jurisdictions—have, to date, proven highly reluctant to permit the peeling away of multiple legal doctrines and strategies that effectively distance multinational enterprises from liability for harms in their global supply chains.[51] Indeed, there has yet to be a single case decided on its merits that holds a lead firm headquartered in a Western developed country liable for the labour rights violations committed by its suppliers and subsidiaries located in developing jurisdictions.[52]

For these reasons, it is proposed that state-based commissions or tribunals, with appropriate mandates and expertise, play a key role in guiding interpretations of the law and resolving HRDD-related disputes at first instance. Regulatory framework should direct parties to negotiated and collaborative solutions wherever possible and facilitate remedy through conciliation, mediation, and arbitration. However, it is also recognised that a specific liability framework is an additional necessary component of HRDD regulation, both for deterrence and to ensure that victims have access to remedy where companies have caused, or contributed to, harm by way of their acts or omissions and administrative/tribunal-based measures have failed.

It is beyond the scope of this book to engage in detailed examination of existing and potential HRDD liability regimes. However, scholars and activists have proposed and contrasted multiple formulations through which responsibility could be assigned for the purposes of establishing liability for harms inflicted because of inadequate due diligence. This includes liability under contract, tort, and criminal law.[53] Scholars have also drawn attention to the relative stringency and effectiveness of approaches taken in due diligence regimes found in other policy areas, such as anti-corruption and illegal logging regulation, in comparison to extant approaches adopted in HRDD regulation.[54]

To the extent that HRDD laws provide for, and/or recognise, judicial avenues for redress, they must include measures to address the multiple and formidable barriers faced by workers and trade unions that seek access to justice if they are to be meaningful. This includes measures that have been proven in labour and

[51] Judy Fudge and Guy Mundlak, 'Peeling the Onion: On Choices Judges Make in Transnational Labour Litigation' in Brian Langille and Anne Trebilcock (eds), *Possible Futures of Global Social Justice: Essays in Honour of Francis Maupain* (Hart Publishing 2023).

[52] ibid. See also Nicolas Bueno and Claire Bright, 'Implementing Human Rights Due Diligence through Corporate Civil Liability' (2020) 69 International and Comparative Law Quarterly 789.

[53] See eg Bueno and Bright (n 52); Hila Shamir and Tamar Barkly, 'Corporate Responsibility' in Hila Shamir and Maayan Niezna (eds), *An Alternative Anti-Trafficking Action Plan; A Proposed Model Based on a Labor Approach to Trafficking* (Tel Aviv University 2022) TraffLab Research Group Policy Paper 121–23.

[54] See eg Genevieve LeBaron and Andreas Ruhmkorf, 'Steering CSR through Home State Regulation: A Comparison of the Impact of the UK Bribery Act and Modern Slavery Act on Global Supply Chain Governance' (2017) 8 Global Policy 15; Hannah Harris and Justine Nolan, 'Outsourcing the Enforcement of Modern Slavery: Overcoming the Limitations of a Market-Based Disclosure Model' (2021) 64 Journal of Industrial Relations 223.

human rights law to assist victims in accessing redress, such as shifting the burden of proof[55] and enabling collective redress and representation of victims by trade unions.[56] Labour scholars have also called for recognition of joint and vicarious liability in the context of redress for breach of HRDD obligations.[57] This doctrine enables distribution of responsibility according to the breach of human rights among actors in the supply chain and is found in labour laws in various national jurisdictions, as well as being proposed transnationally.[58] Drawing on approaches in extant labour and corporate laws, labour scholars have also called for the inclusion of provisions imposing individual liability of corporate officeholders in case of violations in certain circumstances to ensure that HRDD obligations are taken seriously within companies.[59]

VII. Strengthening OECD National Contact Points

This study has argued that the OECD has successfully established itself as a leading actor in transnational labour governance when it comes to HRDD and its implementation. It has also been observed that the OECD's efforts to establish its authority in the field have entailed the adoption of measures to strengthen the visibility, relevance, and functionality of its system of National Contact Points (NCPs) as a key mechanism through which OECD due diligence standards are interpreted and applied.[60] However, as dispute resolution mechanisms, these NCPs continue to suffer from serious and well-documented deficiencies. Below, I argue that securing substantial improvement to the structure and operation of the OECD NCPs, as well as state measures to support the effectiveness of these mechanisms, constitutes an important complementary step to building more robust regulatory architectures for HRDD at the national level.[61]

A key theme throughout this book has been that interpretive authority—and the nature of the institutional forums through which it is exercised—matters. As a forum for dispute resolution, the OECD NCP system has a number of strengths. These strengths include accessibility and informality, a detailed body of standards upon which to draw (the OECD Guidelines for Multinational Enterprises (OECD

[55] See Marshall and others, 'Mandatory Human Rights Due Diligence' (n 41); Christopher M. Roberts, 'Reversing the Burden of Proof before Human Rights Bodies' (2022) 25 International Journal of Human Rights 1682.

[56] Marshall and others, 'Mandatory Human Rights Due Diligence' (n 41).

[57] ibid.

[58] See eg Mark Anner, Jennifer Bair, and Jeremy Blasi, 'Toward Joint Liability in Global Supply Chains: Addressing the Root Causes of Labor Violations in International Subcontracting Networks' (2013) 35 Comparative Labor Law & Policy Journal 1; LeBaron (n 8) 168.

[59] Marshall and others, 'Mandatory Human Rights Due Diligence' (n 41).

[60] See Chapter 6.

[61] For a brief discussion of the role of NCPs under the *OECD Guidelines for Multinational Enterprises*, see Chapter 6.

Guidelines for MNEs) and related due diligence guidance), and a relatively high level of legitimacy arising from its state-based nature.[62] Moreover, in the absence of alternative and accessible national or transnational forums through which to bring disputes concerning corporate HRDD responsibilities, the NCP system is likely to continue to constitute an important, if not the only, state-based non-judicial mechanism through which HRDD standards and their implementation by specific companies may be contested and resolved.

As noted in Chapter 5, OECD NCPs already play a unique role in interpreting HRDD standards embodied in the OECD Guidelines for MNEs and related guidance. NCPs are being asked to resolve an increasing number of complaints concerning corporate non-compliance with the due diligence obligations in the OECD Guidelines for MNEs, including with respect to labour rights. In resolving these complaints, NCPs are interpreting and applying HRDD in a range of important ways. They have, for example, provided a degree of clarity in relation to the application of the Guidelines to a diverse range of businesses and business models. This includes, for example, complex corporate structures (specifically headquarters, subsidiaries, franchise companies, and holding companies),[63] platform companies,[64] MSIs,[65] the economic activities of state actors,[66] minority shareholders,[67] and international sporting organisations.[68]

OECD NCPs are proving to be an important, albeit flawed, mechanism through which trade unions and civil society organisations can challenge the adequacy of HRDD undertaken by companies in specific circumstances. Such challenges have, on occasion, resulted in clear determinations that a company has failed to engage in adequate HRDD. In the 2014 case of *PWT Group and the NGOs Clean Clothes Campaign Denmark and Active Consumers*, for example, the Danish NCP was asked to consider allegations that clothing company PWT Group had failed to carry out due diligence in relation to its supplier located in the Rana Plaza building at the time of the building's collapse in 2013. While mediation was unsuccessful, the Danish NCP, in its final statement, concluded that PWT was directly linked to the supplier and that it had failed to take appropriate measures to identify, prevent,

[62] Shelley Marshall, 'OECD National Contact Points: Better Navigating Conflict to Provide Remedy to Vulnerable Communities' (2016) Corporate Accountability Research.

[63] OECD, 'Stocktaking Report on the OECD Guidelines for Multinational Enterprises' (2022) 21 <https://mneguidelines.oecd.org/stocktaking-exercise-on-the-oecd-guidelines-for-multinational-enterprises.htm> accessed 20 October 2022.

[64] *AhTop and Airbnb* (French NCP 2020).

[65] See eg *IDI, EC, and LICADHO v Bonsucro* (UK NCP 2019); *Roundtable for Sustainable Palm Oil and TUK Indonesia: Land Conflict in Indonesia* (Swiss NCP 2018).

[66] See eg Both Ends v Atradius (Dutch NPC 2016); Danish NCP v Danish Ministry of Defence (Danish NCP 2018).

[67] *Lok Shakti Abhiyan and others v ABP* (Dutch NCP 2012); *Lok Shakti Abhiyan and others v Government Pension Fund—Global* (Norwegian NCP 2012).

[68] *Fédération Internationale de Football Association (FIFA) Building and Wood Workers' International (BWI)* (Swiss NCP 2017).

or remedy adverse impacts linked to the supplier's operations in regard to employees' human and labour rights, including occupational health and safety.[69]

In other cases, trade union complaints lodged with NCPs concerning business compliance with the due diligence provisions in the OECD Guidelines for MNEs have resulted in the facilitation of negotiated outcomes between the parties. In the 2017 case of *Fédération Internationale de Football Association (FIFA) and Building and Wood Workers' International (BWI)*, for example, a complaint submitted by BWI to the effect that FIFA had failed to conduct adequate HRDD in relation to human rights violations of migrant workers related to the construction of facilities for the FIFA 2022 World Cup in Qatar resulted in a successful mediation between the parties. In the agreement mediated by the Swiss NCP, FIFA accepted its responsibility to use its leverage on relevant actors in Qatar to mitigate risks of labour rights violations and undertook to establish a complaint mechanism for workers. The parties also agreed on a series of follow-up activities and to subsequent meetings under the auspices of the NCP. By way of another example, in the more recent case of *Four Trade Unions v APG Asset Management*, the International Union of Food, Agricultural, Hotel, Restaurant, Catering, Tobacco and Allied Workers' Associations (IUF), the European Federation of Food, Agriculture and Tourism Trade Unions (EFFAT–IUF), the Service Employees International Union (SEIU), and the União Geral dos Trabalhadores (UGT) submitted a complaint to the Dutch NCP against McDonald's Corporation, and APG Assets Management in the Netherlands and Norges Bank Investment Management (NBIM) in Norway. The complainants alleged that the companies had failed to exercise due diligence with respect to gender-based violence and harassment in the global operations of McDonald's Corporation. In the case against APG considered by the Dutch NCP, the parties reached an agreement which included a commitment by APG to better integrate gender-based violence and harassment considerations into their due diligence policies and practices and underscored the importance of engaging with workers and trade unions when undertaking due diligence.[70]

The NCP system has also enabled some clarification as to important but ambiguous terms in the OECD Guidelines for MNEs and related guidance, such as 'meaningful stakeholder engagement'. For example, in 2019, following an unsuccessful complaint filed by the IUF alleging violations of farm workers' rights to freedom of association in the British American Tobacco supply chain in the United States,[71] the Trade Union Advisory Committee to the OECD (TUAC) submitted a request for clarification to the OECD Investment Committee as to whether

[69] 'Specific Instance Notified by Clean Clothes Campaign Denmark and Active Consumers regarding the activities of PWT Group: Final Statement' (Danish NCP 2016).

[70] 'Final Statement NCP Specific Instance 4 Trade Unions (IUF, EFFAT–IUF, SEIU, UGT) vs APG Asset Management' (Dutch NCP 2022).

[71] *British American Tobacco (BAT) and the International Union of Food, Agricultural, Hotel, Restaurant, Catering, Tobacco and Allied Workers' Associations (IUF)* (British NCP 2019).

industry-led or multi-stakeholder processes used by companies to conduct due diligence in respect of human and labour rights issues fulfil the requirements of the OECD Guidelines for MNEs if they fail to include engagement with trade unions.[72] In a clarification issued in 2021, the OECD Investment Committee emphasised that a company should engage with workers with respect to all specific activities that impact, or could impact, upon them. It should prioritise meaningful engagement with bona fide trade unions, where these exist, when conducting due diligence with respect to employment and industrial relations, occupational health and safety, and human rights, as well as any remediation process supporting due diligence. When examining due diligence steps taken by a company which involve participation in industry-led or multi-stakeholder initiatives, NCPs should consider whether these initiatives include meaningful engagement with worker representatives, including with bona fide trade unions, as a priority, where these exist.

This small sample of developments suggests that OECD NCPs can, where appropriately structured and resourced, play a valuable role in clarifying HRDD expectations and resolving disputes between parties with divergent interpretations of due diligence. This conclusion is consistent with the broader academic literature on OECD NCPs, which emphasises their *potential* to perform an important transnational dispute resolution function and provide greater access for victims of corporate-related human rights abuses.[73] However, it is widely recognised that, at present, there is considerable variation in the quality and effectiveness of NCPs across countries. This variation is borne out by the statistics: while the OECD NCPs have received over 380 cases concerning non-compliance with Guidelines since 2011, these cases are distributed very unevenly across the network. Six NCPs have received over twenty cases each, and sixteen NCPs have received fewer than five. Eleven NCPs are yet to receive a case.[74]

Addressing longstanding and widely recognised deficiencies in the OECD NCP system is an important complementary measure to the attainment of robust HRDD laws at the national level. These deficiencies include, but are not limited to, an absence of adequate minimum standards stipulated in the Procedural Guidance attached to the OECD Guidelines for MNEs, lack of visibility and accessibility, inadequate structuring and resourcing by member states, insufficient protections against reprisals for those who seek to use the mechanism, and an absence of

[72] OECD, 'Engagement with Trade Unions in Due Diligence Processes Conducted by Industry-Led or Multi-Stakeholder Initiatives: Clarification by the OECD Investment' (2021) <https://mneguidelines.oecd.org/engagement-with-trade-unions-in-due-diligence-processes-conducted-by-industry-led-or-multi-stakeholder-initiatives.pdf> accessed 13 September 2022.

[73] See eg Kinnari Bhatt and Gamze Erdem Türkelli, 'OECD National Contact Points as Sites of Effective Remedy: New Expressions of the Role and Rule of Law within Market Globalization?' (2021) 6 Business and Human Rights Journal 423; Samantha Balaton-Chrimes and Fiona Haines, 'Redress and Corporate Human Rights Harms: An Analysis of New Governance and the POSCO Odisha Project' (2017) 14 Globalizations 596; Marshall, 'OECD National Contact Points' (n 62).

[74] OECD, 'Stocktaking Report' (n 63) 72.

sanctions for companies that fail to participate in proceedings or have decisions made against them.[75]

Both individual OECD member states and the OECD as a whole have important roles to play in improving the operation of what is proving to be an important mechanism for the interpretation of due diligence obligations in transnational labour governance. OECD NCPs could be made more effective through the introduction of stronger minimum standards concerning NCP structure and functions in the Procedural Guidance. Ongoing monitoring and the exertion of pressure from within the OECD are necessary to secure improvements in the institutional structure, resourcing, and functioning of specific NCPs. Political will is also needed at the state level to ensure appropriate structuring, resourcing, and operation of these mechanisms. States should also be ensuring that there are meaningful sanctions for companies that fail to engage in NCP processes in good faith or are found to have breached the Guidelines.[76]

VIII. Conclusion

This chapter has sought to contribute to alternative visions of human rights due diligence as transnational labour law. Building on analyses in previous chapters, it has focused on measures that could be implemented at the national level and on measures that could assist in more effective implementation and enforcement of the considerable body of HRDD standards emanating from the OECD. This focus is not intended to detract from the importance of pursuing improvements to many of the other approaches and mechanisms that together make up the crowded multi-scalar field of transnational labour governance.

At its core, this chapter has suggested an alternative role for the state in HRDD regulation. The role of states should lie not in promulgating detailed and prescriptive HRDD standards but in establishing broad and supportive legislative and administrative frameworks within which rights are embedded and industry-specific standards and multi-stakeholder agreements can be formulated, adjusted, and enforced. This chapter has also called for significant improvements to the OECD NCP system. This longstanding system is far from transformative. It suffers from multiple and well-documented deficiencies. However, and with state support, NCPs are positioned optimally to play an important role in interpreting, and securing the

[75] See Marshall, 'OECD National Contact Points' (n 62); OECD, 'Summary of Public Submissions: Stocktaking Exercise on the OECD Guidelines for Multinational Enterprises, OECD Public Consultation, March 2021–April 2022' (2022) <https://mneguidelines.oecd.org/stocktaking-exercise-on-the-oecd-guidelines-for-multinational-enterprises-summary-of-public-submissions.pdf> accessed 5 September 2022.

[76] This includes, for example, by way of exclusion from public procurement opportunities and subsidies. See further Marshall, 'OECD National Contact Points' (n 62).

implementation of, HRDD. Optimistically, it is suggested that the developments examined in this book—including expansion of the OECD's standard-setting role in transnational labour governance and normative shifts evinced in the rise of HRDD legislation at the national level—may also have helped to create a more conducive environment to securing tangible improvements in the operation of this unique mechanism.

9
Conclusion
A Pyrrhic Victory? Human Rights Due Diligence and Transnational Labour Law

In June 2021, the global community celebrated ten years of the United Nations Guiding Principles on Business and Human Rights (UNGPs). This anniversary prompted a stocktaking exercise from UN leaders, governments, and stakeholders. Many contributors spoke of the remarkable momentum surrounding human rights due diligence (HRDD) over the past decade, pointing to its incorporation into normative frameworks at the international and national levels.[1] Indeed, the UN Working Group on Business and Human Rights described HRDD—the requirement that businesses identify, prevent, and mitigate their adverse impacts and account for how they address them—as likely the most influential contribution of the UNGPs.[2] The developments examined in this book attest to the concept's broad and rapid ascension in global governance. Numerous international instruments now urge businesses to adopt HRDD so that they can know and show that they are respecting workers' rights in their operations and supply chains. An increasing number of national jurisdictions require companies to report on, or in some cases engage in, labour rights due diligence efforts. Civil society and business use the term as a *lingua franca* when calling for, or otherwise speaking of, responsible business practices when it comes to labour standards in their supply chains.

The preceding chapters of this book examined contests that have taken place over the meaning and status of HRDD and explored the implications of the concept for transnational labour governance. This analysis has revealed that there is little to suggest that HRDD is being legalised in a manner that meets the expectations initially accorded to the concept by the international trade union movement and other labour rights activists. Nor is it being legalised in ways that render it a particularly potent mechanism of transnational labour law. Drawing on legal endogeneity theory, my analysis has revealed that, faced with the challenging task

[1] UN (United Nations), 'Stocktaking on the 10th Anniversary of the UNGPs' (*Office of the High Commissioner for Human Rights*) <www.ohchr.org/en/special-procedures/wg-business/stocktaking-10th-anniversary-ungps> accessed 5 October 2021.

[2] UNGA (United Nations General Assembly), 'Guiding Principles on Business and Human Rights at 10: Taking Stock of the First Decade: Report of the Working Group on the Issue of Human Rights and Transnational Corporations and Other Business Enterprises' (22 April 2021) UN Doc A/HRC/47/39 [19].

Human Rights Due Diligence and Labour Governance. Ingrid Landau, Oxford University Press. © Ingrid Landau 2023.
DOI: 10.1093/oso/9780198876069.003.0009

of adopting and elaborating on HRDD, policymakers at the global and national levels have largely deferred to managerial understandings of the concept. This dynamic has shorn HRDD of much of its transformative potential.

Most HRDD-related regulatory initiatives today provide significant room for corporate management to determine the scope and nature of due diligence undertaken and to privilege process over outcome. Critically, these regulatory initiatives are also failing to ensure that companies adequately consider and respect those workers' human rights that are considered in transnational labour law to be of central importance to increasing the collective agency of workers, including rights to freedom of association and collective bargaining. Rather than being a powerful corrective against the shortcomings of private labour governance approaches, HRDD so far appears to be applying a technical and apolitical veneer to questions around the corporate management of labour rights in supply chains and thus potentially impeding, rather than facilitating, the capacity of workers and their organisations to challenge corporate practices. In this respect, this study echoes the cautionary notes voiced by other scholars against the presumption that adoption of public regulation that integrates and complements private governance initiatives will necessarily strengthen compliance and generally lead to improvements in corporate practices.[3]

This study has also sought to draw attention to some of the broader implications of the concept's ascension for transnational labour governance as a field of law, activism, and scholarship. HRDD is shaping transnational labour governance in unintended and, to date, largely unacknowledged ways. By privileging risk and professional expertise, the concept is driving an expanding market for due diligence-related services and products that is being occupied (and, indeed, in part being driven) by for-profit intermediaries. Ongoing efforts by civil society to embed HRDD as a legally enforceable duty, along with the concept's genealogy in legal due diligence, are positioning national courts to assume a greater role in judging the adequacy of corporate efforts to respect workers' rights in transnational supply chains.

The final shift precipitated by HRDD's rise concerns the relative authority and influence of two prominent intergovernmental organisations in the field. The Organisation for Economic Co-operation and Development (OECD) has successfully drawn on its perceived technical competence and authority to pursue a broad standard-setting agenda with respect to HRDD. It has significantly expanded the volume and breadth of its work in this area and now claims a position as a strategic leader in defining what responsible business conduct means and how it can be implemented by businesses and states. In contrast, the International Labour

[3] See eg Genevieve LeBaron and Andreas Ruhmkorf, 'Steering CSR through Home State Regulation: A Comparison of the Impact of the UK Bribery Act and Modern Slavery Act on Global Supply Chain Governance' (2017) 8 Global Policy 15, 19.

Organization (ILO)—the UN agency long regarded as the authoritative intergovernmental organisation (IGO) with respect to international labour standards—has been much slower to embrace the concept. Despite sustained efforts by the international labour movement, non-governmental organisations (NGOs), and some states to elaborate on HRDD within the organisation, the ILO has struggled to find its own role and voice with respect to HRDD and what the concept means for business, as well as for states and workers. Business has played an influential role in these dynamics, supporting efforts by the OECD to produce yet more non-binding guidance while resisting (indeed, thwarting) ILO ambitions to establish itself as the natural authority on HRDD when it comes to internationally recognised workers' human rights.

This book has focused on the first decade or so of HRDD's ascension in transnational labour governance. HRDD remains a relatively novel concept and the multiscale processes by which it is being elaborated upon and legalised are still very much underway. Thus, there are many aspects of HRDD that merit ongoing academic attention and scrutiny.

For a start, empirical studies of business implementation of HRDD remain limited in number and scope.[4] Synthesising extant studies in 2018, the UN Working Group on Business and Human Rights observed that while a 'small but growing' number of large corporations in different sectors have issued policy statements expressing their commitment to respect human rights in line with the UNGPs, business practice continues to exhibit 'many gaps and challenges' when it comes to HRDD.[5] The Working Group identified a number of ways in which, despite growing awareness and commitment by business, HRDD was not being 'understood properly'. Issues included misconstruction of risk; failure to identify most significant risks first; a 'tick-the-box' approach to risk assessment; and businesses taking a reactive, rather than a proactive, approach to their adverse human rights impacts. Corporate performance was found 'particularly weak' on HRDD's 'taking action' and 'tracking of responses' components.[6] Further quantitative and qualitative research on business implementation—including within different sectors and different locales—is critical to informing discussion over the adequacy of existing approaches (including new laws) and proposals for reform.

This study has focused on the towers of global and national lawmaking rather than the trenches of everyday translation, implementation, and contestation. From above, as Tim Bartley reminds us, one can see only 'blurry structures—that is,

[4] See eg Robert McCorquodale and others, 'Human Rights Due Diligence in Law and Practice: Good Practices and Challenges for Business Enterprises' (2017) 2 Business and Human Rights Journal 195.

[5] UNGA, 'Report of the Working Group on the Issue of Human Rights and Transnational Corporations and other Business Enterprises: Note by the Secretary-General'(16 July 2018) UN Doc A/73/163 [25].

[6] ibid [25]–[30].

broad contours of rule-making, legitimation, and convergence'.[7] One cannot see how businesses targeted by these norms are translating or operationalising them, how auditors and others are judging compliance, or how workers and their representatives are leveraging global norms in pursuit of their agendas.[8] Little is known about how HRDD is being translated and operationalised at the ground level, whether by corporate actors, workers and trade unions, NGOs, or intermediaries.

Even if, as argued in this book, HRDD is not being legalised in a way that effectively empowers or protects labour, it may, nonetheless, be providing useful 'points of countervailing political leverage' as actors exploit the gap between corporate discourse and practice.[9] Empirically examining the extent to which, and how, HRDD, as a norm and in its various national legal forms, may be facilitating contestation in specific contexts—as well as driving intensified connections and collaborations between actors in various jurisdictions—would appear to be another important task for scholars going forwards. Such research may help us to understand the ways in which HRDD is influencing the accountability politics that predominate in transnational labour governance.[10]

With the rise of HRDD, transnational labour governance is becoming more highly intermediated. This book has underscored the need for further scholarly attention to intermediary authority and accountability. The presence of for-profit intermediaries in labour governance is not a new phenomenon; for example, private labour initiatives have long relied on monitoring and certification by auditors.[11] However, HRDD is driving an unprecedented expansion of professional management consultancies, risk advisory services, and law firms in the field. Steps are now being taken to conceptualise and empirically examine the role of intermediaries in transnational labour governance. However, further research is needed into how intermediaries who translate HRDD understand their roles, how they exercise their functions, and with what effects. Important questions arise as to the extent to which, and how, professional services firms (PSFs) may shape HRDD practices to accord with their own interests and/or defer to, rather than challenge, company practices in order to preserve important client relationships.[12]

[7] Tim Bartley, *Rules without Rights: Land, Labour, and Private Authority in the Global Economy* (OUP 2018) 4. See also Sally Engle Merry, *Human Rights and Gender Violence: Translating International Law into Local Justice* (University of Chicago Press 2006) 3.

[8] Bartley, *Rules without Rights* (n 7) 4.

[9] For an example of local labour rights advocates leveraging symbolic commitments in corporate social responsibility (CSR) policies, see Tim Bartley and Niklas Egels-Zandén, 'Beyond Decoupling: Unions and the Leveraging of Corporate Social Responsibility in Indonesia' (2016) 14 Socio-Economic Review 231.

[10] Peter Evans, 'Fighting Marginalization with Transnational Networks: Counter-Hegemonic Globalization' (2000) 29 Contemporary Sociology 230.

[11] Axel Marx and Jan Wouters, 'Rule Intermediaries in Global Labor Governance' (2017) 670 Annals of the American Academy of Political and Social Science 189.

[12] Kenneth W Abbott, David Levi-Faur, and Duncan Snidal, 'Enriching the RIT Framework' (2017) 670 Annals of the American Academy of Political and Social Science 280, 284.

For example, recent empirical research into audit regimes has shown that external auditors do not always act objectively but rather respond to, and protect, commercial interests. These actors may be deployed by businesses as mechanisms to legitimise business models and construct an illusion of governance effectiveness and compliance. Attention should also be paid to what may be lost in the process of 'translating' HRDD into managerial discourse and further business opportunities.[13] Whether certain intermediaries themselves are, or should be, subject to formal accountability mechanisms and how this could be done merits further attention from scholars and policymakers.[14]

The trend towards the legalisation of HRDD has also raised the stakes when it comes to contests over the appropriate role for, and credibility of, multi-stakeholder initiatives (MSIs) in transnational labour governance. States, which have long tended to remain at arms length from these initiatives, are now being compelled to engage with difficult questions around the role of MSIs in mandatory HRDD and what role the state itself should play in supporting these initiatives and in assisting parties to evaluate MSI credibility and effectiveness.[15] These developments will, no doubt, open up further sites of contest—at both international and national levels—between actors in transnational labour governance who hold different views on the legitimacy of different MSIs and the approaches they adopt. The nature of these contests and their outcomes constitute a further area that merits academic scrutiny.

For understandable reasons, much of the attention from activists and scholars has, to date, focused on securing a treaty on business and human rights at the UN and national HRDD laws. However, a range of IGOs are now engaging with HRDD and, through various mechanisms, shaping the take-up of the concept by states and businesses. Specifically, this study has called for more attention to be paid to the OECD as a transnational labour regulator. To date, this organisation has received little academic attention from the discipline and, indeed, generally. The small literature that exists on the OECD's influence on labour governance has tended to focus on the organisation's influence on domestic labour market regulation or on the OECD Guidelines for Multinational Enterprises. However, this low-profile global governance agency is exerting significant interpretive authority over standards of responsible business conduct in the global economy. Little is known about how the organisation works in practice. How are normative instruments produced by the

13 Fiona Haines, Kate Macdonald, and Samantha Balaton-Chrimes, 'Contextualising the Business Responsibility to Respect: How Much is Lost in Translation?' in Radu Mares (ed), *The UN Guiding Principles on Business and Human Rights: Foundations and Implementation* (Koninklijke Brill 2012).

14 Ingrid Landau and Tess Hardy, 'Transnational Labour Governance in Global Supply Chains: Asking Questions and Seeking Answers on Accountability' in Guillaime Delautre, Elizabeth Echeverria Manrique, and Colin Fenwick (eds), *Decent Work in a Globalized Economy: Lessons from Public and Private Initiatives* (ILO 2021) 63–64.

15 See eg OECD, 'The Role of Sustainability Initiatives in Mandatory Due Diligence: Note for Policy Makers' (2022) <https://mneguidelines.oecd.org/the-role-of-sustainability-initiatives-in-mandatory-due-diligence-note-for-policy-makers.pdf> accessed 15 October 2022.

organisation negotiated? Which actors are included, and which are excluded? How effective are the mechanisms through which the OECD seeks to influence states and private actors? To what extent are national HRDD laws drawing on, or even formally embedding, OECD due diligence instruments and with what implications? There is a need for research into the accountability dynamics and challenges of this influential global institution. Detailed analysis of the quasi-jurisprudence of the OECD National Contact Points (NCPs) is also critical to better understanding both the nature of the OECD as a transnational labour regulator and trajectories of HRDD in transnational governance.

Ultimately, I have sought, in this book, to take an approach to HRDD that is both critical and pragmatic. HRDD continues to hold out the possibility (albeit a diminishing one) of opening up corporate processes to external scrutiny and participation and strengthening corporate respect for workers' rights. It has also enjoyed—and continues to enjoy—a breadth of support and degree of policy momentum that is otherwise absent in transnational labour governance. Despite its shortcomings, it may still deliver tangible improvements for workers. It remains too early to tell, for example, whether HRDD laws in Europe are capable of being leveraged effectively by trade unions, civil society, and others to hold businesses to account for working conditions in their supply chains. There would appear, however, a real possibility that HRDD's legalisation will ultimately reinforce existing private governance approaches and further entrench those very business models and power dynamics that lead to labour exploitation in the first place. There is also a risk that ongoing momentum surrounding HRDD in transnational governance may overshadow, or detract from, efforts to expand other more promising approaches and mechanisms in transnational labour governance.

Amid the daily grind of labour activism—whether it be organising, campaigning, negotiating, or participating in policy and law reform processes at multiple levels—it can be difficult to find the time to pause and reflect on the changing landscape. It is hoped that this study, by charting the trajectory of HRDD in its first decade and revealing the subtle ways the concept is influencing transnational labour governance, may assist in this important task.

Bibliography

Abbott KW and Snidal D, 'Hard and Soft Law in International Governance' (2000) 54 International Organization 421.

Abbott KW and Snidal D, 'Taking Responsive Regulation Transnational: Strategies for International Organizations' (2013) 7 Regulation & Governance 95.

Abbott KW and others, 'The Concept of Legalization' (2000) 54(3) International Organization 401.

Abbott KW and others, 'Orchestration: Global Governance through Intermediaries' in KW Abbott and others (eds), *International Organizations as Orchestrators* (CUP 2015).

Abbott KW, Levi-Faur D, and Snidal D, 'Enriching the RIT Framework' (2017) 670(1) ANNALS of the American Academy of Political and Social Science 280.

Abbott KW, Levi-Faur D, and Snidal D, 'Introducing Regulatory Intermediaries' (2017) 670(1) ANNALS of the American Academy of Political and Social Sciences 6.

Abbott KW, Levi-Faur D, and Snidal D, 'Theorizing Regulatory Intermediaries: The RIT Model' (2017) 670(1) ANNALS of the American Academy of Political and Social Science 14.

Act on Living Wages, 'Memorandum of Understanding between ACT Corporate Signatories and IndustriALL Global Union on Establishing within Global Supply Chains Freedom of Association, Collective Bargaining, and Living Wages' (2017) <https://actonlivingwages.com/app/uploads/2021/04/Memorandum-of-Understanding-English.pdf> accessed 10 February 2022.

AFWA (Asia Floor Wage Alliance) and others, 'Precarious Work in the Gap Global Value Chain' (23 May 2016) <www.globallaborjustice.org/wp-content/uploads/2018/05/Precarious-Work-in-the-GAP-Global-Value-Chain.pdf> accessed 20 September 2018.

Alston P, '"Core Labour Standards" and the Transformation of the International Labour Rights Regime' (2004) 15(3) European Journal of International Law 457.

Amnesty International, 'Comments in Response to the UN Special Representative of the Secretary General on Transnational Corporations and Other Business Enterprises: Guiding Principles—Proposed Outline' (4 October 2010) <www.amnesty.org/en/documents/IOR50/001/2010/en> accessed 5 October 2022.

Amnesty International and others, 'Joint Civil Society Statement on the Draft Guiding Principles on Business and Human Rights' (*International Federation for Human Rights*, January 2011) <www.fidh.org/IMG/pdf/Joint_CSO_Statement_on_GPs.pdf> accessed 5 October 2022.

Anner M, 'Corporate Social Responsibility and Freedom of Association Rights: The Precarious Quest for Legitimacy and Control in Global Supply Chains' (2012) 40(4) Politics & Society 609.

Anner M, Bair J, and Blasi J, 'Toward Joint Liability in Global Supply Chains: Addressing the Root Causes of Labor Violations in International Subcontracting Networks' (2013) 35 Comparative Labor Law & Policy Journal 1.

Arthurs HW, 'Corporate Self-Regulation: Political Economy, State Regulation and Reflexive Labour Law' in C Estlund and B Bercusson (eds), *Regulating Labour in the Wake of Globalisation* (Hart Publishing 2007).

Ashwin S and others, 'Spillover Effects across Transnational Industrial Relations Agreements: The Potential and Limits of Collective Action in Global Supply Chains' (2020) 73(4) Industrial and Labour Relations Review 995.

Australian Government, 'Commonwealth Modern Slavery Act 2018: Guidance for Reporting Entities' (*Statutory Guidance*, September 2019) <https://modernslaveryregister.gov.au/resources/> accessed 10 September 2022.

Avant DD, Finnemore M, and Sell SK, 'Conclusion: Authority, Legitimacy, and Accountability in Global Politics' in DD Avant, M Finnemore, and SK Sell (eds), *Who Governs the Globe?* (CUP 2012).

Ayres I and Braithwaite J, *Responsive Regulation: Transcending the Deregulation Debate* (OUP 1992).

Baars G, '"It's Not Me, It's the Corporation": The Value of Corporate Accountability in the Global Political Economy' (2016) 4 London Review of International Law 127.

Baccaro L and Mele V, 'For Lack of Anything Better? International Organizations and Global Corporate Codes' (2011) 89(2) Public Administration 451.

Baccaro L and Mele V, 'Pathology of Path Dependency? The ILO and the Challenge of New Governance' (2012) 65(2) Industrial and Labour Relations Review 195.

Backer LC, 'Multinational Corporations, Transnational Law: The United Nation's Norms on the Responsibilities of Transnational Corporations as Harbinger of Corporate Responsibility in International Law' (2006) 37(2) Columbia Human Rights Law Review 287.

Backer LC, 'Rights and Accountability in Development ("RAID") v DAS AIR and Global Witness v Afrimex: Small Steps towards an Autonomous Transnational Legal System for the Regulation of Multinational Corporations' (2009) 10(1) Melbourne Journal of International Law 258.

Backer LC, 'On the Evolution of the United Nations "Protect-Respect-Remedy Project": The State, the Corporation and Human Rights in a Global Governance Context' (2011) 9(1) Santa Clara Journal of International Law 37.

Bair J and Palpacuer F, 'The Institutionalisation of Supply Chain CSR' in K Tsutsui and A Lim (eds), *Corporate Social Responsibility in a Globalizing World* (CUP 2015).

Balaton-Chrimes S and Haines F, 'Redress and Corporate Human Rights Harms: An Analysis of New Governance and the POSCO Odisha Project' (2017) 14 Globalizations 596.

Baldwin, R, 'Regulation: After "Command and Control"' in K Hawkins (ed), *The Human Face of Law: Essays in Honour of Donald Harris* (OUP 1997).

Baldwin R and Black J, 'Driving Priorities in Risk-Based Regulation: What's the Problem?' (2016) 43 Journal of Law and Society 565.

Barnett MN and Finnemore, M, 'The Politics, Power, and Pathologies of International Organizations' (1999) 53(4) International Organization 699.

Bartley T, 'Certifying Forests and Factories: States, Social Movements, and the Rise of Private Regulation in the Apparel and Forest Products Fields' (2003) 31(3) Politics & Society 433.

Bartley T, 'How Foundations Shape Social Movements: The Construction of an Organizational Field and the Rise of Forest Certification' (2007) 54(3) Social Problems 229.

Bartley T, *Rules without Rights: Land, Labor and Private Authority in the Global Economy* (OUP 2018).

Bartley T and Egels-Zandén N, 'Beyond Decoupling: Unions and the Leveraging of Corporate Social Responsibility in Indonesia' (2016) 14(2) Socio-Economic Review 231.

Baumann-Pauly D and others, 'Industry-Specific Multi-Stakeholder Initiatives that Govern Corporate Human Rights Standards: Legitimacy Assessments of the Fair Labor Association and the Global Network Initiative' (2017) 143 Journal of Business Ethics 771.

Beau de Lomenie T and Cossart S, 'Stakeholders and the Duty of Vigilance' (2017) 50 Revue Internationale de la Compliance et de l'Ethique des Affaires 1.

Bell C and Cavanaugh K, '"Constructive Ambiguity" or Internal Self-Determination? Self-Determination, Group Accommodation, and the Belfast Agreement' (1998) 22 Fordham International Law Journal 1345.

Benford RD and Snow DA, 'Framing Processes and Social Movements: An Overview and Assessment' (2000) 26 Annual Review of Sociology 211.

Bhatt K and Türkelli GE, 'OECD National Contact Points as Sites of Effective Remedy: New Expressions of the Role and Rule of Law within Market Globalization?' (2021) 6 Business and Human Rights Journal 423.

BIAC (Business and Industry Advisory Council to the OECD), 'Responsible Business Conduct: The OECD Guidelines for Multinational Enterprises' (*BIAC*, June 2015).

BIAC, 'OECD Due Diligence Guidance for Responsible Business Conduct: BIAC Contribution' (2018) <https://mneguidelines.oecd.org/BIAC-Due-Diligence-Guidance-Contribution-2018.pdf> accessed 20 October 2022.

BIAC, 'Business at OECD (BIAC) In Brief' (2022) <https://25159535.fs1.hubspotusercontent-eu1.net/hubfs/25159535/website/documents/pdf/Business%20at%20OECD%20(BIAC)%20in%20Brief%2009%202022.pdf> accessed 20 October 2022.

Bilchitz D, 'A Chasm between "Is" and "Ought"? A Critique of the Normative Foundations of the SRSG's Framework and the Guiding Principles' in S Deva and D Bilchitz (eds), *Human Rights Obligations of Business: Beyond the Corporate Responsibility to Respect?* (CUP 2013).

Birkey RN and others, 'Mandated Social Disclosure: An Analysis of the Response to the California Transparency in Supply Chains Act of 2010' (2018) 152 Journal of Business Ethics 827.

Black J, 'Critical Reflections on Regulation' (2002) 27 Australian Journal of Legal Philosophy 1.

Black J, 'Constructing and Contesting Legitimacy and Accountability in Polycentric Regulatory Regimes' (2008) 2(2) Regulation & Governance 137.

Black J, 'Forms and Paradoxes of Principles-Based Regulation' (2008) 3 Capital Markets Law Journal 425.

Black J, 'The Role of Risk in Regulatory Processes' in R Baldwin, M Cave, and M Lodge (eds), *The Oxford Handbook of Regulation* (OUP 2010).

Black J, '"Says Who?" Liquid Authority and Interpretive Control in Transnational Regulatory Regimes' (2017) 9(2) Information Technology 286.

Blackett A, 'Global Governance, Legal Pluralism and the Decentered State: A Labor Law Critique of Codes of Corporate Conduct' (2001) 8 Indiana Journal of Global Legal Studies 401.

Blackett A and Trebilcock A, 'Conceptualizing Transnational Labour Law' in A Blackett and A Trebilcock (eds), *Research Handbook on Transnational Labour Law* (Edward Elgar 2015).

Brabant S and Savourey E, 'A Closer Look at the Penalties Faced by Companies' (2017) 50 Revue Internationale de la Compliance et de l'Éthique des Affaires—Supplément à la Semaine Juridique Enterprise et Affaires 1.

Brabant S and Savourey E, 'France's Corporate Duty of Vigilance Law: A Closer Look at the Penalties Faced by Companies' (2017) 50 Revue Internationale de la Compliance et de l'Éthique des Affaires—Supplément à la Semaine Juridique Enterprise et Affaires 1.

Brabant S and Savourey E, 'From Global Toolbox to Local Implementation: The IBA Practical Guide on Business and Human Rights for Business Lawyers' (2017) 2(2) Business and Human Rights Journal 343.

Brabant S and Savourey E, 'Law on the Corporate Duty of Vigilance: A Contextualised Approach' (2017) 50 Revue Internationale de la Compliance et de l'Éthique des Affaires—Supplément à la Semaine Juridique Enterprise et Affaires 1.

Braithwaite J and Drahos P, *Global Business Regulation* (CUP 2000).

Braithwaite J and Parker C, 'Regulation' in M Tushnet and P Cane (eds), *The Oxford Handbook of Legal Studies* (OUP 2003).

Brès L and Gond JP, 'The Visible Hand of Consultants in the Markets for Virtue: Translating Issues, Negotiating Boundaries and Enacting Responsive Regulations' (2014) 67(11) Human Relations 1347.

Bright C, 'Mapping Human Rights Due Diligence Regulations and Evaluating their Contribution in Upholding Labour Standards in Global Supply Chains' in G Delautre, E Manrique, and C Fenwick (eds), *Decent Work in a Globalized Economy: Lesson from Public and Private Initiatives* (International Labour Organization 2021).

Bueno N, 'Multinational Enterprises and Labour Rights: Concepts and Implementation' in JR Bellace and B Haar (eds), *Research Handbook on Labour, Business and Human Rights* (Edward Elgar 2019).

Bueno N and Bright C, 'Implementing Human Rights Due Diligence through Corporate Civil Liability' (2020) 69 International and Comparative Law Quarterly 789.

Buhmann K, 'The Development of the "UN Framework": A Pragmatic Process towards a Pragmatic Output' in R Mares (ed), *The UN Guiding Principles on Business and Human Rights: Foundations and Implementation* (Koninklijke Brill 2012).

Buhmann K, 'Public Regulators and CSR: The "Social Licence to Operate" in Recent United Nations Instruments on Business and Human Rights and the Juridification of CSR' (2016) 136(4) Journal of Business Ethics 699.

Buhmann K, 'Analysing OECD National Contact Point Statements for Guidance on Human Rights Due Diligence: Method, Findings and Outlook' (2018) 36(4) Nordic Journal of Human Rights 390.

Buhmann K, 'Neglecting the Proactive Aspect of Human Rights Due Diligence? A Critical Appraisal of the EU's Non-Financial Reporting Directive as a Pillar One Avenue for Promoting Pillar Two Action' (2018) 3(1) Business and Human Rights Journal 23.

Burrow S, 'Letter from Burrow S to Ruggie JG' (*ITUC*, 27 May 2011) <www.ituc-csi.org/IMG/pdf/Letter_to_Mr_John_G_Ruggie_.pdf> accessed 5 October 2022.

Burrow S, 'Global Supply Chains: What Does Labour Want?' (*OpenDemocracy*, 31 May 2016) <www.opendemocracy.net/en/beyond-trafficking-and-slavery/global-supply-chains-what-does-labour-want> accessed 28 September 2022.

'Business and Human Rights: Together at Last? A Conversation with John Ruggie' (2011) 35 Fletcher Forum of World Affairs 117.

Büthe T and Mattli W, *The New Global Rulers: The Privatization of Regulation in the World Economy* (Princeton UP 2011).

Cabrelli D, 'Liability for the Violations of Human Rights and Labour Standards in Global Supply Chains: A Common Law Perspective' (2019) 10(2) Journal of European Tort Law 108.

Carroll P and Kellow A, *The OECD: A Study of Organisational Adaptation* (Edward Elgar 2011).

Cashore B, 'Legitimacy and the Privatization of Environmental Governance: How Non-State Market-Driven (NSMD) Governance Systems Gain Rule-Making Authority' (2002) 15(4) Governance 503.

CCC (Clean Clothes Campaign), 'Position Paper on Human Rights Due Diligence' (March 2016) <https://cleanclothes.org/resources/publications/position-paper-on-human-rights due-diligence> accessed 7 October 2022.

Chambers R and Vastardis AY, 'Human Rights Disclosure and Due Diligence Laws: The Role of Regulatory Oversight in Ensuring Corporate Accountability' (2021) 21 Chicago Journal of International Law 323.

Chuang JA, 'Exploitation Creep and the Unmaking of Human Trafficking Law' (2014) 108(4) American Journal of International Law 609.

Civil Society Statement, 'Proposed EU Corporate Sustainability Due Diligence Directive' (2022) <https://media.business-humanrights.org/media/documents/CSO_statement_CSDDD_EN_bpByp6L.pdf> accessed 20 October 2022.

Coglianese C and Mendelson E, 'Meta-Regulation and Self-Regulation' in R Baldwin, M Cave, and M Lodge (eds), *The Oxford Handbook of Regulation* (OUP 2010).

Connor M, 'Interview with John Ruggie' (*Business Ethics*, 30 October 2011) <https://business-ethics.com/2011/10/30/8127-un-principles-on-business-and-human-rights-interview-with-john-ruggie> accessed 30 September 2022.

Cooney S, 'Testing Times for the ILO: Institutional Reform for the New International Political Economy' (1999) 20(3) Comparative Labor Law & Policy Journal 365.

Cossart S, Chaplier J, and Lomenie TB, 'The French Law on Duty of Care: A Historic Step Towards Making Globalization Work for All' (2017) 2(2) *Business and Human Rights Journal* 317.

Crane A, Matten D, and Moon J, *Corporations and Citizenship: Business, Responsibility and Society* (CUP 2008).

Cullen H, 'The Irresistible Rise of Human Rights Due Diligence: Conflict Minerals and Beyond' (2016) 48(4) George Washington International Law Review 743.

Dahan Y, Lerner H, and Milman-Sivan F, 'The International Labour Organization, Multinational Enterprises, and Shifting Conceptions of Responsibility in the Global Economy' in A Marx and others (eds), *Global Governance of Labour Rights: Assessing the Effectiveness of Transnational Public and Private Regulatory Initiatives* (Edward Elgar 2015).

Dahan Y, Lerner H, and Milman-Sivan F, 'The Guiding Principles for Business and Human Rights: Labour Violations and Shared Responsibility' (2016) 34(4) International Journal of Comparative Labour Law and Industrial Relations 425.

Dashwood HS, *The Rise of Global Corporate Social Responsibility: Mining and the Spread of Global Norms* (CUP 2012).

Davidov G, *The Idea of Labour Law* (OUP 2016).

Davidov G, 'Distributive Justice and Labour Law' in H Collins, G Lester, and V Mantouvalou (eds), *Philosophical Foundations of Labour Law* (OUP 2018).

Davis R, 'Legislating for Human Rights Due Diligence: How Outcomes for People Connect to the Standard of Conduct' (*Shift*, 2021) <https://shiftproject.org/hrdd-outcomes-standard> accessed 5 October 2022.

De Schutter O, 'Towards Mandatory Due Diligence in Global Supply Chains' (*ITUC*, 2020) <www.ituc-csi.org/IMG/pdf/de_schutte_mandatory_due_diligence.pdf> accessed 10 September 2021.

Deva S, 'Treating Human Rights Lightly: A Critique of the Consensus Rhetoric and the Language Employed by the Guiding Principles' in S Deva and D Bilchitz (eds), *Human Rights Obligations of Business: Beyond the Responsibility to Respect* (CUP 2012).

Deva S, 'Business and Human Rights: Alternative Approaches to Transnational Regulation' (2021) 17 Annual Review of Law and Social Science 139.

Dezalay Y and Garth BG, 'Legitimating the New Legal Orthodoxy' in Y Dezalay and BG Garth (eds), *Global Prescriptions: The Production, Exportation and Importation of a New Legal Orthodoxy* (University of Michigan Press 2002).

Dezalay Y and Garth BG, 'Introduction: Constructing Transnational Justice' in Y Dezalay and BG Garth (eds), *Lawyers and the Construction of Transnational Justice* (Routledge 2012).

Diller JM, 'International Labour Law and the Challenge of Pluralism in the International Order' (2013) 10(2) Manchester Journal of International Economic Law 128.

Diller JM, 'Pluralism and Privatization in Transnational Labour Regulation: Experience of the International Labour Organization' in A Blackett and A Trebilcock (eds), *Research Handbook on Transnational Labour Law* (Edward Elgar 2015).

DiMaggio PJ and Powell WW, 'The Iron Cage Revisited: Institutional Isomorphism and Collective Rationality in Organizational Fields' in WW Powell and PJ DiMaggio (eds), *The New Institutionalism in Organizational Analysis* (University of Chicago Press 1991).

Djelic ML and Sahlin-Andersson K, 'Reordering the World: Transnational Regulatory Governance and Its Challenges' in D Levi-Faur (ed), *The Oxford Handbook of Governance* (OUP 2012).

Doorey DJ, 'Who Made That? Influencing Foreign Labour Practices through Reflexive Domestic Disclosure Regulation' (2005) 43 Osgoode Hall Law Journal 353.

Doorey DJ, 'Lost in Translation: Rana Plaza, Loblaw, and the Disconnect Between Legal Formality and Corporate Social Responsibility' (*Social Science Research Network*, 13 September 2018) <http://ssrn.com/abstract=3265826> accessed 20 September 2021.

Dostal JM, 'Campaigning on Expertise: How the OECD Framed EU Welfare and Labour Market Policies—and Why Success Could Trigger Failure' (2004) 11(3) Journal of European Public Policy 440.

Downie C, *The Politics of Climate Change Negotiations: Strategies and Variables in Prolonged International Neg*otiations (Edward Elgar 2014).

Drahos P, 'Regulatory Globalisation' in P Drahos (ed), *Regulatory Theory: Foundations and Applications* (ANU Press 2017).

Drimmer JC and Phillips NJ, 'Sunlight for the Heart of Darkness: Conflict Minerals and the First Wave of SEC Regulation of Social Issues' (2012) 6 Human Rights and International Legal Discourse 131.

Drouin RC, 'Freedom of Association in International Framework Agreements' in A Blackett, and A Trebilcock (eds), *Research Handbook on Transnational Labour Law* (Edward Elgar 2015).

Dukes R, *The Labour Constitution: The Enduring Idea of Labour Law* (OUP 2014).

Eberlein B and Grande E, 'Beyond Delegation: Transnational Regulatory Regimes and the EU Regulatory State' (2005) 12 Journal of European Public Policy 89.

Eberlein B and others, 'Transnational Business Governance Interactions: Conceptualization and Framework for Analysis' (2014) 8 Regulation & Governance 1.

Ebert FC, 'A Public Law Perspective on Labour Governance by International Financial Institutions' (2020) 17 International Organizations Law Review 105.

Ebert FC and Novitz T, 'Introduction: International Institutions, Public Governance and Future Regulation of Work: Taking Stock at the International Labour Organization's Centenary' (2020) 17 International Organizations Law Review 1.

ECCJ, 'Comparing Corporate Due Diligence and Liability Laws and Legislative Proposals in Europe' (28 May 2020) <https://corporatejustice.org/news/comparing-corporate-due-diligence-and-liability-laws-and-legislative-proposals-in-europe> accessed 27 April 2023.

ECCJ, 'Map: Corporate Accountability Legislative Progress in Europe' (25 January 2022) <https://corporatejustice.org/publications/map-corporate-accountability-legislative-progress-in-europe> accessed 10 September 2022.

Eccleston R, 'The OECD and Global Economic Governance' (2011) 65(2) Australian Journal of International Affairs 243.

Edelman LB, 'Legal Ambiguity and Symbolic Structures; Organizational Mediation of Civil Rights Law' (1992) 97 American Journal of Sociology 1531.

Edelman LB, *Working Law: Courts, Corporations, and Symbolic Civil Rights* (Chicago UP 2016).

Edelman LB and Talesh SA, 'To Comply or Not to Comply—That Isn't the Question: How Organizations Construct the Meaning of Compliance' in C Parker and VL Nielsen (eds), *Explaining Compliance: Business Responses to Regulation* (Edward Elgar 2011).

Edelman LB, Abraham SE, and Erlanger HS, 'Professional Construction of Law: The Inflated Threat of Wrongful Discharge' (1992) 26(1) Law & Society Review 47.

Egels-Zandén N and Merk J, 'Private Regulation and Trade Union Rights: Why Codes of Conduct Have Limited Impact on Trade Union Rights' (2014) 123(3) Journal of Business Economics 461.

Empson L and others, 'Researching Professional Services Firms: An Introduction and Overview' in L Empson and others (eds), *The Oxford Handbook of Professional Services Firms* (OUP 2015).

Esbenshade J, *Monitoring Sweatshops: Workers, Consumers, and the Global Apparel Industry* (Temple UP 2004).

Estlund C, 'A Return to Governance in the Law of the Workplace' in D Levi-Faur (ed), *The Oxford Handbook of Governance* (OUP 2012).

Estlund C, 'Enforcement of Private Transnational Labor Regulation: A New Frontier in the Anti-Sweatshop Movement' in F Cafaggi (ed), *Enforcement of Transnational Regulation: Ensuring Compliance in a Global World* (Edward Elgar 2012).

ETI (Ethical Trading Initiative), 'Freedom of Association in Company Supply Chains: A Practical Guide' (2013) <www.ethicaltrade.org/sites/default/files/shared_resources/foa_in_company_supply_chains.pdf> accessed 25 September 2022.

ETI, 'Human Rights Due Diligence Framework' (19 May 2016) <www.ethicaltrade.org/resources/human-rights-due-diligence-framework> accessed 28 September 2022.

ETUC (European Trade Union Confederation), 'ETUC Position for a European Directive on Mandatory Human Rights Due Diligence and Responsible Business Conduct' (2019) <www.etuc.org/en/document/etuc-position-european-directive-mandatory-human-rights-due-diligence-and-responsible> accessed 28 September 2022.

ETUC, 'ETUC Initial Analysis of the Commission's Proposal for a Directive on Corporate Sustainability Due Diligence and Updated Roadmap for ETUC Actions in 2022–2023' (2022) <www.etuc.org/en/document/etuc-initial-analysis-commissions-proposal-directive-corporate-sustainability-due> accessed 28 September 2022.

European Commission, 'Proposal for a Directive of the European Parliament and of the Council on Corporate Sustainability Due Diligence and Amending Directive' (2022).

European Commission, 'Proposal for a Directive on Corporate Sustainability Due Diligence and Annex 2022' (2022) <https://ec.europa.eu/info/publications/proposal-directive-corporate-sustainable-due-diligence-and-annex_en> accessed 5 October 2022.

European Parliament, 'Resolution of 10 March 2021 with Recommendations to the Commission on Corporate Due Diligence and Corporate Accountability' (2021).

European Parliament, 'Directive as Regards Disclosure of Non-Financial and Diversity Information by Certain Large Undertakings and Groups' (2014).

European Parliament, 'Regulation Laying Down Supply Chain Due Diligence Obligations for Union Importers of Tin, Tantalum and Tungsten, Their Ores, and Gold Originating from Conflict-Affected and High-Risk Areas' (19 May 2017).

Evans A, 'Overcoming the Global Despondency Trap: Strengthening Corporate Accountability in Supply Chains' (2020) 27(3) Review of International Political Economy 658.

Evans P, 'Fighting Marginalization with Transnational Networks: Counter-Hegemonic Globalization' (2000) 29(1) Contemporary Sociology 230.

Fasterling B, 'Human Rights Due Diligence as Risk Management: Social Risk versus Human Rights Risk' (2017) 2(1) Business and Human Rights Journal 1.

Fasterling B and Demuijnck G, 'Human Rights in the Void? Due Diligence in the UN Guiding Principles on Business and Human Rights' (2013) 116 Journal of Business Ethics 799.

Fenwick C and Novitz T (eds), *Human Rights at Work: Perspectives on Law and Regulation* (Hart Publishing 2010).

FIDH (International Federation for Human Rights), 'Open Letter to OECD Investment Committee on the Review Process of the OECD Guidelines for Multinational Enterprises' (28 April 2011) <www.fidh.org/en/issues/globalisation-human-rights/Open-Letter-to-OECD-Investment> accessed 20 October 2022.

Finnegan B, 'Responsibility Outsourced: Social Audits, Workplace Certification and Twenty Years of Failure to Protect Workers Rights' (*American Federation of Labor–Congress of Industrial Organizations*, April 2013).

Finnemore M and Sikkink K, 'International Norm Dynamics and Political Change' (1998) 52(4) International Organization 887.

Fisher E, 'Risk and Governance' in D Levi-Faur (ed), *Oxford Handbook of Governance* (OUP 2012).

Ford J and Nolan J, 'Regulating Transparency on Human Rights and Modern Slavery in Corporate Supply Chains: The Discrepancy between Human Rights Due Diligence and the Social Audit' (2020) 26(1) Australian Journal of Human Rights 27.

Ford M and Gillan M, 'The Global Union Federations in International Industrial Relations: A Critical Review' (2015) 57(3) Journal of Industrial Relations 456.

Foort SV, 'Due Diligence and Supply Chain Responsibilities in Specific Instances' (2019) 4 Erasmus Law Review 61.

Fransen L, *Corporate Social Responsibility and Global Labor Standards: Firms and Activists in the Making of Private Regulation* (Routledge 2012).

Fransen L, 'Multi-Stakeholder Governance and Voluntary Programme Interactions: Legitimation Politics in the Institutional Design of Corporate Social Responsibility' (2012) 10(1) Socio-Economic Review 163.

Fransen L and Burgoon B, 'Introduction to the Special Issue: Public and Private Labor Standards Policy in the Global Economy' (2017) 8(53) Global Policy 5.

Fransen L and LeBaron G, 'Big Audit Firms as Regulatory Intermediaries in Transnational Labour Governance' (2019) 13(2) Regulation & Governance 260.

Friedland R and Alford RR, 'Bringing Society Back in: Symbols, Practices, and Institutional Contradictions' in W Powell and PJ DiMaggio (eds), *The New Institutionalism in Organizational Analysis* (University of Chicago Press 1991).

Fudge J, 'The New Discourse of Labor Rights: From Social to Fundamental Rights?' (2007) 29 Comparative Labor Law & Policy Journal 29.

Fudge J, 'Modern Slavery, Unfree Labour and the Labour Market: The Social Dynamics of Legal Characterization' (2017) 27 Social & Legal Studies 1.

Fudge J and Mundlak G, 'Peeling the Onion: On Choices Judges Make in Transnational Labour Litigation' in B Langille and A Trebilcock (eds), *Possible Futures of Global Social Justice: Essays in Honour of Francis Maupain* (Hart Publishing 2023).

Fudge J and Strauss K (eds), *Temporary Work, Agencies and Unfree Labour: Insecurity in the New World of Work* (Routledge 2014).

Gearhart J, 'Global Supply Chains: Time for a Convention on Decent Work' (*Huffpost*, 2 June 2016) <www.huffpost.com/entry/global-supply-chains-time_b_10228772> accessed 27 April 2023.

Gereffi G and Mayer F, 'Globalization and the Demand for Governance' in G Gereffi (ed), *The New Offshoring of Jobs and Global Development* (International Labour Organization 2006).

Gilad S, 'It Runs in the Family: Meta-Regulation and Its Siblings' (2010) 4 Regulation & Governance 485.

Gilad S, 'Institutionalizing Fairness in Financial Markets: Mission Impossible?' (2011) 5(3) Regulation & Governance 309.

Gilad S, 'Beyond Endogeneity: How Firms and Regulators Co-Construct the Meaning of Regulation' (2014) 36 Law & Policy 134.

Gladstone A, 'Worker Driven Social Responsibility Agreements: A New Future in Labor Rights Protections' (2020) 44 Fordham International Law Journal 549.

Glimcher I, 'Arbitration of Labor and Human Rights: The Bangladesh Experience' (2019) 52 International Law and Politics 231.

Global Unions, 'Draft Guiding Principles for the Implementation of the United Nations' "Protect, Respect and Remedy" Framework: Global Unions' Response' (January 2011) <https://media.business-humanrights.org/media/documents/files/media/documents/ruggie/global-unions-response-re-guiding-principles-jan-2011.pdf> accessed 27 April 2023.

Goodman R and Jinks D, *Socializing States: Promoting Human Rights through International Law* (OUP 2013).

Greer BT and Purvis JG, 'Corporate Supply Chain Transparency: California's Seminal Attempt to Discourage Forced Labour' (2016) 20(1) International Journal of Human Rights 55.

Gunningham N and Grabosky P, *Smart Regulation: Designing Environmental Policy* (OUP 1998).

Haas PM, 'Epistemic Communities' in D Bodansky, J Brunnée, and E Hey (eds), *The Oxford Handbook of International Environmental Law* (OUP 2008).

Hadwiger F, 'Global Framework Agreements: Achieving Decent Work in Global Supply Chains?' (2015) 7(1) International Journal of Labour Research 8.

Haines F, Macdonald K, and Balaton-Chrimes, S, 'Contextualising the Business Responsibility to Respect: How Much is Lost in Translation?' in R Mares (ed), *The UN Guiding Principles on Business and Human Rights: Foundations and Implementation* (Koninklijke Brill 2012).

Halliday TC, 'Recursivity of Global Normmaking: A Sociolegal Agenda' (2009) 5 Annual Review of Law and Society 263.

Halliday TC and Block-Lieb S, 'Global Duelists: The Recursive Politics of the Text in International Trade Law' in A Perry-Kessaris (ed), *Socio-Legal Approaches to International Economic Law: Text, Context, Subtext* (Routledge 2013).

Halliday TC and Carruthers BG, 'The Recursivity of Law: Global Norm Making and National Lawmaking in the Globalization of Corporate Insolvency Regimes' (2007) 112(4) American Journal of Sociology 1135.

Halliday TC and Shaffer G, *Transnational Legal Orders* (CUP 2015).

Hamdani K and Ruffing L, 'Lessons from the UN Centre on Transnational Corporations for the Current Treaty' in S Deva and D Bilchitz (eds), *Building a Treaty on Business and Human Rights: Context and Contours* (CUP 2017).

Hardy T, '"It's Oh So Quiet?" Employee Voice and the Enforcement of Employment Standards in Australia' in A Bogg and T Novitz (eds), *Voices at Work: Continuity and Change in the Common Law World* (OUP 2014).

Harris H and Nolan J, 'Outsourcing the Enforcement of Modern Slavery: Overcoming the Limitations of a Market-Based Disclosure Model' (2021) 64 Journal of Industrial Relations 223.

Hassel A, 'The Evolution of a Global Labor Governance Regime' (2008) 21(2) Governance 231.

Heijden J, 'Brighter and Darker Sides of Intermediation: Target-Oriented and Self-Interested Intermediaries in the Regulatory Governance of Buildings' (2017) 670(1) ANNALS of the American Academy of Political and Social Science 207.

Helfen M and Sydow J, 'Negotiating as Institutional Work: The Case of Labor Standards and International Framework Agreements' (2013) 34(8) Organization Studies 1073.

Henne, K, *Testing for Athletic Citizenship: Regulating Doping and Sex in Sport* (Rutgers UP 2015).

Henne K, 'Multi-Sited Fieldwork in Regulatory Studies' in P Drahos (ed), *Regulatory Theory: Foundations and Applications* (ANU Press 2017).

Hepple B, *Labour Laws and Global Trade* (Hart Publishing 2005).

Holly G and Lysgaard SA, 'Legislating for Impact: Analysis of the Proposed EU Corporate Sustainability Due Diligence Directive' (*Danish Institute for Human Rights*, 2022) <www.humanrights.dk/publications/legislating-impact-analysis-proposed-eu-corporate-sustainability-due-diligence> accessed 20 October 2022.

HRW (Human Rights Watch) 'UN Human Rights Council: Weak Stance on Business Standards' (16 June 2011) <www.hrw.org/news/2011/06/16/un-human-rights-council-weak-stance-business-standards> accessed 5 October 2022.

HRW, 'Human Rights in Supply Chains: A Call for a Binding Global Standard on Due Diligence' (30 May 2016) <www.hrw.org/report/2016/05/30/human-rights-supply-chains/call-binding-global-standard-due-diligence> accessed 7 October 2022.

HRW, 'Submission to the OECD on the Draft Due Diligence Guidance for Responsible Business Conduct' (9 February 2017) <www.hrw.org/news/2017/02/09/submission-oecd-draft-due-diligence-guidance-responsible-business-conduct> accessed 25 September 2021.

Human Rights Council, 'Human Rights and Transnational Corporations and Other Business Enterprises' (6 July 2011) UN Doc A/HRC/RES/17/4.

Hutter BM, *Regulation and Risk: Occupational Health and Safety on the Railways* (OUP 2001).

Hutter BM and Jones CJ, 'From Government to Governance: External Influences on Business Risk Management' (2007) 1 Regulation & Governance 27, 34.

IBA (International Bar Association), 'Practical Guide on Business and Human Rights for Business Lawyers' (2016) <www.ibanet.org/MediaHandler?id=D6306C84-E2F8-4C82-A86F-93940D6736C4> accessed 10 June 2021.

IndustriALL Global Union, 'IndustriALL Signs Global Framework Agreement with ASOS' (2 October 2017) <www.industriall-union.org/industriall-signs-global-framework-agreement-with-asos> accessed 27 April 2023.

ILO (International Labour Organization), 'Promotion at the National Level / Promotion by Tripartite Appointed National Focal Points' <www.ilo.org/empent/areas/mne-declaration/WCMS_570379/lang--en/index.htm> accessed 20 October 2022.

ILO, 'Tripartite Declaration of Principles concerning Multinational Enterprises and Social Policy' (1977).

ILO, 'Towards the ILO Centenary: Realities, Renewal and Tripartite Commitment—Report of the Director-General' (2013) ILC.102/DG/1A.

ILO, 'How to Do Business with Respect for Children's Right to Be Free from Child Labour: ILO–IOE Child Labour Guidance Tool for Business' (*ILO International Programme on the Elimination of Child Labour and International Organisation of Employers*, 2015).

ILO, 'World Employment and Social Outlook' (2015).

ILO, 'Decent Work in Global Supply Chains' (2016).

ILO, 'Decision on the Eighth Item on the Agenda: Proposed Modalities to Review the Tripartite Declaration of Principles concerning Multinational Enterprises and Social Policy' (2016).

ILO, 'Meeting of Experts to Promote Decent Work and Protection of Fundamental Principles and Rights at Work for Workers in Export Processing Zones' (November 2017) <https://labordoc.ilo.org/discovery/fulldisplay/alma994969691802676/41ILO_INST:41ILO_V2> accessed 27 April 2023.

ILO, 'Recommendation Concerning Employment and Decent Work for Peace and Resilience' (2017).

ILO, 'Recommendations of the Tripartite Ad Hoc Working Group concerning the Review of the Tripartite Declaration of Principles Concerning Multinational Enterprises and Social Policy Text, Annex and Addenda and the Interpretation Procedure' (2017).

ILO, *Tripartite Declaration of Principles Concerning Multinational Enterprises and Social Policy* (5th edn, ILO 2017).

ILO, 'Cross-Border Social Dialogue: Report for discussion at the Meeting of Experts on Cross-border Social Dialogue' (12–15 February 2019) MECBS8/18/23/2019.

ILO, 'Meeting of Experts on Cross-Border Social Dialogue' (February 2019) <www.ilo.org/wcmsp5/groups/public/---ed_dialogue/---dialogue/documents/meetingdocument/wcms_700599.pdf> accessed 27 April 2023.

ILO, 'Final Report: Meeting of Experts on Cross-border Social Dialogue' (2020).

ILO, 'Note on the Proceedings, Technical Meeting on Achieving Decent Work in Global Supply Chains' (2020).

ILO Governance and Tripartism Department, 'Final Report: Meeting of Experts on Cross-Border Social Dialogue' (Geneva, 12–15 February 2020) MECBSD/2019/5 (19 September 2019).

ILO Governance and Tripartism Department, 'Note on the Proceedings, Technical Meeting on Achieving Deent Work in Global Supply Chains' (Geneva, 25–28 February 2020) TMDWSC/2020/7 (5 October 2020).

ILO Governing Body, 'Decision on the Eighth Item on the Agenda: Proposed Modalities to Review the Tripartite Declaration of Principles Concerning Multinational Enterprises and Social Policy' (*ILO*, 24 March 2016).

ILO Governing Body, 'Proposed Modalities to Review the Tripartite Declaration of Principles Concerning Multinational Enterprises and Social Policy' (*ILO*, 24 February 2016) GB.326/POL/8.

ILO Governing Body, 'Follow-Up to the Resolution Concerning Decent Work in Global Supply Chains: Roadmap for the Programme of Action' (*ILO*, 20 February 2017) GB.329/INS/3/2.

ILO Governing Body, 'Recommendations of the Tripartite Ad Hoc Working Group Concerning the Review of the Tripartite Declaration of Principles Concerning Multinational Enterprises and Social Policy Text, Annex and Addenda and the Interpretation Procedure' (*ILO*, 6 March 2017) GB.329/POL/7.

International Labour Conference (103rd Session), 'Reports of the Committee on Decent Work in Global Supply Chains: Resolution and Conclusions Submitted for Adoption by the Conference' (*ILO*, 2016) ILC105-14-1.

International Labour Conference (103rd Session), 'Reports of the Committee on Decent Work in Global Supply Chains: Summary of Proceedings' (*ILO*, 2016) ILC105-PR14-2(Rev).

International Labour Conference (105th Session), 'Decent Work in Global Supply Chains—Report' (*ILO*, 2016) ILC.105/IV.

IOE (International Organisation of Employers), 'UN Guiding Principles on Business and Human Rights: Employers' Guide' (February 2012) <www.ioe-emp.org/fileadmin/ioe_documents/publications/Policy%20Areas/business_and_human_rights/EN/_2012-02__UN_Guiding_Principles_on_Business_and_Human_Rights_-_Employers__Guide.pdf> accessed 5 October 2022.

IOE, 'IOE's Main Points Following the 2nd Meeting of the Tripartite Ad-Hoc Working Group to Review the ILO MNE Declaration' (2017) <http://uscib.informz.net/uscib/data/images/Main%20points%20from%202nd%20meeting%20of%20WG%20review%20of%20ILO%20MNE%20Declaration_FINAL.pdf> accessed 20 September 2018.

IOE, International Chamber of Commerce, and BIAC (Business and Industry Advisory Committee), 'Joint Statement on Business and Human Rights to the United Nations Human Rights Council' (30 May 2011) <https://iccwbo.org/content/uploads/sites/3/2011/05/Joint-Statement-on-Business-Human-Rights-to-the-United-Nations-Human-Rights-Council.pdf> accessed 5 October 2022.

ITUC (International Trade Union Confederation), 'The United Nations "Protect, Respect and Remedy" Framework for Business and Human Rights and the United Nations Guiding Principles for Business and Human Rights: Briefing Note for Trade Unionists' (April 2012) <www.ituc-csi.org/IMG/pdf/12-04-21_ruggie_briefing_note_mk_3.pdf> accessed date 27 April 2023.

ITUC, 'The United Nations "Protect, Respect, Remedy" Framework for Business and Human Rights and the United Nations Guiding Principles for Business and Human Rights: A Guide for Trade Unionists' (May 2012) <www.ituc-csi.org/IMG/pdf/12-04-23_ruggie_background_fd.pdf> accessed 5 October 2022.

ITUC, 'Global Unions Welcome Next Steps in Binding Treaty Process to End Corporate Impunity' (11 December 2020) <www.ituc-csi.org/global-unions-welcome-treaty-next-step> accessed 28 September 2022.

ITUC, IndustriALL, Clean Clothes Campaign, and Uni Global Union, 'The UN Guiding Principles on Business and Human Rights and the Human Rights of Workers to Form or Join Trade Unions and to Bargain Collectively' (*ITUC*, November 2012) <www.ituc-csi.org/IMG/pdf/12-11-22_ituc-industriall-ccc-uni_paper_on_due_diligence_and_foa.pdf> accessed 20 September 2021.

Jakovleski V, Jerbi S, and Biersteker T, 'The ILO's Role in Global Governance: Limits and Potential' (2019) 11 International Development Policy 82.

Kahn-Freund O, *Labour and the Law* (3rd edn, Stevens 1972).

Keck M and Sikkink K, *Activists beyond Borders: Advocacy Networks in International Politics* (Cornell UP 1998).

Kennedy D, 'The International Human Rights Movement: Part of the Problem?' (2001) 3 European Human Rights Law Review 245, 261.

Kennedy D, *A World of Struggle: How Power, Law and Expertise Shape Global Political Economy* (Princeton UP 2016).

Kinley D, Nolan J, and Zerial, N, 'The Politics of Corporate Social Responsibility: Reflections on the United Nations Human Rights Norms for Corporations' (2007) 25(1) Companies and Securities Law Journal 30.

Koenig-Archibugi M, 'Global Regulation' in R Baldwin, M Cave, and M Lodge (eds), *The Oxford Handbook of Regulation* (OUP 2010).

Kolben K, 'Labor Rights as Human Rights?' (2010) 50 Virginia Journal of International Law 449.

Krajewski M and Faracik B, 'Substantive Elements of Potential Legislation on Human Rights Due Diligence' (*Briefing Policy No 1, Policy Department for External Relations, European Parliament*, June 2020).

Krajewski M, Tonstadt K, and Wohltmann, F, 'Mandatory Human Rights Due Diligence in Germany and Norway: Stepping, or Striding, in the Same Direction?' (2021) 6 Business and Human Rights Journal 550.

Krawiec KD, 'Cosmetic Compliance and the Failure of Negotiated Governance' (2003) 81 Washington University Law Quarterly 487.

Krisch N, 'Liquid Authority in Global Governance' (2017) 9(2) International Theory 237.

Kytle B and Ruggie JG, 'Corporate Social Responsibility as Risk Management: A Model for Multinationals' (2005) Corporate Social Responsibility Initiative Harvard University Working Paper 10/2005, 2 <www.hks.harvard.edu/sites/default/files/centers/mrcbg/programs/cri/files/workingpaper_10_kytle_ruggie.pdf> accessed 3 October 2022.

Landau I, 'Game Changer? Human Rights Due Diligence and Corporate Respect for Workers' Rights in a Global Economy' in J Howe, A Chapman, and I Landau (eds), *The Evolving Project of Labour Law* (Federation Press 2017).

Landau I, 'Human Rights Due Diligence and the Risk of Cosmetic Compliance' (2019) 20(1) Melbourne Journal of International Law 221.

Landau I and Hardy T, 'Transnational Labour Governance in Global Supply Chains: Asking Questions and Seeking Answers on Accountability' in G Delautre, EE Manrique, and C Fenwick (eds), *Decent Work in a Globalized Economy: Lessons from Public and Private Initiatives* (ILO 2021).

Landau I and Marshall S, 'Should Australia be Embracing the Modern Slavery Model of Regulation?' (2018) 46 Federal Law Review 313.

Leary V, 'The Paradox of Workers' Rights as Human Rights' in L Compa and S Diamond (eds), *Human Rights, Labor Rights and International Trade* (University of Pennsylvania Press 2003).

LeBaron G, *Combatting Modern Slavery: Why Labour Governance Is Failing and What We Can Do About It* (Wiley 2020).

LeBaron G and Rühmkorf A, 'Steering CSR through Home State Regulation: A Comparison of the Impact of the UK Bribery Act and Modern Slavery Act on Global Supply Chain Governance' (2017) 8(3) Global Policy 15.

LeBaron G and Rühmkorf A, 'The Domestic Politics of Corporate Accountability Legislation: Struggles over the 2015 UK Modern Slavery Act' (2019) 17(3) Socio-Economic Review 709.

LeBaron G, Lister J, and Dauvergne P, 'Governing Global Supply Chain Sustainability through the Ethical Audit Regime' (2017) 14(6) Globalizations 958.

Locke R, *The Promise and Limits of Private Power: Promoting Labor Standards in a Global Economy* (CUP 2013).

Locke R, Amengual M, and Mangla A, 'Virtue Out of Necessity? Compliance, Commitment, and the Improvement of Labor Conditions in Global Supply Chains' (2009) 37(3) Politics & Society 319.

Lofland JD, 'Analytic Ethnography: Features, Failings, and Futures' (1995) 24 Journal of Contemporary Ethnography 30.
Mahon R and McBride S, 'Conclusion' in R Mahon and S McBride (eds), *The OECD and Transnational Governance* (University of British Columbia Press 2008).
Mahon R and McBride S, 'Introduction' in R Mahon and S McBride (eds), *The OECD and Transnational Governance* (University of British Columbia Press 2008).
Mahon R, and McBride S, 'Standardizing and Disseminating Knowledge: The Role of the OECD in Global Governance' (2009) 1(1) European Political Science Review 83.
Mares R, 'Business and Human Rights after Ruggie: Foundations, the Art of Simplification and the Imperative of Cumulative Progress' in R Mares (ed), *The UN Guiding Principles on Business and Human Rights: Foundations and Implementation* (Koninklijke Brill 2012).
Mares R (ed), *The UN Guiding Principles on Business and Human Rights: Foundations and Implementation* (Koninklijke Brill 2012).
Marshall S, 'OECD National Contact Points: Better Navigating Conflict to Provide Remedy to Vulnerable Communities' (2016) Non-Judicial Redress Mechanism Report Series No 16, Corporate Accountability Research.
Marshall S, *Living Wage: Regulatory Solutions to Informal and Precarious Work in Global Supply Chains* (OUP 2019).
Marshall S and others, 'Mandatory Human Rights Due Diligence: Risks and Opportunities for Workers and Unions' (Royal Melbourne Institute of Technology University Business and Human Rights Centre, TraffLab European Research Council, and Labour Equality and Human Rights (LEAH) Research Group, Monash Business School, 2023).
Marx A and Wouters J, 'Redesigning Enforcement in Private Labour Regulation: Will It Work?' (2015) 155(3) International Labour Review 435.
Marx A and Wouters J, 'Rule Intermediaries in Global Labor Governance' (2017) 670(1) ANNALS of the American Academy of Political and Social Science 189.
Mayer F and Gereffi G, 'Regulation and Economic Globalization: Prospects and Limits of Private Governance' (2010) 12(3) Business and Politics 1.
McBarnet D, 'It's Not What You Do But the Way That You Do It: Tax Evasion, Tax Avoidance and the Boundaries of Deviance' in D Downes (ed), *Unravelling Criminal Justice* (MacMillan 1992).
McCorquodale R and Nolan J, 'The Effectiveness of Human Rights Due Diligence for Preventing Business Human Rights Abuses' (2021) 68 Netherlands International Law Review 455.
McCorquodale R and others, 'Human Rights Due Diligence in Law and Practice: Good Practices and Challenges for Business Enterprises' (2017) 2(2) Business and Human Rights Journal 195.
Mehra A, 'Always in All Ways: Ensuring Business Respect for Human Rights' in C Rodriquez-Garavito (ed), *Business and Human Rights: Beyond the End of the Beginning* (CUP 2017).
Melish TJ, 'Putting "Human Rights" Back into the UN Guiding Principles on Business and Human Rights: Shifting Frames and Embedding Participation Rights' in C Rodriquez-Garavito (ed), *Business and Human Rights: Beyond the End of the Beginning* (CUP 2017).
Melish TJ and Meidinger, E, 'Protect, Respect, Remedy and Participate: "New Governance" Lessons for the Ruggie Framework' in R Mares (ed), *The UN Guiding Principles on Business and Human Rights: Foundations and Implementation* (Koninklijke Brill 2012).
Merry SE, *Human Rights and Gender Violence: Translating International Law into Local Justice* (Chicago University Press 2006).
Morgan G and Quack S, 'Global Networks or Global Firms? The Organizational Implications of the Internationalization of Law Firms' in A Ferner, J Quintanilla, and C

Sánchez-Runde (eds), *Multinationals, Institutions and the Construction of Transnational Practice* (Palgrave Macmillan 2006).

Mundlak G, 'Human Rights and Labor Rights: Why Don't the Two Tracks Meet?' (2012) 34 Comparative Labour Law and Policy Journal 217.

Murphy H and Kellow A, 'Forum Shopping in Global Governance: Understanding States, Business and NGOs in Multiple Arenas' (2013) 4(2) Global Policy 139.

Murray J, 'A New Phase in the Regulation of Multinational Enterprises: The Role of the OECD' (2001) 30(3) Industrial Law Journal 255.

Nieuwenkamp R, 'The OECD Guidelines for Multinational Enterprises on Responsible Business Conduct: Soft Law with Hard Consequences' (2013) 4 Dovenschmidt Quarterly 171.

Niforou C, 'International Framework Agreements and Industrial Relations Governance: Global Rhetoric versus Local Realities' (2012) 50 British Journal of Industrial Relations 352.

Nolan J, 'The Corporate Responsibility to Respect Human Rights: Soft Law or Not Law?' in S Deva and D Bilchitz (eds), *Human Rights Obligations of Business: Beyond the Corporate Responsibility to Respect?* (CUP 2015).

Nolan J, 'Human Rights and Global Corporate Supply Chains: Is Effective Supply Chain Accountability Possible?' in S Deva and D Bilchitz (eds), *Building a Treaty on Business and Human Rights: Context and Contours* (CUP 2017).

OECD (Organisation for Economic Co-operation and Development), 'Our Global Reach', <oecd.org/about/members-and-partners> accessed 20 October 2022.

OECD, 'Partners and Stakeholders' <http://mneguidelines.oecd.org/workingwithstakeholdersandpartners.htm> accessed 10 October 2022.

OECD, *OECD Guidelines for Multinational Enterprises* (OECD Publishing 2000).

OECD, 'Annual Report on the OECD Guidelines for Multinational Enterprises 2010: Corporate Responsibility: Reinforcing a Unique Instrument' (3 December 2010).

OECD, 'OECD Declaration on International Investment and Multinational Enterprises' (2011).

OECD, *OECD Guidelines for Multinational Enterprises* (OECD Publishing 2011).

OECD, 'Establishment of a Working Party on Responsible Business Conduct' (15 February 2013).

OECD, 'Annual Report on the OECD Guidelines for Multinational Enterprises 2013: Responsible Business Conduct in Action' (4 December 2013).

OECD, *OECD Due Diligence Guidance for Responsible Supply Chains of Minerals from Conflict-Affected and High-Risk Areas* (3rd edn, OECD Publishing 2016).

OECD/FAO (Food and Agriculture Organization), *OECD–FAO Guidance for Responsible Agricultural Supply Chains* (OECD Publishing 2016).

OECD, 'Specific Instance Notified by Clean Clothes Campaign Denmark and Active Consumers regarding the activities of PWT Group: Final Statement' (2016).

OECD, *OECD Due Diligence Guidance for Meaningful Stakeholder Engagement in the Extractives Sector* (OECD Publishing 2017).

OECD, *OECD Due Diligence Guidance for Responsible Supply chains in the Garment and Footwear Sector* (OECD Publishing 2017).

OECD, 'Public Consultation on the Due Diligence Guidance for Responsible Business Conduct: Compilation of Responses' (2017) 20 <https://mneguidelines.oecd.org/OECD-Due-Diligence-Guidance-for-RBC-Public-Consultation-Responses.pdf> accessed 5 October 2022.

OECD, *Responsible Business Conduct for Institutional Investors* (OECD Publishing 2017).

OECD, *OECD Due Diligence Guidance for Responsible Business Conduct* (OECD Publishing 2018).

OECD, 'Annual Report on the OECD Guidelines for Multinational Enterprises 2019' (2020).

OECD, 'National Contact Points for Responsible Business Conduct: Providing Access to Remedy—20 Years and the Road Ahead' (2020) <https://mneguidelines.oecd.org/NCPs-for-RBC-providing-access-to-remedy-20-years-and-the-road-ahead.pdf> accessed 20 October 2022.

OECD, 'Terms of Reference for an Update of the OECD Guidelines for Multinational Enterprises' (4 May 2020) Investment Division, Directorate for Financial and Enterprise Affairs.

OECD, 'Engagement with Trade Unions in Due Diligence Processes Conducted by Industry-Led or Multi-Stakeholder Initiatives: Clarification by the OECD Investment' (2021) <https://mneguidelines.oecd.org/engagement-with-trade-unions-in-due-diligence-processes-conducted-by-industry-led-or-multi-stakeholder-initiatives.pdf> accessed 13 September 2022.

OECD, 'Standard-Setting Review: Five Year Report (2016–2021)' (21 May 2021) C/MIN(2021)9.

OECD, 'Driving, Supporting and Promoting Responsible Business Practices through Government Policies' (2022) <https://mneguidelines.oecd.org/public-consultation-draft-oecd-recommendation-on-the-role-of-government-in-promoting-responsible-business-conduct.htm> accessed 20 October 2022.

OECD, 'Stocktaking Report on the OECD Guidelines for Multinational Enterprises' (2022) <https://mneguidelines.oecd.org/stocktaking-exercise-on-the-oecd-guidelines-for-multinational-enterprises.htm> accessed 20 October 2022.

OECD, 'Summary of Public Submissions: Stocktaking Exercise on the OECD Guidelines for Multinational Enterprises, OECD Public Consultation, March 2021–April 2022' (2022) <https://mneguidelines.oecd.org/stocktaking-exercise-on-the-oecd-guidelines-for-multinational-enterprises-summary-of-public-submissions.pdf> accessed 5 September 2022.

OECD, 'The Role of Sustainability Initiatives in Mandatory Due Diligence: Note for Policy Makers' (2022) <https://mneguidelines.oecd.org/the-role-of-sustainability-initiatives-in-mandatory-due-diligence-note-for-policy-makers.pdf> accessed 15 October 2022.

OECD Watch, 'Advisory Groups' <www.oecdwatch.org/oecd-ncps/stakeholders> accessed 10 October 2022.

OECD Watch, 'OECD Watch Comments on the OECD Due Diligence Guidance for Responsible Business Conduct and the Due Diligence Companion' (February 2017) <www.oecdwatch.org/wp-content/uploads/sites/8/2017/02/OECD-Watch-comments-on-the-OECD-Due-Diligence-Guidance-for-Responsible-Business-Conduct-and-Due-Dilligence-Companion.pdf> accessed 10 October 2022.

O'Rourke D, 'Monitoring the Monitors: A Critique of PricewaterhouseCoopers Labor Monitoring' (*Massachusetts Institute of Technology*, 2000) <https://nature.berkeley.edu/orourke/PDF/pwc.pdf> accessed 3 October 2022.

O'Rourke D, 'Outsourcing Regulation: Analyzing Nongovernmental Systems of Labor Standards and Monitoring' (2003) 31(1) Policy Studies Journal 1.

Ougaard, M, 'Civil Society and Patterns of Accountability in the OECD' in JA Scholte (ed), *Building Global Democracy? Civil Society and Accountable Global Governance* (CUP 2011).

Paiement P, 'Jurisgenerative Role of Auditors in Transnational Labor Governance' (2018) 13(3) Regulation & Governance 280.

Palombo D, 'The Duty of Care of the Parent Company: A Comparison between French Law, UK Precedents and the Swiss Proposals' (2019) 4(2) Business and Human Rights Journal 265.

Papadakis K (ed), *Shaping Global Industrial Relations: The Impact of International Framework Agreements* (ILO Publication/Palgrave Macmillan 2011).

Parker C and Howe J, 'Ruggie's Diplomatic Project and Its Missing Regulatory Infrastructure' in R Mares (ed), *The UN Guiding Principles on Business and Human Rights: Foundations and Implementation* (Martinus Nijhoff 2012).

Patz C, 'The EU's Draft Corporate Sustainability Due Diligence Directive: A First Assessment' (2022) 7 Business and Human Rights Journal 291.

Perry-Kessaris A, 'What Does It Mean to Take a Socio-Legal Approach to International Economic Law?' in A Perry-Kessaris (ed), *Socio-Legal Approaches to International Economic Law: Text, Context, Subtext* (Routledge 2013).

Phillips N, LeBaron G, and Wallin S, 'Mapping and Measuring the Effectiveness of Labour-Related Disclosure Requirements for Global Supply Chains' (2018) ILO Working Paper 32/2018, ILO Research Department.

Power M, 'The Risk Management of Everything' (2004) 5 Journal of Risk Finance 58.

Power M, *Organized Uncertainty: Designing a World of Risk Management* (OUP 2007).

Poynton C, 'Five Questions for Business and Human Rights Leaders: Irit Tamir, Oxfam America' (*ArticleOne*, 6 June 2016) <http://articleone.squarespace.com/insights/2016/6/2/irittamir> accessed 28 April 2023.

Quack, S, 'Law, Expertise and Legitimacy in Transnational Economic Governance: An Introduction' (2010) 8(1) Socio-Economic Review 3.

Quijano G and Lopez C, 'Rise of Mandatory Human Rights Due Diligence: A Beacon of Hope or a Double-Edged Sword?' (2021) 6 Business and Human Rights Journal 241.

Rawling, M, 'A Generic Model of Regulating Supply Chain Outsourcing' in C Arup and others (eds), *Labour Law and Labour Market Regulation: Essays on the Construction, Constitution and Regulation of Labour Markets and Work Relationships* (Federation Press 2006).

Reinecke J and Donaghey J, 'When Industrial Democracy Meets Corporate Social Responsibility—A Comparison of the Bangladesh Accord and Alliance as Responses to the Rana Plaza Disaster' (2018) 56 British Journal of Industrial Relations 14.

Reinecke J and Donaghey J, 'Towards Worker-Driven Supply Chain Governance: Developing Decent Work through Democratic Worker Participation' (2021) 57 Journal of Supply Chain Management 14.

Roberts CM, 'Reversing the Burden of Proof Before Human Rights Bodies' (2022) 25 International Journal of Human Rights 1682.

Rosen RE, 'Risk Management and Corporate Governance: The Case of Enron' (2003) 35 Connecticut Law Review 1157.

Ruggie JG, 'Report of the Special Representative of the Secretary-General on the Issue of Human Rights and Transnational Corporations and Other Business Enterprises Further Steps Towards the Operationalization of the "Protect, Respect and Remedy" Framework' (*UN DigitalLibrary*, 2010).

Ruggie JG, 'Special Representative of the UN Secretary-General for Business and Human Rights, 'Remarks at OECD Investment Committee' (*OECD Investment Committee*, 4 October 2010) <https://media.business-humanrights.org/media/documents/files/reports-and-materials/Ruggie-remarks-to-OECD-Investment-Committee-4-Oct-2010.pdf> accessed 10 October 2022.

Ruggie JG, *Just Business: Multinational Corporations and Human Rights* (WW Norton 2013).

Ruggie JG, 'Letter from Ruggi JG to Ryder G' (*Business and Human Rights Resource Centre*, 30 May 2016) <www.business-humanrights.org/en/latest-news/letter-from-john-ruggie-to-guy-ryder-regarding-supply-chains-in-the-context-of-the-un-guiding-principles> accessed 18 September 2020.

Ruggie JG and Nelson T, 'Human Rights and the OECD Guidelines for Multinational Enterprises: Normative Innovations and Implementation Challenges' (2015) 22(1) Brown Journal of World Affairs 99.

Safarty GA, 'Shining Light on Global Supply Chains' (2015) 56(2) Harvard International Law Journal 419.

Salzman J, 'Labor Rights, Globalization and Institutions: The Role and Influence of the Organization for Economic Cooperation and Development' (2000) 21(4) Michigan Journal of International Law 769.

Savourey E and Brabant S, 'The French Law on the Duty of Vigilance: Theoretical and Practical Challenges since Its Adoption' (2021) 6(1) Business and Human Rights Journal 141.

Scheper C, '"From Naming and Shaming to Knowing and Showing": Human Rights and the Power of Corporate Practice' (2015) 19 International Journal of Human Rights 737.

Schilling-Vacaflor A and Lenschow A, 'Hardening Foreign Corporate Accountability through Mandatory Due Diligence in the European Union? New Trends and Persisting Challenges' (2021) 17 Regulation & Governance 677.

Scholte JA, 'Global Governance, Accountability and Civil Society' in JA Scholte (ed), *Building Global Democracy? Civil Society and Accountable Global Governance* (CUP 2011).

Scott C, 'Standard-Setting in Regulatory Regimes' in R Baldwin, M Cave, and M Lodge (eds), *The Oxford Handbook of Regulation* (OUP 2010).

Shaffer G, 'Transnational Legal Process and State Change' (2012) 37(2) Law & Social Inquiry 229.

Shaffer G, 'How the World Trade Organization Shapes Regulatory Governance' (2015) 9(1) Regulation & Governance 1.

Shamir H and Barkly T, 'Corporate Responsibility' in H Shamir and M Niezna (eds), *An Alternative Anti-Trafficking Action Plan; A Proposed Model Based on a Labor Approach to Trafficking* (Tel Aviv University 2022) TraffLab Research Group Policy Paper.

Shamir R, 'Capitalism, Governance, and Authority: The Case of Corporate Social Responsibility' (2010) 6 Annual Review of Law and Society 531.

Shavin C, 'Unlocking the Potential of the New OECD Due Diligence Guidance on Responsible Business Conduct' (2018) 4(1) Business and Human Rights Journal 1.

Shift, 'Implications of the UN Guiding Principles on Business and Human Rights for the Fair Labor Association' (July 2012) <https://shiftproject.org/resource/implications-of-the-guiding-principles-for-the-fair-labor-association> accessed 28 September 2022.

Shift and UN OHCHR (United Nations Office of the High Commissioner for Human Rights), 'Enforcement of Mandatory Due Diligence: Key Design Considerations for Administrative Supervision' (*Shift*, 2021) Policy Paper <https://shiftproject.org/wp-content/uploads/2021/10/Enforcement-of-Mandatory-Due-Diligence_Shift_UN-Human-Rights_Policy-Paper-2.pdf> accessed 5 October 2022.

Sinclair A and Dinshaw F, 'Paper Promises? Evaluating the Early Impact of Australia's Modern Slavery Act' (*Human Rights Law Center*, 2022) <www.hrlc.org.au/reports/2022/2/3/paper-promises-evaluating-the-early-impact-of-australias-modern-slavery-act> accessed 10 September 2022.

Sinclair A and Nolan J, 'Modern Slavery Laws in Australia: Steps in the Right Direction?' (2020) 5(1) Business and Human Rights Journal 164, 169.

Smits JM, 'Enforcing Corporate Social Responsibility Codes Under Private Law: On the Disciplining Power of Legal Doctrine' (2017) 24(1) Indiana Journal of Global Legal Studies 99.

Snyder F, 'The Effectiveness of European Community Law: Institutions, Processes, Tools and Techniques' (1993) 56(1) Modern Law Review 19.

Sobczak A, 'Are Codes of Conduct in Global Supply Chains Really Voluntary? From Soft Law Regulation of Labour Relations to Consumer Law' (2015) 16(2) Business Ethics Quarterly 167.

Spitzer M, 'Human Rights, Global Supply Chains and the Role of Tort' (2019) 10(2) Journal of European Tort Law 95.

Standing G, 'The ILO: An Agency for Globalization' (2008) 39(3) Development and Change 355.

Suchman MC, 'Managing Legitimacy: Strategic and Institutional Approaches' (1995) 20(3) Academy of Management Review 571.

Suddaby R and Greenwood R, 'Colonizing Knowledge: Commodification as a Dynamic of Jurisdictional Expansion in Professional Services Firms' (2001) 54(7) Human Relations 933.

Sydow J and others, 'Implementation of Global Framework Agreements: Towards a Multi-Organizational Practice Perspective' (2014) 20(4) Transfer 489.

Talesh S, 'How Dispute Resolution System Design Matters: An Organizational Analysis of Dispute Resolution Structures and Consumer Lemon Laws' (2012) 46 Law & Society Review 463.

Talesh S, 'Rule-Intermediaries in Action: How State and Business Stakeholders Influence the Meaning of Consumer Rights in Regulatory Governance Arrangements' (2015) 37(1) Law & Policy 1.

Taylor CR, 'The Dodd–Frank Death Knell' (2018) 49(3) Loyola University Chicago Law Journal 655.

Taylor M, 'The Ruggie Framework: Polycentric Regulation and the Implications for Corporate Social Responsibility' (2011) 5(1) Nordic Journal of Applied Ethics 9.

Thomas H and Anner M, 'Dissensus and Deadlock in the Evolution of Labour Governance: Global Supply Chains and the International Labour Organization (ILO)' (2023) 184 Journal of Business Ethics 33.

Thomas H and Turnbull P, 'From Horizontal to Vertical Labour Governance: The International Labour Organization (ILO) and Decent Work in Global Supply Chains' (2018) 71(4) Human Relations 536.

Thouvenin JM, 'Diffusion and Leveraging of Transnational Labour Norms by the OECD' in A Blackett and A Trebilcock (eds), *Research Handbook on Transnational Labour Law* (Edward Elgar 2015).

Tobin J, 'Seeking to Persuade: A Constructive Approach to Human Rights Treaty Interpretation' (2010) 23 Harvard Human Rights Journal 1.

Torres-Cortés F and others, 'Study on Due Diligence Requirements through the Supply Chain. Final Report' (*European Commission, Directorate-General for Justice and Consumers*, 2020) <http://data.europea.eu/doi/10.2838/39830> accessed 22 October 2022.

Trebilcock A, 'Due Diligence on Labour Issues: Opportunities and Limits of the UN Guiding Principles on Business and Human Rights' in A Blackett and A Trebilcock (eds), *Research Handbook on Transnational Labour Law* (Edward Elgar 2015).

TUAC (Trade Union Advisory Committee), 'Implementing the OECD Due Diligence Guidance' (28 May 2018) <https://tuac.org/wp-content/uploads/2018/05/140PS_E_10_duediligence.pdf> accessed 10 October 2022.

TUAC, 'About TUAC' (2022) <https://tuac.org/about> accessed 20 October 2022.

TUC (Trade Union Congress), 'Implementing the UN Guiding Principles on Business and Human Rights' (24 October 2012) <www.tuc.org.uk/research-analysis/reports/implementing-un-guiding-principles-business-and-human-rights> accessed 20 September 2020.

UK Home Office, 'Transparency in Supply Chains Etc: A Practical Guide' (*Statutory Guidance* 29 October 2015).

UK Home Office, 'Transparency in Supply Chains: A Practical Guide' (2021) <www.gov.uk/government/publications/transparency-in-supply-chains-a-practical-guide/transparency-in-supply-chains-a-practical-guide> accessed 20 October 2022.

UN (United Nations), 'Report of the Special Representative of the Secretary-General on the Issue of Human Rights and Transnational Corporations and other Business Enterprises, Interim Report of the Special Representative of the Secretary-General on the Issue of Human Rights and Transnational Corporations and Other Business Enterprises' (22 February 2006) UN Doc E/CN.4/2006/97.

UN, 'Report of the Special Representative of the Secretary-General on the Issue of Human Rights and Transnational Corporations and Other Business Enterprises, Protect, Respect and Remedy: A Framework for Business and Human Rights' (7 April 2008) UN Doc A/HRC/8/5.

UN, 'Report of the Special Representative of the Secretary-General on the Issue of Human Rights and Transnational Corporations and Other Business Enterprises, Business and Human Rights: Further Steps towards the Operationalization of the "Protect, Respect and Remedy" Framework' (9 April 2010) UN Doc A/HRC/14/27.

UN, 'Report of the Special Representative of the Secretary-General on the Issue of Human Rights and Transnational Corporations and Other Business Enterprises, John Ruggie, "Guiding Principles on Business and Human Rights: Implementing the United Nations 'Protect, Respect and Remedy' Framework"' (21 March 2011) UN Doc A/HRC/17/31.

UN, 'Stocktaking on the 10th Anniversary of the UNGPs' (*OHCHR*, 2021) <www.ohchr.org/en/special-procedures/wg-business/stocktaking-10th-anniversary-ungps> accessed 5 October 2021.

UNCTC (United Nations Centre for Transnational Corporations), 'The United Nations Code of Conduct on Transnational' Corporations (1986).

UNGA (United Nations General Assembly), 'Report of the Working Group on the Issue of Human Rights and Transnational Corporations and other Business Enterprises: Note by the Secretary-General' (16 July 2018) UN Doc A/73/163.

UNGA, 'Guiding Principles on Business and Human Rights at 10: Taking Stock of the First Decade: Report of the Working Group on the Issue of Human Rights and Transnational Corporations and Other Business Enterprises' (22 April 2021) UN Doc A/HRC/47/39.

UNHRC, 'The UN Guiding Principles on Business and Human Rights at 10' (*Office of the UNHCR*, June 2021) <www.ohchr.org/EN/Issues/Business/Pages/UNGPsBizHRsnext10.aspx> accessed 27 April 2023.

UNHRC Open-Ended Intergovernmental Working Group on Transnational Corporations and Other Business Enterprises with Respect to Human Rights, 'Legally Binding Instrument to Regulate, in International Human Rights Law, the Activities of Transnational Corporations and Other Business Enterprises: Third Revised Draft' (*Office of the High Commissioner of Human Rights*, 17 August 2021) <www.ohchr.org/en/hr-bodies/hrc/wg-trans-corp/igwg-on-tnc> accessed 23 October 2022.

UN OHCHR (United Nations Office of the High Commissioner for Human Rights), 'Guiding Principles on Business and Human Rights: Implementing the United Nations 'Protect, Respect, and Remedy' Framework' (2011).

UN OHCHR, 'OHCHR Feedback on the Proposal for a Directive of the European Parliament and of the Council on Corporate Sustainability Due Diligence' (2022) <www.ohchr.org/sites/default/files/2022-05/eu-csddd-feedback-ohchr.pdf> accessed 20 October 2022.

United Nations Global Compact and Business for Social Responsibility, 'Supply Chain Sustainability: A Practical Guide for Continuous Improvement' (2nd edn, United Nations 2015) <www.unglobalcompact.org/library/205> accessed 20 September 2021.

UN Sub-Commission on the Promotion and Protection of Human Rights, 'Norms on the Responsibilities of Transnational Corporations and Other Business Enterprises with Regard to Human Rights' (*United Nations*, 26 August 2003).

Van Ho T and Terwindt C, 'Assessing the Duty of Care for Social Auditors' (2019) 27 European Review of Private Law 379.

Venkatesan R, 'The UN Framework on Business and Human Rights: A Workers' Rights Critique' (2019) 157 Journal of Business Ethics 635.

Verité, 'Compliance Is Not Enough: Best Practices in Responding to the California Transparency in Supply Chains Act' (2011) <www.verite.org/sites/default/files/VTE_WhitePaper_California_Bill657FINAL5.pdf> accessed 23/03/2016> accessed 27 April 2023.

Vogel D, *The Market for Virtue: The Potential and Limits of Corporate Social Responsibility* (Brookings Institute Press 2005).

Voiculescu A, 'Human Rights, Corporate Social Responsibility and International Economic Law: Strong Answers to Strong Questions?' in A Perry-Kessaris (ed), *Socio-Legal Approaches to International Economic Law* (Taylor and Francis 2013).

Wheeler S, 'Corporate Respect for Human Rights: As Good as It Gets?' in A Perry-Kessaris (ed), *Socio-Legal Approaches to International Economic Law: Text, Context Subtext* (Routledge 2013).

Wilde-Ramsing J, Vanpeperstraete B, and Hachfeld D, 'Legislating Human Rights Due Diligence: Respecting Rights and Ticking Boxes' (*SOMO*, 2022) Clean Clothes Campaign, ECCHR, Public Eye, and Centre for Resaerch on Multinational Corporations (SOMO) Briefing Paper <www.somo.nl/respecting-rights-or-ticking-boxes> accessed 20 October 2022.

Woodward R, 'Towards Complex Multilateralism? Civil Society and the OECD' in R Mahon and S McBride (eds), *The OECD and Transnational Governance* (University of British Columbia Press 2008).

Woodward R, *The Organisation for Economic Cooperation and Development* (OUP 2009).

Woody KE, 'Conflict Minerals Legislation: The SEC's New Role as Diplomatic and Humanitarian Watchdog' (2012) 81 Fordham Law Review 1315.

Worker Rights, 'Combating Gender-Based Violence in Lesotho' (*Worker Rights Consortium*, 2022) <www.workersrights.org/issues/gender-based-violence-and-discrimination/gender-based-violence-in-lesotho> accessed 25 October 2022.

Zajak S and Scheper C, 'The Dual Nature of Transparency: Corporatization and Democratization of Global Production Networks' in S Berger and D Owetschkin (eds), *Contested Transparencies, Social Movements and the Public Sphere* (Palgrave Macmillan 2019).

Index

For the benefit of digital users, indexed terms that span two pages (e.g., 52–53) may, on occasion, appear on only one of those pages.